THE PERSISTENCE OF
INNOVATION IN
GOVERNMENT

INNOVATIVE GOVERNANCE IN THE 21ST CENTURY

ANTHONY SAICH
Series editor

This is the eighth volume in a series that examines important issues of governance, public policy, and administration, highlighting innovative practices and original research worldwide. All titles in the series will be copublished by the Brookings Institution Press and the Ash Center for Democratic Governance and Innovation, housed at Harvard University's John F. Kennedy School of Government.

Decentralizing Governance: Emerging Concepts and Practices
G. Shabbir Cheema and Dennis A. Rondinelli, eds. (2007)

Innovations in Government: Research, Recognition, and Replication
Sandford Borins, ed. (2008)

The State of Access: Success and Failure
of Democracies to Create Equal Opportunities
Jorrit de Jong and Gowher Rizvi, eds. (2008)

Unlocking the Power of Networks: Keys to High-Performance Government
Stephen Goldsmith and Donald F. Kettl, eds. (2009)

Ports in a Storm: Public Management in a Turbulent World
John D. Donahue and Mark H. Moore, eds. (2012)

Agents of Change: Strategy and Tactics for Social Innovation
Sanderijn Cels, Jorrit de Jong, and Frans Nauta (2012)

The PerformanceStat Potential: A Leadership Strategy for Producing Results
Robert D. Behn (2014)

The Persistence of Innovation in Government
Sandford F. Borins (2014)

The Persistence of Innovation in Government

Sandford F. Borins

Ash Center for Democratic Governance and Innovation
John F. Kennedy School of Government
Harvard University

BROOKINGS INSTITUTION PRESS
Washington, D.C.

The Brookings Institution is a private nonprofit organization devoted to research, education,
and publication on important issues of domestic and foreign policy. Its principal purpose is to
bring the highest quality independent research and analysis to bear on current and emerging
policy problems. Interpretations or conclusions in Brookings publications should be
understood to be solely those of the authors.

Library of Congress Cataloging-in-Publication data
Borins, Sandford F., 1949–
    The persistence of innovation in government / Sandford F. Borins.
        pages   cm. —   (Innovative governance in the 21st century)
    Includes bibliographical references and index.
    ISBN 978-0-8157-2560-2 (pbk. : alk. paper) 1. Political planning—United States.
2. Public administration—United States. 3. Administrative agencies—United States—
Management. 4. Organizational change—United States. 5. Government productivity—
United States. I. Title.
    JK468.P64B724 2014
    320.60973—dc23   2014008492

9 8 7 6 5 4 3 2 1

Printed on acid-free paper

Typeset in Adobe Garamond

Composition by R. Lynn Rivenbark
Macon, Georgia

For Alexander Stefan Borins and Nathaniel Benjamin Borins
—innovative thinkers, and very persistent

Contents

Acknowledgments   ix

1   Public Sector Innovation: Still, and Again   1

2   Emergence and Diversity: Public Sector Innovation Research   11

3   The Class of 2010   40

4   Present at the Creation   61

5   Innovation Stories: Real People, Real Challenges, Real Outcomes   86

6   Creating Public Value, Receiving Public Recognition   108

7   From Data to Stories: Innovation Patterns in the Six Policy Areas   143

8   Summing Up, Looking Forward: Awards, Practitioners,
    and Academics   180

Appendix: Initial Application and Semifinalist Application
    Questionnaires   207

References   211

Index   217

Acknowledgments

This book represents the latest product of my long-standing and extraordinarily fruitful research relationship with the Ash Center for Democratic Governance and Innovation at the Harvard Kennedy School. In recent years, the Ash Center has supported my involvement as editor of the 2008 book *Innovations in Government: Research, Recognition, and Replication* and as organizer of a seminar series in the 2009–10 academic year. I then received support for research on narratives about public sector innovation, on the determinants of the selection of semifinalists in the Innovations in American Government Awards, and on a comparative analysis of semifinalists in 2010 with those of two decades ago that I discussed in my 1998 book, *Innovating with Integrity*. These three research projects became the genesis of this book, and without that generous research support this book would not have been possible.

Relationships, of course, depend on people, and three people at the Ash Center have been particularly helpful: Professor Tony Saich, director of the Ash Center, for his support; Marty Mauzy, executive director, and Christina Marchand, associate director for outreach. I thank them for their interest and encouragement. In addition, Christina organized my frequent visits to the Harvard Kennedy School, made application data available, answered my questions about selection procedures, and read and commented on the manuscript.

The Department of Management at the University of Toronto, Scarborough also supported my research with a one-course reduction in my teaching load when I was completing the manuscript.

Professor Richard Walker of the City University of Hong Kong, a distinguished and prolific public sector innovation scholar, collaborated with me on statistical analysis of the determinants of the selection of semifinalists in the Innovations in

American Government Awards. I have incorporated much of our coauthored paper in chapter 6. I appreciate his statistical expertise and research collaboration.

Two research assistants helped me immensely with the data generation and analysis. Kaylee Chretien, originally an undergraduate at the University of Toronto, Scarborough and now a public servant at Public Works and Government Services Canada, coded the Innovations in American Government Awards applications. Elizabeth Lyons, a doctoral student in strategic management at the University of Toronto's Rotman School of Management, analyzed the data generated by the coded applications. Both did work that was careful, thoughtful, and prompt.

My spouse, Beth Herst, a literary scholar and playwright, read the manuscript and made numerous suggestions that clarified my arguments and improved how I expressed them. I am deeply grateful for her contribution to the book and consider myself very lucky that this intellectual collaboration is sustained by, and also enriches, our marriage.

Two anonymous reviewers made numerous suggestions. I considered all of them carefully and have taken many of them on board.

As I was completing the research and writing the book I made presentations at the Australian National University, Canberra; Institute of Public Administration of Australia, Melbourne; Organization for Economic Cooperation and Development, Paris; Roskilde University Political Science Department, Denmark; Ash Center for Democratic Governance and Innovation, Harvard University; the 2013 Public Management Research Conference, Madison, Wisconsin; and the Strategic Management Department, Rotman School of Management. The questions and comments of all these audiences were helpful in formulating my argument and explaining the supporting evidence.

Finally, I appreciate the efforts of the team at Brookings Institution Press—senior acquisitions editor Chris Kelaher, managing editor Janet Walker, art coordinator Susan Woollen, and copy editor Katherine Scott—in helping me produce a volume that conveys with clarity and precision ideas that are expressed in both words and numbers.

1

Public Sector Innovation: Still, and Again

Innovation as a phenomenon within the public sector persists. Despite skepticism about whether large, hierarchical, monopolistic government agencies can initiate and embrace change, there is extensive evidence that they can, they do, and they will. Because innovators persist. In the face of the obstacles inherent to the process, in spite of the risk of failure, in spite of the time, energy, vision, skill, networking, preparation, accommodation, persuasion, education, and improvisation required to bring an innovation to fruition, public servants continue to try new ways to create public value. Innovation has also outlasted the theoretical controversies and political backlash of the 1980s, when the New Public Management *was* new and government was the problem, the all-too-brief limelight of Reinventing Government in the 1990s, and the security and financial crises of the new century, when government started to look more like the only possible solution.

Innovation awards also persist, bringing wider recognition to these efforts among practitioners, scholars, and the general public and encouraging new generations of change agents, experimenters, and "local heroes." Twenty-five years after their inception, the Harvard Kennedy School's Innovations in American Government Awards receive over five hundred applications every year, two-thirds of them new, all of them evidence of an enduring fact. The academic study of public sector innovation clearly persists. Researchers worldwide are producing a continual stream of work, seeking new data sources, and asking new questions. And my own personal interest in innovation persists. Twenty years after first studying innovation awards applicants, I continue to find that they provide an important body of information and experience for grappling with this persistent, and shifting, subject. For if public sector innovation endures, and it clearly does, it still does not stay the same.

1

In many ways this book is a return—to a subject, to a methodology, and to data I have engaged with extensively, in my book *Innovating with Integrity: How Local Heroes are Transforming American Government* (Borins 1998) and in numerous articles that followed it. Technically, it is even a replication. Like the earlier work, this study will analyze applications to the Innovations in American Government Awards program run by the Ash Center for Democratic Governance and Innovation at the Harvard Kennedy School. Like the earlier work, this too will employ rigorous statistical analysis, aggregating data to identify trends and anomalies and using regression analysis to test hypotheses about the relationships among characteristics of public sector innovations. And it will also try to convey something of the character and specificity of individual innovations, innovators, and their processes through secondary, disaggregated, qualitative observation.

Within the social sciences, replication tends to be endorsed in theory more often than it is embraced in practice. No one questions the desirability of repeating research as a test of its initial validity or broader applicability. But replicating other scholars' work can be felt to suggest a lack of imagination or initiative and generates none of the excitement of discovery. Most researchers, understandably, prefer to strike out for themselves. If they are revisiting others' data, they do so in their own way, choosing their own methodologies and providing their own interpretations. The one exception occurs when findings are considered controversial or have proved to have a major impact on public policy. The recent reanalysis of Rogoff and Rinehart's data about financially induced recessions comes to mind as a pertinent current example.[1] When replication does occur, it is most often undertaken by the original scholar, because he or she believes in the ongoing value of the research and has better access to the original data and methodology. Replication of this type often appears as subsequent editions of a book. The study of innovation has a distinguished exemplar: the late Everett Rogers's *Diffusion of Innovations*, published in five editions between 1962 and 2003. Rogers originally developed a conceptual model of diffusion. He then applied it to a growing number of phenomena in his subsequent editions.

I do not see this book as a second edition of *Innovating with Integrity*, however, nor would I call it simply a replication. To explain why, it is necessary to recap something of the history of public sector innovation, as a practice and as an object of study, retracing the evolution of my own thinking and writing about the subject as part of that larger story. Initially, innovation was closely tied to the Reinventing Government movement, the term most often used in the United States, or the New Public Management (NPM) as the phenomenon was known internationally, with NPM and innovation evolving simultaneously in the last fifteen

---

1. Paul Krugman, "The Excel Depression," *New York Times*, April 18, 2013.

years of the previous century. The governments of the United Kingdom and New Zealand in the mid-1980s pioneered NPM ideas and practices. David Osborne, first in *Laboratories of Democracy* (1990) and then together with Ted Gaebler in *Reinventing Government* (1992), analyzed and publicized the innovations that were bubbling up, primarily at the state and local levels in the United States. *Reinventing Government* derived ten principles of a new paradigm of government from approximately fifty government innovations with which the authors were familiar. The Harvard Kennedy School's Innovations in State and Local Government Award, instituted in 1986, offered external recognition to encourage innovative public servants to share information about the programs they had initiated. The program was also intended to counteract the "government is the problem" rhetoric and policies espoused by the Reagan administration. Indeed, some of the early winners were discussed in *Reinventing Government,* and David Osborne has been a longtime member of the national selection committee. (A word of explanation regarding the proliferation of award program names: the John F. Kennedy School of Government's State and Local Government Awards program was expanded in 1995 to include applications from the federal government, and consequently was renamed the Innovations in American Government Awards, the name that is still in use today. In 2007 the school began referring to itself as the Harvard Kennedy School (HKS). For convenience I will generally refer to the awards program as the HKS Awards and distinguish particular iterations of it by date or date span.)

Much of the debate among practitioners and academics about the merits of NPM focused on high-level, government-wide structural reforms such as service charters, disaggregation of government departments into a cluster of single-purpose (or at least tightly focused) agencies, fixed-term contracts between agency heads and ministers, and the replacement of cash-basis accounting with accrual accounting. But it was clear even then that "big reforms and big ideas" were not necessarily the whole story. Pollitt and Bouchaert (2000, 191) concluded their magisterial comparative study of high-level reforms with the recognition that the reform movement necessarily included local innovations, what they called "micro-improvements." The proliferation of such improvements was, they felt, a direct result of the cultural shifts within the public sector represented by NPM, and fostering them was a crucial component of any successful reform strategy:

> And yet there is another side to public management reform, which has a more solid and sensible persona. The pressure, the rhetoric, the loosening of the old ways—all these have combined to give many public servants the opportunity to make changes which make local sense to *them.* Such "improvements" may occasionally be self-serving, but often they are substantially other-directed and result in gains in productivity, service quality,

transparency, fairness, or some other important value. . . . One of the major limitations of our approach—and the approaches of many others who have concentrated on big reforms and big ideas—is that they capture very little of this micro-improvement. As some of the most successful reform leaders in several countries have recognized, a crucial ingredient of a successful reform strategy is that it should create and sustain conditions in which small improvements—many of them unforeseen and unforeseeable—can flourish.

Despite this resounding endorsement of local innovation by two major scholars, critics of NPM did not spare it. They argued that the entrepreneurial public servants who initiated innovations were engaging primarily in self-promotion, rule-breaking, and power politics, ignoring traditional public service values such as probity and deference to political authority. Larry Terry (1998), who made this argument most forcefully, concluded that the innovators' "penchant for rule-breaking and manipulating public authority for private gain has been, and continues to be, a threat to democratic governance." NPM advocates countered, with leading scholars like Robert Behn (1998) arguing that innovative public servants were taking the lead in policy areas on which elected politicians were not focusing their attention and that legislation often did not provide clear direction for public servants, a fact that forced them to take the initiative.

Although the very title of my 1998 book might be seen as an implicit admission of the possibility of innovation *without* integrity, I explicitly joined the debate about public sector entrepreneurship with an article published in *Public Administration Review* (Borins 2000a) entitled "Loose Cannons and Rule Breakers, or Enterprising Leaders? Some Evidence about Innovative Public Managers." The article used data from the HKS Awards in the 1990s to demonstrate that the applicants did not behave like loose cannons or rule-breakers; rather, they combined initiative and creativity with traditional public service values, such as respect for the law and due process.[2]

The vigor, and even occasional vitriol, of the New Public Management debate has long since abated—changes in political leadership (Bush replacing Clinton and Obama replacing Bush), the emergence of new policy priorities (homeland security, climate change, and economic renewal in response to the global financial crisis), and changing research interests all playing their part. Perhaps the most lasting legacy of NPM has been a focus on defining and measuring the results that public sector programs and activities are intended to achieve. This has been facilitated by the information technology (IT)revolution that has enabled govern-

---

2. The editor of *Public Administration Review* at the time was Larry Terry. Although he disagreed with my thesis, he was supportive of my article, publishing it as the lead in the issue in which it appeared. His respect for and encouragement of open debate was exemplary. Larry Terry died at too early an age in 2006.

ments to readily gather, analyze, and post their performance data online. Kamensky (2013) succinctly summarizes this trend as the evolution from "Reinventing Government" to "Moneyball Government." To a certain extent the NPM battle has mutated, with former enthusiasts emerging as advocates of performance measurement and performance management and former skeptics redefining themselves as critics of the performance management revolution.

Nothing ages faster than yesterday's "new." But if the New Public Management controversies are now history, interest in public sector innovation has if anything grown stronger among both practitioners and scholars. Today's much more challenging policy agenda has led governments to welcome public entrepreneurship and commentators to celebrate the achievements of innovative public servants, rather than impugn their motives. Governments look both within the public service and to civil society generally for innovative solutions to policy problems and for better ways of providing service, and they will likely continue to do so. Within the public sector, innovation awards programs, most notably the HKS Awards, are still in operation and continue to receive hundreds of applications, providing scholars with an ongoing source of qualitative and quantitative information. This new urgency has its parallel in the private sector, with the question of innovation now a pressing one for private sector managers and business school researchers alike. Innovative corporate "visionaries" and "geniuses" are routinely featured in the popular media and some management scholarship for their defiance of conventional corporate wisdom and ability to "think outside the box." (Within the private sector business advice genre, "innovation" often seems to have become today's TQM, shorthand for a comprehensive reconceptualization of practice focused on new product development.)

It is the data from the HKS Awards that have formed the persistent throughline in my own study of public management innovation. *Innovating with Integrity* drew on systematic statistical analysis and thematic qualitative analysis of a large sample of 217 semifinalists in the HKS Awards between 1990 and 1994. I quickly followed this with a number of articles applying its analysis to additional, albeit smaller, data sets (Borins 2000a, 2000b, 2001a, 2001b). These included 104 HKS Awards finalists between 1995 and 1998, 33 of the best applicants between 1990 and 1994 to the Institute of Public Administration of Canada's Innovative Management Awards, and 83 applications to the Commonwealth Association of Public Administration and Management's (CAPAM) Commonwealth International Innovations Awards in 1998 and 2000.[3] The subsequent

---

3. "Commonwealth" here refers to the Commonwealth of Nations, the voluntary association of fifty-three countries that formerly were parts of the British Empire. The sample included applications from Canada, Australia, Singapore, New Zealand, the United Kingdom, Malta, India, Malaysia, South Africa, and Jamaica.

articles detailed an innovation process similar to that observed in the United States and discussed in *Innovating with Integrity*.

Of course, this time period was the beginning of the Web era, and it is not surprising that approximately one-third of the award applications I analyzed involved some form of information technology. This led me into a parallel exploration of IT as a facilitator of public sector innovation. I convened an international team of scholars to chronicle the progress and explore the implications of the Internet as medium of transaction with citizens (Gov 1.0) and its use for policy development, public consultation, and democratic dialogue (Gov 2.0) in Canada, the United States and the United Kingdom. We published our findings in *Digital State at the Leading Edge* (Borins and others 2007).

At the same time, I continued my active research on, and teaching of, professionally authored narratives relating to the American and British public sectors, culminating in my 2011 book, *Governing Fables: Learning from Public Sector Narratives* (Borins 2011). This, too, has been a long-standing, persistent intellectual interest of mine, but one that I had initially conceived as quite separate from my work on innovation. Increasingly, however, the two streams—narrative and innovation—converged. This was literally the case in 2008, when I edited a festschrift celebrating the twentieth anniversary of the HKS Awards, *Innovations in Government*, while researching and writing *Governing Fables*. The festschrift included chapters studying public sector innovations in the United States, the United Kingdom, and Brazil, as well as a history of the HKS Awards program and an evaluation of the body of research it has supported. Carrying over something of the narrative perspective of my other project to my engagement with my colleagues' work enabled me to see as narratives the HKS Awards semifinalist applications, which respond to a comprehensive questionnaire about the program's antecedents, origins, implementation, overcoming of obstacles, and achievements. I undertook a pilot project, employing a narratological methodology and perspective to analyze the varied retellings of the stories of the thirty-one finalists in 2008 and 2009.

This fusion of innovation and narrative research was a difficult but immensely rewarding venture. It was published in the *Journal of Public Administration Research and Theory* in 2011 (Borins 2012). By returning me to the HKS Awards database, albeit with a markedly different perspective, it also served to convince me that, almost two decades after the first applications I studied, the time had come for a comprehensive reexamination of innovations undertaken by applicants to the program. The Ash Center for Democratic Governance and Innovation at HKS concurred and generously provided funding. The approach we decided on was an analysis of applications to the 2010 awards. This time, however, in addition to studying the detailed questionnaires submitted by the semifinalists—

which had been my database in previous research—I also collected and analyzed the data from a large sample of the much more succinct initial applications, which included both those chosen as semifinalists and those that were not. Data about initial applicants enabled me to ask additional questions: What differentiates those selected as semifinalists from those that were not? Do the semifinalists demonstrate characteristics similar to the group from which they were selected? Are certain characteristics more frequently represented because the HKS Awards judges impose their own views of what constitutes public sector innovation?

So I would seem to have come full circle. Yet it is a return with a difference. *Innovating with Integrity* was undoubtedly a product of the Reinventing Government or NPM moment. Indeed, I've been surprised to realize in retrospect the extent to which the book was shaped by the debates of the time, seeking the salience of reinvention themes among the applications I studied and presenting evidence about the integrity of the innovators themselves to refute the charges of self-interest, and worse, being leveled against them. That was then. We have already considered the changes to the policy context of public sector innovation: the emerging new priorities of security, climate change, and management of the global financial crisis of 2008–09. And these have led to shifts in public attitudes, too. The academic context has changed equally dramatically. An extensive body of research on public sector innovation has emerged in the last fifteen years that simply did not exist before. And it, too, must leave its mark on this new study. Different data, different contexts, and different methodologies (particularly the incorporation of narrative-related concepts and perspectives)—all these enable *The Persistence of Innovation in Government* to ask new questions and find new answers. Not only what has stayed the same but, no less important, what has changed?

The Persistence of Innovation in Government was written for both academic and practitioner audiences. The intended academic audience is particularly scholars exploring public sector innovation. The review of this growing field of research, the analysis of a new data source dealing with the process of public sector innovation, and my situating this new research within the field should all be of interest to such scholars. The practitioner audience is more diverse, including would-be innovators at the political and civil service level in any government, public servants with a mandate for innovation (for example, those involved in the growing number of innovation units or labs, particularly in local government in the United States), and public servants who are involved with innovation awards, either as applicants, judges, or managers. Though the book discusses various aspects of the HKS Awards process, it will be relevant to those involved with other innovation awards as well.

Some authors separate the "technical" material intended primarily for academics from the conclusions derived from it and aimed at practitioners. I have not wanted to entrench either those divisions or the assumptions on which they are based. Instead, I have included either in the text or as footnotes less technical, more intuitive accounts of the statistical methodology and results, offering an alternative entry point. Writing for multiple readerships always increases the risk of pleasing none. The goal of keeping these two public management communities in dialogue justifies taking this risk.

Overview

The book begins with the scholarly context, adopting a thematic approach to the burgeoning academic literature. Chapter 2 offers a selective survey of studies based on applications to innovation awards, studies about whether innovations are launched on the basis of deliberate planning or through a process of incremental groping, studies of policy entrepreneurs and entrepreneurship, and studies, some inspired by Rogers's diffusion of innovation model, of the determinants of innovation in public sector organizations. My interest is not simply to catalogue scholarship that is relevant to or supportive of the hypotheses I will go on to offer (the default goal of many literature reviews), but rather to chart the dimensions of a field of inquiry that scarcely existed two decades ago. In addition to providing a context for my study, it introduces other studies that my study either corroborates or contradicts.

Chapter 3 launches the discussion of the applications to the 2010 innovation awards, contrasting them with previous applications, especially those studied in *Innovating with Integrity*. Its aim is to present a portrait of these innovative programs, including their characteristics, age, size, sources of funding, and organizational structure and accountability relationships. These characteristics are what I have elsewhere (Borins 2006) referred to as the "building blocks" of an innovation, and it is not unusual for an innovation to encompass several. The chapter compares the building blocks for the entire sample with those observed for each of the six policy areas that make it up and discusses in detail the statistical methodology I use for comparing the characteristics of the different innovation data sets.

The focus then shifts to the actual process of innovating. Chapter 4 begins with the applicant innovators' self-reporting on whether they thought they were doing something entirely new, as opposed to adding features to a previous innovation, either their own or launched elsewhere. From there I consider the profile of the innovations' initiators, differentiated both by rank and gender, before moving on to consider the factors leading to the innovation. This includes a discussion of the analytical process involved, in particular whether that process employed deliberate planning or incremental groping. It concludes with secondary analysis of the relationships among the characteristics presented. Did some initiators tend to work together? Were there certain external circumstances that brought particular initiators to the fore? What were the determinants of planning and incremental groping, the two alternative approaches to initiating an innovation? Were certain initiators more likely to plan and others more likely to employ incrementalism? Were certain contexts more likely to lead to incrementalism and others to planning?

Chapter 5 discusses the stories of the innovations, in particular regarding the implementation of change. It identifies the sources of resistance to the innovations and, equally, the tactics innovators used to respond to them, as well as the frequency with which they were successful. The chapter also discusses ongoing criticism of the innovations and correlates criticism with the organizational viewpoint of the critic. The chapter then reverses perspective and reports on what the innovators themselves identified as the shortcomings of their innovations, their self-criticisms. It concludes by outlining the archetypal innovation story that emerges from the data.

This archetypal story of change and resistance to change leads naturally to consideration of the impact of the innovations. Chapter 6 begins by presenting the applicants' own assessments of their programs' impact as well as of their most important achievement. While this was sometimes the same as the reported impact (for example, replying that the achievement was that the innovation was implemented well), it was often something quite different, indicating a broader philosophical or organizational agenda. The chapter then moves to examine external evaluations of the innovations and the media attention, replication, and awards (other than the HKS Awards) they received. After creating indexes for evaluating media attention, replication, and awards, I use multiple regression analysis to identify factors explaining the semifinalists' scores on each. I conclude by applying this approach to the HKS Awards itself, attempting to determine statistically why certain initial applications were chosen as semifinalists and then why the top twenty-five programs and six finalists were chosen from among them. This analysis attempts to determine whether the program was in fact selecting semifinalists and finalists on the basis of its own stated criteria, and it makes explicit a theme that runs throughout the book: the importance of awards programs such as the HKS in encouraging, recognizing, and diffusing public sector innovation and enabling scholarly research about it.

To this point, the focus of analysis is the entire data sample, both of initial and semifinalist applications. Chapter 7 shifts to consider the subsamples represented by the six policy areas defined by the HKS Awards staff: Governance and Management; Transportation, Infrastructure, and Environment; Education and Training; Community and Economic Development; Health and Social Services; and

Criminal Justice and Public Safety. The analysis demonstrates how innovations in the six areas in 2010 differ from one another as well as from those in the corresponding policy area in the early 1990s as presented in *Innovating with Integrity*. Much of that book was devoted to a detailed discussion of innovations in each policy area. Although this chapter does not go into comparable detail, it does identify trends that illuminate significant changes within each policy area over two decades.

Chapter 8, the conclusion to the book, also serves as a point of departure. The chapter begins by mapping the landscape of contemporary public sector innovation, summarizing both the shifts and continuities previous chapters have explored in detail. It then looks forward, addressing the book's academic and practitioner audiences separately. Distilling the previous chapters' findings into a set of precepts for would-be public sector innovators, chapter 8 offers its own contribution to the persistence of innovation. Detailing the research possibilities offered by innovation awards programs such as the Harvard Kennedy School's, it also suggests new avenues for public sector innovation scholarship, in both methodology and focus. In effect, the concluding chapter looks forward to the book—hopefully by a scholar other than me—that will need to be written to update the findings of this one. The certainty that such an updating will be necessary is the final assertion of my belief in the truth of the present book's title.

2

Emergence and Diversity: Public Sector Innovation Research

Ｉt is always instructive, if sometimes a little humbling, to re-read one's earlier work. Revisiting *Innovating with Integrity,* I was struck by the relative brevity of its literature review. Fifteen years ago, a conscientious survey of relevant scholarship included Osborne and Gaebler's best-selling *Reinventing Government* (1992) as well as the Clinton administration's high-profile National Performance Review, commonly known as the Gore Report (1993), the academic critiques of both that became part of the New Public Management debate, and some key private sector literature such as Kanter's (2000) encyclopedic review of the literature on innovation. A very few books and articles had been published on public sector innovation specifically, all of them employing only case study methods. Naturally, I referred to them. And that exhausted the field.

Since then, the academic study of public management innovation has emerged as a thriving field of research, generating a diverse and growing literature. This makes it not only possible but also necessary to limit this current review to empirical research on innovation in the public sector only, ignoring the sprawling literature on the private sector. In any event, scholars studying public sector innovation whom I cite here have already reviewed the private sector literature in their publications, and there is no need to duplicate their efforts. As Potts and Kastelle (2010) argue in their article laying out an agenda for research in public sector innovation, there is good reason to differentiate between the two: private sector innovation is fundamentally driven by profit maximization; consequently, the financial interests of the owners of the firm and the innovators within the firm are closely aligned. In the public sector, however, a considerable amount of innovation is mandated by politicians seeking to serve or impress the electorate. The interests of the politicians and the public servants who implement these innovations are less closely aligned—indeed, they can be widely disparate. A recent article coauthored by an eminent scholar of private sector innovation, Clayton Christensen, illustrates the pitfalls of failing to differentiate. When Christensen turned his attention to the public sector, he demonstrated a fundamental lack of familiarity with the unique public sector context. He and his coauthors (Sahni, Wessel, and Christensen 2013) restricted their attention to cost-reducing technological innovations, ignoring administrative or policy innovations. They advocated closing down outdated public sector infrastructure, not recognizing that the public sector cannot fire the customer and must serve the entire population, which may require keeping outdated infrastructure in operation. They supported the use of non-monetary incentives such as recognition to reward successful public sector innovators, but had nothing to say about the more difficult problem of protecting unsuccessful public sector innovators from public criticism and termination (Borins 2013).

I further limit my focus to articles in academic journals or books with academic publishers, rather than professional reports, which constitute a different genre and are governed by different conventions. Because the literature has proliferated, I will not attempt to review every relevant article, but will choose representative ones, particularly for more prolific authors.

Empirical studies tend to adopt an instrumental approach to the literature they cite, mining it for support for the set of hypotheses the author will be testing but making no attempt to map the scholarly terrain as a whole. The academic literature on public sector innovation is not monolithic. It comprises clusters of subliteratures with some researchers often moving between them. Some clusters are simply abandoned as scholarly attention is turned elsewhere. Yet for all this diversity, there is a "big picture" taking shape—and it is this picture I seek to outline here. My approach is both thematic and roughly chronological. This assumes that there is a reasonable chance researchers working in a particular cluster would have read research predating their own and are responding to or incorporating its results and approaches. They are, in essence, working as small epistemic communities, some overlapping and others quite separate.

I have classified these communities in two ways, by their dominant methodology and by the focus of their research (see table 2-1). The two most commonly used methodologies are case studies and statistical analysis. The case studies may be either individual or comparative analysis of several cases. They are historical narratives, developed initially from documents in the public domain, that are supplemented by semi-structured interviews with a variety of people currently or previously associated with the innovation being studied, as well as any internal documents that interviewees may make available.

Statistical analysis is the creation of data sets concerning some aspect of public management innovation and the subsequent analysis of those sets using methods

Table 2-1. *Categories of Innovation Literature*

	Focus of research		
Methodology	*The innovation*	*Public sector entrepreneurship*	*Innovative organizations*
Case study	Behn (1988,1991) Golden (1990) Barzelay (1992) Straussman (1993) Deyle (1994) Levin and Sanger (1994) Moore (1995) Borins (2000c) Walker (2003) Bovaird and Loffler (2009) Cels, de Jong, and Nauta (2012)	Roberts and King (1991, 1992, 1996) Howard (2001) Bartlett and Dibben (2002) Bernier and Hafsi (2007) Petchey, Williams, and Carter (2008)	Schall (1997) Light (1998) Donahue (2008) Carstensen and Bason (2012)
Statistical	Borins (1991, 1998, 2000a, 2000b, 2001a, 2001b, 2006) Walker, Jeanes, and Rowlands (2002) Walker (2006) Berry and Berry (2007) Hartley and Downe (2007) Farah and Spink (2008) Hartley (2008) Wu, Ma, and Yang (2013)	Teske and Schneider (1994) Mintrom (1997) Mintrom and Vergari (1998) Carter and Scott (2004) Considine, Lewis, and Alexander (2009) Mack, Green, and Vedlitz (2008) Teodoro (2011)	Osborne (1998) Lonti and Verma (2003) Boyne and others (2005) Vigoda-Gadot and others (2008) Osborne, Chew, and McLaughlin (2008) Damanpour and Schneider (2008) Walker (2008) Damanpour, Walker, and Avellaneda (2009) Salge (2010) Walker, Damanpour, and Devece (2010) Salge and Vera (2012) Bernier, Hafsi, and Deschamps (2012) Nolan (2012) Walker (2014)

Source: Author's compilation.

of increasing complexity: descriptive statistics, bivariate correlations, multiple regression analysis, factor analysis, and structural equation modeling.

Any innovation, however it is studied, has three components: a program that is either doing something new or doing something differently; agents who are responsible for implementing the program; and an organizational context within which the program is implemented. Each of these is an essential aspect of any innovation, yet researchers tend to focus on just one, in effect making it the variable to be tracked and explained. Some researchers scrutinize the innovation itself: the factors explaining its inception, its evolution, and the outcomes it has achieved. (This book clearly falls within this category.) Others, on the premise that their subjects will demonstrate traits that distinguish them from their fellow public servants, focus on the people who play a major role in launching and sustaining one or more innovations. These scholars refer to their subjects as public sector entrepreneurs, which makes their work analogous to private sector researchers who study exceptional figures such as Steve Jobs, Richard Branson, and Mark Zuckerberg, the scope of whose achievements sets them apart from other managers or corporate leaders. A third community of scholars focuses on innovative organizations, attempting to distinguish organizations that easily and successfully adopt and launch innovations from those that do not. Studies of public sector entrepreneurship and innovation organizations map readily onto the second and third columns of table 2-1.

Other means of characterizing the constituent scholarly communities further refine table 2-1's categories by asking how researchers choose to frame their work—as extensions of, commentary upon, or refutation of the work of others—and the sources of their data. This would introduce categories for research using innovation awards programs, studying either the applicants to the program or the award process itself; studies commenting upon or responding to Robert Behn's influential theory opposing "managing by planning" and "managing by groping along"; and research on the diffusion of innovations. The first two of these map most closely onto research about innovations themselves, although they may well overlap with studies of individuals and their organizational contexts. Research about the diffusion of innovation probes the interaction between an innovation and an organization that may or may not adopt it, and the agents within the organization that affect the decision. Thus, it maps onto all three columns of the table. This overlap is worth noting. It is a necessary reminder of the complex and multifactoral nature of innovation as an agent-driven process occurring within a highly specific organizational, interpersonal, and political, context—a fact to which I shall return repeatedly in the course of my analysis. Finally, the numerous entries in every cell of table 2-1 make clear the thematic and methodological diversity of the field.

In the sections that follow I present and discuss research being done in five principal clusters:

1. Research using innovation awards
2. Research about management by groping along
3. Research about public sector entrepreneurship
4. Research about the diffusion of innovations
5. Research about innovative organizations

Research Using Innovation Awards

This book belongs firmly to the research cluster applying statistical methods to the applications to an innovation awards program. It makes sense, therefore, to begin our survey there. Innovation awards programs produce written applications and through the judging process rank those that have most closely met the program's criteria. The written applications and subsequent interviews of the applicants can serve as the basis for research. In fact, when the Innovations in State and Local Government Awards program was first designed by the Ford Foundation and the Harvard Kennedy School, research was considered to be as important as granting awards (Walters 2008). Thus, the program not only encouraged public servants who had successfully implemented positive change to tell their stories and be recognized for their efforts, but it was also building a bank of these stories for researchers to use.

Early research based on innovation awards generally consisted of case studies. Michael Barzelay's *Breaking through Bureaucracy* (1992) was a detailed study of the state of Minnesota's Striving Toward Excellence in Performance (STEP) program, an HKS Awards winner. But Barzelay went beyond the details of the program to identify its principles and on that basis to theorize New Public Management (although he did not use the term) as a reduction in central agency controls and an increase in operating department discretion. Mark Moore's (1995) highly influential book *Creating Public Value: Strategic Management in Government* incorporated several comprehensive cases of public sector turnarounds, most notably those led by Lee Brown in the Houston Police Department and Harry Spence in the Boston Housing Authority. Moore used these as a basis for deducing management lessons. Moore's cases were not taken from the files of the HKS Awards, but his use of case material and style of analysis were very similar to Barzelay's.

Martin Levin and Mary Bryna Sanger (1994, 104–09) also used the HKS Awards files, but in a different manner than Barzelay. They sampled thirty-five winners between 1986 and 1991. Unlike their predecessors, they did not undertake detailed studies of individual cases. Instead, they enumerated characteristics of the innovations, innovative processes, and management styles of the entire group, which were then set out in tables. This may have looked like a move toward a different, more quantitative methodology, except that Levin and Sanger presented their tables as checklists, did not total them, and made little effort to integrate them fully into their analysis.

At that time, having read Barzelay, Moore, and Levin and Sanger, I sought to take public sector innovation research in a more quantitative direction. Following an initial study of 57 applicants to the Institute of Public Administration of Canada's (IPAC) first award for Innovative Management in 1990 (Borins 1991), I undertook a much larger study of a sample of 217 semifinalists in the HKS Awards program, which was published as *Innovating with Integrity* (Borins 1998). The Canadian study contained only descriptive statistics regarding key variables; the book went beyond this and looked for causal relationships among them (discussed in detail in later chapters). *Innovating with Integrity* set a direction for my research that I pursued with other quantitative studies of applications to the Commonwealth International Innovation Awards (Borins 2001a) and to the 1995–1998 HKS Awards (Borins 2000a). It also established a precedent and a methodology for other scholars pursuing quantitative research using applications to innovation award programs.

A noteworthy feature of this research cluster is its international character, including work studying data from Brazil, China, and the Commonwealth (particularly Canada, Singapore, Malaysia, and India). Farah and Spink (2008) studied applications to a Brazilian innovation awards program that received the support of the Ford Foundation. The program was launched in 1997 and ran for a decade. The authors conceived of innovation awards programs as action research, in the sense that they were attempting to determine if there were "a lot of interesting things happening" in the public sector. Farah and Spink proposed as a shared motto for all innovation awards programs "If you [the applicant] think what you are doing is innovative, we are at least prepared to listen" (74). Some of Farah and Spink's quantitative results were very close to my own: They found that organizational collaboration was involved in 80 percent of the applications they analyzed (83). The main reason for innovating was to take the initiative in solving an existing problem (84), or, as they put it, "When push comes to shove, [the innovations] are about people getting out there and trying to solve problems" (92). Fifty-six percent of the award-winning applications had been transferred to other organizations (86). These recurring results will be discussed more fully in later chapters.

Wu, Ma, and Yang (2013) studied eighty-three award winners and finalists in a Chinese local government innovation awards program between 2001 and 2008. They found management, service, and collaborative innovations to be the main types in China and noted that there was a lower incidence of technological, governance, and collaborative innovation in China than in the more economically advanced countries to which they compared their results.

Bernier, Hafsi, and Deschamps (2012) have built a database using applications to the IPAC Award for Innovative Management for the last two decades. Their research interest is less the characteristics of the innovations themselves than the characteristics of the governmental environment that produces the applications: the size of the organization, the state of the economy (unemployment rate, government surplus or deficit), and the type of government (whether it was a parliamentary majority or minority). This is a clear instance of research that overlaps several of the general categories defined earlier.

In a recent doctoral dissertation, Nolan (2012) surveyed all 152 applicants to the Commonwealth Association for Public Administration and Management's (CAPAM's) Commonwealth International Innovation Awards by sending a short questionnaire asking the CEO of the submitting organization to identify the key people associated with the innovation, and then sending them a longer questionnaire.[1] A unique feature of this study was Nolan's decision to incorporate into this longer questionnaire Avolio and Bass's (2009) multifactor leadership questionnaire, which had not previously been applied to research on public sector innovation. Nolan's questionnaire received 169 replies from 61 organizations, 89 percent of which were in Singapore, Malaysia, and India. Nolan's research focused on the organization's leadership style and the degree to which it was supportive of innovation. His main finding was that senior leaders in the public sector organizations surveyed displayed many of the traits associated with transformational leadership as measured by the Avolio-Bass instrument, but that their behavior did not impact innovation directly. Rather, the leaders did so indirectly by creating a climate supportive of innovation, by encouraging creativity, tolerating differences, providing resources, and protecting risk takers. Here, too, the set of applications to an innovation awards program has provided a means of probing questions of organizational structure and personal agency and their role in the innovation process.

Though research using applications to innovation awards has taken a quantitative turn, case study methodology continues to be used. Cels, de Jong, and Nauta (2012) chose an international sample of eight innovations—three in the United States, three in Europe, one in Canada, and one in Japan—that had been recognized by innovation awards and provided comprehensive narratives of the process by which they were implemented. The objective of this comparative qualitative research was to develop generalizations about strategies and tactics for introducing innovations and building support for them.

---

1. I was a member of Nolan's dissertation committee.

A related stream of research involves the study of public sector awards programs, of which innovation awards are one type. There was a proliferation of new awards programs in the 1990s; some papers attempted to explain the increase, to categorize the programs (competitive versus threshold, innovation versus quality), and to examine the cost-benefit calculus of jurisdictions or nonprofits initiating programs and organizations deciding whether or not to apply (Borins 2000c, Bovaird and Loffler 2009). In England, Jean Hartley and several coauthors have comprehensively studied the Beacons Scheme, a national awards program designed to encourage innovation and excellence in local government. Because there is a well-defined universe of 388 English local governments, Hartley and Downe (2007) were able to analyze the frequency of applications over time and found that a reasonable percentage of governments apply, that larger governments are more likely to apply than smaller ones, and that applicants that do not win awards still continue to apply. Regarding the administration of the program, they found that increasing the benefits of applying boosts the application rate and that the provision of feedback as part of the application process is seen by applicants as helpful. They also proposed a set of criteria to assess the effectiveness of any awards program.

Hartley (2008) compared the Beacons Scheme to the HKS Awards and found that the former puts more emphasis on excellence—the overall performance of the local government that is applying—than on innovation, in contrast to the latter, which gives awards strictly on the basis of innovation. Her paper outlined a model of diffusion characterized by interaction among the source organization, recipient organization, the enabling process of interorganizational communication, and the environmental context. She found that face-to-face contact, in particular "open days" held by award winners, most effectively disseminated their innovations and best practices (177). There is a double benefit to research that scrutinizes the mechanisms and outcomes of the awards programs themselves, for it can feed back into the design of the programs and, by increasing the number of applicants or the effectiveness of the program's design, enrich the potential data pool for subsequent research. The literature on public sector awards programs is relevant to chapters 3 and 6 of this book, about assessing the future prospects and effectiveness of the HKS Awards.

All the researchers cited here except Nolan and me have measured the frequency with which government units apply to awards programs. This is easy to do when the government units are well defined, whether they are the 388 English local governments used by Hartley or Canada's federal government and 10 provinces used by Bernier and his colleagues. Given the size and complexity of American government, with more than 50,000 local jurisdictions, as well as the large number of annual applications to the HKS Awards, I have not tried to establish the frequency with which different jurisdictions generate applications as a way of measuring their innovativeness. I have preferred to maintain a focus on the innovations themselves and analyze the rich trove of data about their characteristics, processes, outcomes, and external recognition found in the semifinalist applications.

The ongoing research in this cluster has proved to be fruitful, with new studies continuously appearing that are diverse both methodologically and thematically. Case studies and statistical analyses and studies of innovations and the awards that recognize them all coexist and are mutually relevant. Public sector innovation as a unique phenomenon continues to attract scholarly attention and leads to a rich and growing literature.

Research on Management by "Groping Along"

This research cluster is unusual in two respects: it is dominated by a single thesis—the notion of "groping along"—and this thesis has been largely abandoned, by both its originator and his interlocutors, despite the continued importance of the theoretical question underlying it in private sector research. In 1988 the American management scholar Robert Behn published an article in the *Journal of Policy Analysis and Management* succinctly titled "Management by Groping Along," followed in 1991 by a book, *Leadership Counts: Lessons for Public Leaders from the Massachusetts Welfare, Training and Employment Program*. He proposed an improvisational model of how successful managers implement change, which he labeled "groping along," in contrast to the careful and at times constraining preparatory groundwork of planning. His advice to managers was clear: "Establish a goal and some intermediate targets. Then get some ideas and try them out. Some will work, some will not. See which ideas move you towards your goals. You will never really know which ones are productive until you experiment with them" (Behn 1988, 652). Behn's evidence for his theory that, in the words of one of his article's section titles, "most managers grope—a lot" (645) consisted of three cases, two of which were early HKS Awards winners: the Massachusetts Department of Revenue's Enhanced Enforcement Program and the Massachusetts Department of Public Welfare's Education and Training Choices Program.

Behn's hypothesis interested a number of other researchers, who chose to test it more broadly. Olivia Golden (1990) applied it to a sample of seventeen human services programs cited by the HKS Awards in 1986 and found support for it. But she also suggested three contexts in which groping might not apply: programs involving large capital investments, programs based on clear causal models, and programs involving complex intergovernmental systems (242). Levin and Sanger (1994) also found that it applied to the thirty-five HKS Awards winners they studied. On the basis of that finding they recommended that public management programs shift their emphasis from teaching students analytical skills to showing them how to "grope along."

Management by groping along did have its critics, however. Straussman (1993), using one case study, found that it didn't apply in a remedial law context in which a judge was supervising policy implementation under a consent decree. Deyle (1994), using two cases, did not find that it applied to the establishment of environmental policy regulations in highly conflicted settings. In *Innovating with Integrity* (Borins 1998, 50–63), I found more instances of comprehensive planning than groping along in a large sample of 217 semifinalists, and also found support for Golden's three hypotheses about when planning is more likely to be used than groping along.

This is precisely the sort of constructive scholarly engagement—a process of testing and refinement—that such a seminal hypothesis should attract. The critics having spoken, it was then up to Behn to take the debate to the next level. Having moved on to other fruitful areas of research—conceptual work on democratic accountability and empirical work on early performance management systems—Behn chose not to engage with his critics. Such a decision is both reasonable and common, as a scholar may well feel that there is more to be gained by moving on than by digging still deeper.[2] Whether because of Behn's decision not to engage further or simply because the debate ran its course, research on "managing by groping along" effectively ceased, with one exception. I continue to look at the incidence of both "groping" and "planning" reported by HKS Awards applicants and continue to seek to determine the reasons why some grope along and others plan. (Chapter 4 includes a discussion of groping versus planning in relation to the 2010 semifinalists.) My reason is simple: the question of incrementalism (Behn's "groping along") versus strategic planning is also a central theoretical question in the private sector strategic management literature, as exemplified by Mintzberg's (2009) career-long research on and advocacy of emergent strategy. I believe strongly that this question retains its relevance for public sector researchers and practitioners alike. Sometimes it is necessary to be a community of one.

Research about Public Sector Entrepreneurship

At the beginning of this chapter's discussion, I indicated my belief in the importance of distinguishing between private and public sector innovation. That being said, it is clear that private sector research can influence (at times subliminally)

---

2. This may well be a question of intellectual style, or indeed personality. Behn may be an instance of Isaiah Berlin's fox, a scholar who has many ideas, rather than a hedgehog, who has one idea, determinedly maintained.

assumptions and approaches adopted by researchers of the public sector. This may be particularly true of the community of scholars exploring issues of "entrepreneurship" among public servants. Although these explorations have produced some valuable insights into the types, approaches, networks, and career trajectories of the change agents they identify as public entrepreneurs and have sparked at least one controversial rebuttal, the concept of public entrepreneurship remains both diffuse and undefined. This may be a case of a borrowed concept with a reasonable claim to relevance being stretched to fit a quite different context, and not quite succeeding.

Nancy Roberts and Paula King (1991) were among the first authors to engage in this area of innovation research. They proposed a definition of public entrepreneurship as "the process of introducing innovation—the generation, translation, and implementation of new ideas—into the public sector." Researchers in both the innovation awards and "groping versus planning" clusters might well claim overlap here, since both groups study the process of introducing innovation. Roberts and King and the researchers who followed them, however, have very explicitly focused their attention on the people most involved in initiating innovations, studying their careers, their personalities, and, in more recent years, the networks in which they operate.

Roberts and King (1991, 1992) intensively studied three educational policy entrepreneurs in Minnesota who promoted the United States' first educational choice law, working as external lobbyists rather than as part of the state's bureaucracy or political system. The authors concluded that the entrepreneurs were less political and power-seeking than typical public sector executives and that they relied on the force of their arguments rather than on any official mandate. Roberts and King (1996) extended this research into a book that emphasized the role of collective entrepreneurship in achieving this educational reform, and set forth a model of radical change in which legislation (as opposed to bureaucratic decisions) is necessary and collective entrepreneurship is essential to its adoption. This model of collective entrepreneurship, it should be noted, is quite foreign to the private sector literature, which tends to favor a heroic narrative of rugged individualism on the part of its visionary leaders. These entrepreneurs have broad powers grounded in their controlling interest in their corporations, while simultaneously inspiring their employees and delighting their shareholders.

Teske and Schneider (1994) studied bureaucratic and political entrepreneurship in municipal government by surveying 1,400 city clerks in suburban American communities and asking them to identify entrepreneurial city managers or politicians. They found that city managers were less likely to be entrepreneurial when the city had a mayor, but that political entrepreneurs were more likely to be found when the community had a mayor's office, when mayoral races were competitive, and when the mayor's term was shorter than average—in other words, when there were electoral incentives at least to appear innovative. From follow-up interviews with the city clerks they found that city managers were more likely to be innovative if they had previously worked in another city and had a broad professional orientation.

Mintrom (1997) and Mintrom and Vergari (1998), continuing Roberts and King's interest in policy entrepreneurs who were engaged in lobbying for school choice legislation, surveyed leading public sector executives in the educational system, as well as academic and other experts in educational policy. They used this survey to identify policy entrepreneurs who were advocates of school reform in twenty-six states. They found that the entrepreneurs' presence and activities raised significantly the probability of legislative approval of school choice (Mintrom 1997). In a further study using event history analysis (a statistical technique discussed on pages 25–26 below with reference to diffusion research), Mintrom and Vergari (1998) found that when school choice policy entrepreneurs consulted external networks of comparable policy entrepreneurs in other states, the likelihood of school choice legislation being considered in their own state's legislature increased. Similarly, when the policy entrepreneurs networked in and around their own state government, the likelihood of school choice legislation being considered increased.

Pursuing a comparable line of inquiry regarding the role of public servants in initiating innovative policy, Howard (2001), in a case study of the implementation of a more generous means test for unemployment benefits in Australia, found that senior public servants, rather than politicians, played the leading role in policy development and implementation. He took this result as a demonstration of policy entrepreneurship on the part of Australian public servants.

Bartlett and Dibben (2002) undertook twelve case studies of local government innovation in the United Kingdom, each including approximately ten semi-structured interviews with the individuals most closely involved with the innovation. On the basis of content analysis of the interviews, they identified "champions" and "sponsors" who worked together to conceptualize and implement the innovations. They concluded that local governments are not simply large bureaucracies that stifle innovation, but that public sector entrepreneurs can indeed play a critical role in implementing innovations.

Focusing on elected officials rather than career public servants, Carter and Scott (2004) discussed foreign policy entrepreneurship: the tendency of individual members of Congress to become involved in and attempt to influence foreign policy issues. Using a data set of 2,600 instances of such foreign policy entrepreneurship, they showed that it has been increasing over time, especially since the end of the cold war. Not surprisingly, they found that this entrepreneurship has become increasingly partisan as well, especially if the majority party in Congress does not hold the White House.

Bernier and Hafsi (2007) used a different definition of public sector entrepreneurship—building a public sector organization or increasing its ability to deliver services and create value—to conceptualize a public sector entrepreneurship cycle. They derived the cycle by generalizing from a number of case studies, particularly those involving public sector corporations in Canada. According to their model, an individual entrepreneur dominates when an organization is young; then, as the organization grows, bureaucratization puts a stop to entrepreneurship. Later on, however, the organization implements systemic entrepreneurship, in which many people are involved in enhancing the organization's ability to deliver new services in new ways, thus overcoming the dysfunctions of bureaucratic rigidity.

Petchey, Williams, and Carter (2008) studied a program of lottery-based U.K. government grants for community cancer care. They found that when funding from the lottery ended, 83 percent of the programs succeeded in locating funding from mainstream agencies. The people who ran these programs came from a variety of backgrounds, some but not all with experience in the National Health Service. They had well-developed contacts within the local community and were able to identify unmet needs, conceptualize responses to these needs, and acquire mainstream funding to support their initiatives. The authors referred to these people as "street-level policy entrepreneurs," thus identifying one more species of public sector entrepreneur.

Mack, Green, and Vedlitz (2008) also cast their definitional net wide, interviewing 111 people involved with the establishment of two telemedicine projects in the United States. None of the interviewees was an elected official or official lobbyist; they were identified through an analysis of documents and then snowball sampling. The authors operationalized the extent that members of the network were entrepreneurial by using as their dependent variable the frequency with which each member of the network was mentioned in interviews with other members. The authors used both personal attributes (age, gender, education, familiarity with telemedicine) and situational attributes (membership in community organizations, the extent of their network of contacts) to explain variation in the dependent variable. The only two personal attributes that were significant were being a health-care professional and being familiar with telemedicine. In contrast, five situational attributes were significant: being an adviser to a health organization, being involved in formal discussions regarding the establishment of a telemedicine network, being involved in local social service organizations, being involved in local business organizations (though this relationship was negative), and having a preference for living in a small community. The authors concluded that individuals with tight links to the community, expertise, and networking skills were the most likely to be effective public entrepreneurs. Their "local pub-lic entrepreneurs" appear to have some common ground with Petchey, Williams, and Carter's "street-level policy entrepreneurs."

Considine, Lewis, and Alexander (2009) surveyed a total of 947 politicians and senior and middle managers in eleven municipalities in the Australian state of Victoria about their attitudes toward public sector innovation and the infor-mal networks with which they were affiliated. They found that in all the munic-ipalities, CEOs were turned to most frequently both for advice and for securing strategic information. Politicians were comparable to middle managers in net-work rankings. The authors also did an interview-based study using 104 key par-ticipants in four of the eleven governments. Paradoxically, this study accorded politicians higher status as innovators than the CEOs, even though the latter had more informal ties. The authors concluded that both formal hierarchical position and informal network relationships are important in explaining innovation.

However different the methods or subjects of study of the entrepreneurship research discussed to this point, the authors all had virtually unalloyed praise for the selfless dedication and achievements of public sector entrepreneurs—particu-larly if they operated outside the bureaucracy—and were interested in conditions that would encourage more such entrepreneurship. Teodoro, in his recent book *Bureaucratic Ambition* (2011), presented a very different perspective. His was a much more skeptical view of entrepreneurial public servants, reflecting the influ-ence of public choice theory, which assumes public servants and politicians to be primarily self-interested agents. He argued that some public servants attempt to advance their careers by moving from agency to agency (what he calls a diagonal career path) and "introduce[e] professionally fashionable policy innovations to [their new] agency" (17) as a means of consolidating their advance. Others, who seek rather to advance *within* their agencies (following vertical career paths), tend to maintain the status quo. Teodoro supported his hypothesis with cross-sectional data on police chiefs and public water utility managers, showing that those who have followed diagonal career paths were more likely to adopt professional inno-vations such as gaining departmental accreditation, for the police chiefs, and implementing water conservation rates, for the utility managers. In his model, innovation is less the result of dedication to improving the functioning of the public service than a tactic to be used in the quest for personal advancement. His focus on the careers of professional public servants does not address the phenom-enon of street-level policy entrepreneurs studied by Petchey, Williams, and Carter and Mack, Green and Vedlitz.

Considering the literature on public sector entrepreneurship as a whole, it is clear that it has evolved to put more emphasis on identifying situational variables to explain the existence of the phenomenon than on the personal attributes of the agents who embody it. Critically, there appears to be no consensus regarding the precise meaning of "public sector entrepreneurship." Consequently, individual studies, while registering valuable self-contained insights, do not build on each other to create a meaningful body of theory. Some studies demonstrate instances of public sector entrepreneurship, often using specific cases to prove that the phenomenon exists. Others identify a wide variety of actors who are public sector entrepreneurs, from Carter and Scott's (2004) American senators and representatives acting as foreign policy entrepreneurs to Howard's (2001) senior Australian public servants to Petchey, Williams, and Carter's (2008) street-level policy entrepreneurs. The more recent literature (Considine, Lewis, and Alexander 2009; Mack, Green, and Vedlitz 2008) has paid considerable attention to these individuals' roles as participants in networks and their mobilization of their networks to bring about change. Unlike the "groping along versus planning" research cluster, this area of research shows no sign of being abandoned, but it shows few signs of scholars making long-term commitments to the creation of common terms of reference and use of a shared methodology for studying public sector entrepreneurship.

Research about the Diffusion of Innovations

This line of research has a clear progenitor, Everett Rogers, who published five editions of his landmark text *Diffusion of Innovations*, the last in 2003.[3] Rogers saw diffusion as the result of interaction between the characteristics of a new product or technology and the population to which it had been introduced. Rogers's research dealt primarily with the diffusion of new technologies or products incorporating new technologies to the general public. His division of the population into groups that form a normal distribution (innovators and early adopters at one tail and laggards at the other, with the early and late majority in the middle) implies that the diffusion process can be mathematically characterized by a logistic curve.

Rogers's approach has been adopted by many other innovation scholars. Political scientists and students of public policy have applied it to the adoption of new policies (lotteries, school choice, hate crime legislation, electricity deregulation) and new management approaches (strategic planning, partnerships) by a group of jurisdictions. One of the most frequently used populations for these diffusion studies is the fifty (or sometimes the geographically contiguous forty-eight) states. In a recent review article, Berry and Berry (2007) referred to fifty-four such studies produced since 1990. The statistical methodology most often used was event

---

3. *Diffusion of Innovations* has been cited more than 48,000 times (Google Scholar, accessed May 8, 2013), making it one of the most cited books in social science. Given the tight focus of his research over his career, Rogers was intellectually a prototypical hedgehog.

history analysis, which employs a categorical dependent variable equal to 0 in years when a jurisdiction has not yet adopted the innovation being studied, and equal to 1 in the year when it was adopted. Once it has been adopted, no further observations for that jurisdiction are included in the data set. Berry and Berry advocated using an exhaustive set of independent variables (not all of which would be expected to display statistical significance in any one study), including the following:

—Motivational factors such as the severity of the policy problem, public opinion, and electoral competition

—Resources available to implement the innovation such as the jurisdiction's level of economic development, the professionalism of its legislators or public servants, and the presence of policy entrepreneurs or advocacy coalitions

—Obstacles to the policy such as its cost and public or political opposition

—Dummy variables representing other policies or the influence of other states

As the numbers make clear, many scholars continue to be actively engaged in pursuing research about the diffusion of innovations in the public sector. This community benefits, too, from a widely accepted model of the diffusion process and statistical methodology to use in applying that model. Diffusion research offers a unique lens through which to view the innovation process. The question it asks—What are the determinants of the diffusion of a particular innovation in a given population?—is different from those asked by scholars characterizing innovations, studying public sector entrepreneurs, or describing innovative organizations. Yet the factors considered by each of these groups will necessarily have an influence on the diffusion process. In chapter 6 of this book, I consider the determinants of the extent of diffusion for the HKS Awards semifinalists and discuss these findings in terms of the factors found to influence diffusion. It is my own acknowledgment of the continued value and vitality of this research stream.

Research about Innovative Organizations

The literature on "game-changing" private sector companies has long shown a fascination with the unique ecosystems they represent yet has, paradoxically, attempted to generalize their success for others to emulate: Apple in the glory days of Steve Jobs's second era as CEO, or, from the prehistory of the technological revolution, Bell Labs in its suburban Murray Hill, New Jersey, campus from the forties into the sixties (Gertner 2012). Researchers on public sector innovation—generally more modest in their aspirations—have also sought to identify and characterize innovative organizations, public sector entities supportive of innovation, as evidenced by the frequency and success with which they adopt or, as needed, adapt innovations. Members of this research community generally favor statistical analysis over case studies. There have been some notable exceptions, however, and I begin with them.

Case Studies

In his 1998 book *Sustaining Innovation*, Paul Light studied twenty-six nonprofit and government organizations in Minnesota that had a reputation for being innovative. Light wanted some large government agencies as part of his sample, but the group ultimately consisted of nonprofits, charter schools, and small state agencies that behaved more like nonprofits. Light also lacked a control group. He noted that all the organizations were well performing and he posited good performance as a prerequisite to innovation. He concluded by setting out what he found to be the four clusters of core values of innovating organizations: trust, demonstrated through internal and external collaboration; honesty, evidenced by a focus on the organization's mission and the creation of a supportive environment for experimentation; rigor in measuring performance and maintaining disciplined management systems; and faith in the organization itself.

Ellen Schall (1997), who led the turnaround at New York City's Department of Juvenile Justice that enabled it to win an HKS Award in 1986, discussed one very specific aspect of maintaining, as opposed to creating, an innovative organization: the succession plan she and her senior staff put in place to perpetuate the department's innovative culture after she left the organization. She ultimately did leave to join the Wagner Graduate School of Public Service at New York University, where she served as dean from 2002 to 2013.

Responding some years later to Light's research, in particular his inability to find a large, innovative public sector organization, John D. Donahue (2008) identified the U.S. Department of Labor under Secretary Robert Reich (who served from 1993 to 1997) as one such. Donahue was then assistant secretary of labor for policy, a political appointment, so his article can be read as the memoir of a participant leavened by his academic experience as a long-time faculty member at the Harvard Kennedy School.[4] Donahue's measure of innovativeness was the number of applications submitted by the Department of Labor to the HKS Awards after they were opened to federal government agencies in 1995. Between 1995 and 1997, the Department of Labor submitted thirty-six applications. Three were winners, one a finalist, and one a semifinalist. This was the strongest performance of any federal agency, even though the Department of Labor, while a large organization, is one of the smaller federal agencies.

---

4. I was aware of the Department of Labor's innovative culture from Reich's (1997) memoir of his term as secretary of labor as well as an interview I did with his second-in-command, Tom Glynn. I invited Donahue to expand on their stories by writing an article for the book I was editing (Borins 2008).

Donahue attributed the department's innovative character to the quality of its political appointees, starting with Reich himself, whom he characterized as a risk taker, a man of passionate conviction, and a charismatic leader. Reich's second-in-command, Deputy Secretary Tom Glynn, was a tough and experienced manager who put in place administrative systems supportive of innovation. These included designating a political appointee responsible for each new initiative, sharing ideas for policy development among the political appointees, and holding daily meetings of the political appointees, chaired by Glynn himself. Openness to innovation also encompassed the permanent public service, through town hall meetings Reich held in the department as well as his frequent visits with staff and the establishment of formal and informal rewards and awards for innovative staff. Reich frequently invited staff members who played major roles in developing a piece of legislation to the White House signing ceremony to meet the president. Donahue's list clearly has a specificity and practical application that Light's more generalized observations lack. These are elements of daily practice, as it were, rather than global commandments.

Carstensen and Bason (2012) documented the ten-year history of MindLab, an initiative by the Danish Ministry of Business Affairs that describes itself as "a cross-governmental innovation unit which involves citizens and businesses in developing new solutions for the public sector" (from their website, www.mind-lab.dk/en)

Their study provides a sustained view of the changing ideas of a government agency committed to encouraging creativity and innovation as to how best to advance that cause. MindLab was created in 2002 and in time became a joint venture of three ministries: Economics and Business Affairs, Taxation, and Employment. Carstensen and Bason note, too, that MindLab increasingly focused on developing expertise to support interorganizational collaboration and to help government understand the perspective of citizens attempting to deal with the complexities of public services. These two themes—collaboration and enabling access—recur repeatedly as we consider the current landscape of public sector innovation.

Statistical Studies

The statistical studies approach the question of what makes an innovative organization from a different perspective. Unlike case studies, which emphasize uniqueness, they survey large numbers of organizations, attempting to find factors that either promote or hinder innovativeness. These studies are primarily cross-sectional, defining a population of organizations and sampling within it at a given point in time. This differentiates them from diffusion studies, which use both temporal and spatial dimensions. Establishing a measure of innovation or innovativeness, these scholars seek to determine how much each organization has achieved in terms of that measure and then, crucially, to explain why. This approach automatically responds to the concern Light expressed about the absence of a control group for the organizations he studied. In some instances, the authors define a set of mutually exclusive and collectively exhaustive types of innovation, sometimes based on typologies used by researchers studying private sector innovation, and then set out to establish the determinants of each type. The innovation typologies they use typically vary from author to author, however, and this makes it hard to compare the findings of different authors.

It is important to note that the majority of these studies were undertaken in the United Kingdom. One of the legacies of New Public Management as practiced in both the Conservative governments of Thatcher and Major and the Labour governments of Blair and Brown was a strong focus on measuring and comparing performance of public sector organizations doing similar work through the use of "league tables." There was a common belief among all these governments that quantitative performance comparisons would lead to improved performance because the organizations at the bottom of the league table would learn from the ones at the top. In addition, quantitative performance data could drive central government decisions regarding funding or regulation of public sector organizations. The availability of such databases for groups of organizations such as local governments and hospitals has encouraged innovation research, resulting in a number of significant contributions to the literature. In addition, the U.K. government's Economic and Social Research Council has provided generous support for researchers to supplement publicly available databases with additional surveys of their own.

Coincidentally, at the same time that Light published his book of comparative case studies of small public sector organizations in Minnesota, Stephen Osborne (1998) published a book on innovation by voluntary and nonprofit organizations in personal social services in the United Kingdom. Osborne's was a quantitative analysis of a survey of 200 such organizations in three localities. He developed a four-fold innovation typology:

1. Total. Innovations that are new to the innovating organization and offer a new service to a new group

2. Expansionary. Innovations offering an existing service to a new group

3. Evolutionary. Innovations offering new services to existing groups

4. Developmental. Innovations improving existing services to existing groups
Among his key findings were that the more innovative organizations were newer, had at least one paid staff member, received most of their funding from government (Osborne 1998, 105), and had a stronger orientation to and more interaction with their external environment (191). Osborne, Chew, and McLaughlin (2008) replicated his original survey a decade later—an extremely valuable scholarly initiative that is unfortunately too rare—and found less total innovative activity (finding new

clients and providing new services) but more incremental development (improving services for existing clients). The authors attributed this to a change in funding policy between the Conservative Party, which was in power at the time of the original survey, 1994, and New Labour, which was in power in 2006, when it was replicated. The former preferred total innovation, especially if it was market-oriented, while the latter preferred continuous improvement (developmental innovation) within a policy context established centrally and reinforced by performance targets.

Osborne's typology was used in Walker, Jeanes, and Rowlands's 2002 study that identified and classified more than 250 innovations launched by British housing associations. Sixty percent were total, expansionary, or evolutionary, and 40 percent were developmental. The authors also found that half were undertaken by housing associations acting on their own and half in partnership with other housing associations, local governments, or private sector organizations. Walker (2003) then drew on this database to develop a set of eleven cases he used to study the innovative process in terms of phases such as gestation, shocks and triggers, and plans and approval. He reached the conclusion that formulaic and sequential management of innovation approaches were "overly simplistic and do not capture the iterative, complex, and inter-organizational way in which innovation needs to be managed by public service organizations" (100).

Boyne and others (2005) studied the determinants of the extent of adoption of one particular innovation, a centrally mandated management improvement program known as Best Value, by seventy-nine local governments in Wales. They found that the program was significantly more likely to be adopted by rural than urban municipalities, when it was concentrated on a limited number of services, and when the managers had prior experience of management reform. Based on the previous results in the literature, the authors had expected size of organization would be positive and significant, but it was not. They concluded that this unexpected result indicated a need to develop more sophisticated measures of the attributes of innovations and of organizations in models that attempt to explain adoption.

Walker (2006) then went on to survey multiple informants regarding 120 English municipalities, using twenty-two possible types of innovations. Factor analysis reduced these to a five-fold typology: new product; technological; technological with a market orientation (such as outsourcing); organizational; and ancillary (involving external collaboration and partnerships). At the time of the survey, three groups of determinants of the extent of adoption of these five types of innovations were posited: socio-economic characteristics of the municipality; characteristics of the municipal government such as its size and its political and managerial leadership; and public pressure for improvement in services. The regression analysis showed that most independent variables were not significant, but that the influence of those that were significant differed among the five innovation types. The one independent variable most consistently significant was public pressure from users and citizens for improvements in service.

In 2008 Walker again turned to a multiple informants survey of seventy-four English local governments. He posited four categories of innovation—service, marketization, organization, and ancillary—and by asking the extent to which each was a major part of a local government's approach to management, organization, or service delivery created dependent variables. Independent variables included both organizational characteristics (centralization, size, performance management systems, slack resources) and environmental characteristics. The surveys were conducted twice, in 2001 and 2002, generating 148 observations and enabling Walker to introduce a lag structure. The regression results again differed considerably for the different types of innovations, leading to the following conclusion:

> The most striking conclusion in this article is that relationships between antecedents and innovation types are relatively complex and need to be understood as such; different antecedents affect different types of innovation, and complementary relationships between innovation types is not perhaps as extensive as previously argued. . . . The findings indicate that relationships between individual variables and innovation type might not be the most useful way to advance knowledge in this field and that approaches based on configurations [of characteristics] are likely to advance the practice and research of public management innovation." (608–11)

Thus, Walker found that the patterns of determinants and organizational contexts for the different types of innovation he identified were different from one another, and were best studied separately. This finding calls into question whether organizational innovativeness can be measured on a single scale.

An important study applying a different theoretical framework to British data was recently undertaken by Salge (2010), a German scholar who completed his doctoral dissertation at Cambridge University. Salge applied Cyert and March's (1963) seminal model of organizational search (in which organizational leaders search for novel solutions when the performance of the organization deteriorates relative to aspiration levels or when excess resources are available) to innovative activity undertaken by U.K. hospitals regulated by the National Health Service. His goal was to test Cyert and March's hypotheses that key drivers of organizational search activity are performance problems and the availability of slack resources. Salge's dependent variable operationalized innovative activity using a measure of research activity, research projects per 100 employees, for the entire population of 154 nonspecialist English public hospitals from 2002 to 2007. This produced 616 observations. His findings were consistent with Cyert and March's model in a number of respects, for example, that hospitals increased their innovative activity when their service performance relative to their aspirations declined; that increases in financial slack increased innovative activity; and that hospitals with higher levels of organizational slack were more likely to undertake research in response to declines in service performance relative to their aspirations than hospitals with lower levels of organizational slack.

Although the largest group of researchers on public sector innovation worked in the United Kingdom, a number of other important studies used data from other countries. Lonti and Verma (2003), using a survey of workplace issues in the Canadian public sector in the late 1990s, analyzed the determinants of the adoption of flexible workplace innovations in Canadian government.[5] They surveyed first-level managers of work units having between 5 and 100 full-time equivalents at the federal level and in five provinces and built a database with 774 observations. They used a list of workplace innovations that included multiskilling, job enlargement, job enrichment, self-directed work teams, employee suggestion programs, employee attitude surveys, and information sharing with employees. A factor analysis demonstrated that the innovations broke down into two clear types: flexible work design and employee involvement mechanisms. They found some significant results: managerial autonomy was the most significant factor explaining the adoption of both groups of practices; perceived public pressure was also a significant driver; and budget constraints were a strong driver of the use of employee involvement practices. This study has unique strengths in its design, in particular its focus on the managers who are most knowledgeable about what is going on in the workplace as opposed to higher-level managers who are more remote from the shop floor, the clear specification of the innovative practices being studied, and its strong results. Though this research was undertaken earlier than many of the others noted here and was considerably more sophisticated than others being undertaken concurrently, it has been virtually ignored by other innovation researchers both within and outside this particular cluster. Geographical chauvinism may be partly to blame: Lonti and Verma used Canadian data, and they were not part of the same local research community as the other authors. Whatever the reason, the fact illustrates a regrettable—and, given the scholars' subject matter, ironic—narrowness of perspective.

Eran Vigoda-Gadot and others (2008) took a somewhat different approach to public sector innovation. Instead of studying public sector organizations directly, they surveyed the attitudes toward public administration innovation of 626 senior and middle managers in the voluntary sector who worked closely with public

---

5. I was a member of Lonti's dissertation committee, which was chaired by Professor Verma.

sector health and social service agencies in eight European countries. Vigoda-Gadot and his coauthors were interested in both the antecedents to and consequences of innovation. Their measure of innovativeness was the voluntary sector managers' assessment of whether the public sector organizations they were familiar with encouraged creativity and developed and offered new services. Hypothesized antecedents to innovation included responsiveness to citizen needs, professionalism, leadership and vision, ethics and morality, and organizational politics (which unlike the others was hypothesized to have a negative effect). The expected consequences included enhancing trust in government, improving the public sector's image, and increasing citizen satisfaction. After testing a variety of structural equation models, Vigoda-Gadot and his colleagues found that the best-fitting model included positive and significant coefficients for both responsiveness and leadership and vision as antecedents, and enhanced trust in government, public sector image, and satisfaction as consequences. This research, analyzing as it does external perceptions of innovativeness, is something of an outlier. Its implications for public sector managers are clear, if unsurprising. Managers wishing their organizations to be perceived as more innovative should be responsive to citizen needs, hire well-qualified leaders, and have a clear vision.

Fariborz Damanpour, a well-known scholar of private sector innovation, and Marguerite Schneider (2008) turned their attention to innovation in municipal government in the United States. They used surveys about innovative practices in U.S. municipalities undertaken by the International City/County Management Association in 1997 and 2003. Despite having combined two surveys at different times there was no temporal linkage between them, so this too was a cross-sectional study. From these surveys, which were completed by city managers for 725 municipalities, the authors developed a set of twenty-five innovations (for example service delivery initiatives, contracting out, outcome-based budgeting) and rated the innovativeness of each city by its aggregate score for adoption of them. The independent variables included expert opinion ratings of the cost, impact, and complexity of each innovation and the characteristics of the city manager—age, education, gender, tenure, attitude toward innovation—completing the questionnaire. This choice of independent variables assumes that the city manager plays a crucial role in stimulating innovation. Some statistically significant findings were that more urbanized and larger municipalities adopted more innovations, that the existence of a mayor decreased innovation adoption, that city managers of medium tenure were the most likely to adopt innovations, and that the city manager's enthusiasm about innovation positively influenced innovation adoption. The authors asked city managers about their political orientation, expecting it would have no influence, but they found that a liberal orientation had a positive influence on innovation adoption.[6] These results do accord city managers a key role in explaining local government innovation. One could ask whether Damanpour and Schneider paid too much attention to city managers and too little to politicians and the rest of the municipal bureaucracy because their paper lacked any independent variables for characteristics of politicians, particularly the mayor, and public servants. Some of the innovations I will discuss in case studies had their impetus in decisions of activist mayors. Though this is case based rather than statistical evidence, it differs from the pattern of Damanpour and Schneider's findings.

Walker (2014) recently published a meta-analysis of seventeen empirical studies of innovations in local government, many of which were discussed earlier. He chose cross-sectional studies where the author was attempting to explain a dependent variable that represented some measure of innovation across local governments. Walker then compiled the independent variables that were frequently used in multiple regression analyses and tabulated their sign and level of statistical significance. In terms of internal characteristics of local governments, he found that organizational size was strongly positive and significant, but did not find, on balance, a strong positive or negative relationship for slack resources. He found administrative capacity—generally measured as the percentage of staff who are administrative or supervisory—to be strongly positive as well. He also found organizational learning, operationalized as either the extent to which the organization employs professionals or the organization's involvement in environmental scanning or in professional organizations, to be another strongly positive influence on innovation. The importance of Walker's meta-analysis is that it assessed the weight of the evidence regarding a number of hypotheses about the determinants of public sector innovation. Surprising results of individual articles (for example, Boyne et al.'s 2005 finding that organization size was not a significant determinant of innovation) may turn out to be outliers and not of great concern when a large number of studies are compared.

A report (Gallup Organization 2010) prepared for the European Commission (EC) *Innobarometer 2010, Analytical Report: Innovation in Public Administration,* merits extended discussion, both for the ambitiousness of the survey it undertook and for its potential to trigger further research. The EC had been publishing reports on private sector innovation for a decade, but the 2010 report was the first to deal with public sector innovation. The report is not an instance of conventional academic research—one of my criteria for inclusion in this review—but it could certainly be used to generate such research. The report was based on a tele-

6. The negative sign on the dummy variable for the existence of a mayor supports the hypothesis that a weak municipal council, dominated by a powerful city manager or municipal CAO, would be more innovative than a council headed by a mayor.

phone survey of 4,000 public sector organizations at the national, regional, and local levels in twenty-seven European Union (EU) countries, with the number of interviews in each country roughly proportional to its population. The interviewees were either senior managers responsible for strategic decisionmaking or general managers, both of whom were assumed to have a good overall understanding of the organization. The survey instrument was very comprehensive, including questions about the characteristics of the organization, its recent service, communication, or process innovations, the organization's workforce and support it receives for innovation, the effects of innovations, drivers of innovation, barriers to innovation, procurement practices, and expectations about both innovation and the drivers of innovation in the next two years.

In its comprehensiveness and topics covered the Innobarometer questionnaire probably aligns better with the HKS Awards process than the survey instrument for any other study discussed here. Its structure, however, is somewhat different: the Innobarometer questionnaire consists entirely of categories developed by the researchers, while almost all of the questions on the HKS questionnaire are open-ended. Given the size of the EU sample, an open-ended questionnaire would have been very expensive and time-consuming to code. In terms of sampling, the Innobarometer study attempted a representative survey of the entire EU public sector, but the HKS Awards questionnaire is completed only by those who choose to apply.

Given the comprehensiveness of the Innobarometer survey, I will review only a few of its results. A full 88 percent of the government agencies surveyed claimed to have implemented at least one type of innovation in the past three years, and the average agency claimed to have implemented four of the nine possible types of innovation included in the survey.[7] Organization size was consistently correlated with greater innovative activity, and national level organizations were consistently more innovative than regional or local organizations. Seventy-five percent of organizations reported that they had developed an innovation on their own, and 65 percent had also developed an innovation in partnership with other public sector organizations. Forty-five percent reported that they had developed an innovation in partnership with private business, and 37 percent, in partnership with a nonprofit. Staff, management, and clients were roughly equal in their contribution of innovative ideas. The main drivers of innovation were new laws and regulations, new policy priorities, mandated new e-government services, and budget cuts. Paradoxically, the most significant barrier to innovation was seen as the lack of financial or human resources. Indeed, the authors of the survey remarked that those who completed the survey had "expectations that do not

---

7. The triad of service, communication, and process innovations was subdivided further into nine categories; for example, service innovations included new services and new methods of providing services or interacting with users.

seem to correspond to the current reality" of budget cuts, which would force innovation upon them. The report also dealt with the impacts of innovation: 76 percent of organizations reported that service innovations improved user access to information, 71 percent reported that service innovations had improved user satisfaction, 62 percent reported that process innovations had improved employee satisfaction, and 62 percent reported that process innovations had reduced costs.

The Innobarometer report was discussed at an Organization for Economic Cooperation and Development (OECD) Expert Workshop on Measuring Public Sector Innovation on February 21, 2013, in Paris, in which I participated. Concern was expressed about the reliability of the data, since the senior managers who completed the survey may have felt they were expected to report innovations, with the result that they duly reported incremental developments or even presented mere feasibility studies of possible initiatives as though they were innovations. The questionnaire, by providing a checklist of categories, does not challenge such reporting. Participants also noted that the activities reported to the Innobarometer survey were much less novel, significant, or effective than the strongest applications to an innovations award, for example the HKS Awards semifinalists.

Despite the concerns about the quality of the data, the Innobarometer database holds great potential for academic research. The report itself presents a series of bivariate tables, but the database could be used for multivariate analysis. An initial project would be analysis of the determinants of organizational innovation, using as dependent variables the various innovation measures and as independent variables a variety of organizational characteristics such as size and level of government, workforce characteristics such as education levels, and workforce practices such as measures to support innovation. Many other studies could be undertaken if this database were made available to the academic community.

A small number of studies have combined organizational performance measures with data on aggregate organizational innovation to see if innovation has an impact on performance. This approach differs from the evaluation of the impact of specific innovations in the context of an innovation award. Damanpour, Walker, and Avellaneda (2009) used as their dependent variable performance scores for U.K. local governments between 2002 and 2005 developed by the Audit Commission, a national government oversight body. The authors surveyed senior and middle managers in these local governments about their perceptions of the extent to which their governments had implemented three types of innovations: service, technological, and administrative. They then aggregated the responses into a measure of perceptions of total innovation. A number of control variables such as organization size, urbanization, service need, and service diversity were also included in the regression. Taking into account the control variables, which were significant, total innovation had a positive impact on organizational performance. The authors also measured the extent to which each government's innovative activity was focused on one or two types of innovation, rather than being spread evenly across all three. They found that focus had a negative and significant impact on performance, implying that too much focus undercut overall innovativeness.

Walker, Damanpour, and Devece (2010) went on to use the same data set in a slightly different way. Their dependent variable in this subsequent article was the Audit Commission performance scores for U.K. local governments in 2005. The authors hypothesized that management innovation affected performance both directly and as mediated by performance management practices. As in the earlier article, the authors surveyed senior and middle managers about their perceptions of the extent to which their organizations were innovative in terms of technological and administrative practices and their perceptions of the extent to which their organizations were using performance management techniques. These techniques included having in place a clear and widely understood framework of mission and values, measuring performance in terms of that mission, and taking action when results deviate from plan. The initial results were ambiguous, in that management innovation had an unexpected negative and nearly significant direct effect on organizational performance, but it had an expected positive direct effect on performance management, and performance management had an expected positive direct effect on organizational performance. The authors then re-specified a structural equation model in which management innovation, mediated by performance management practices, had a positive effect on organizational performance. They interpreted this result to mean that the presence of performance management practices encouraged managers to be innovative. The authors concluded that a more definitive result for the direct effect of innovation on performance might have been ascertained if their data had had a longer lag structure.

Salge and Vera (2012), as in Salge's (2010) previous study, used data about the entire population of 154 nonspecialist English public hospitals from 2002 to 2007 to study the impact of innovation on organizational performance. Their dependent variable was the patient survival rate, a standard measure of hospital quality used globally. Their measure of innovative activity included research and development funding, ongoing research projects per staff member, and publications per staff member, which were all sufficiently correlated that they could be reduced to one common factor. The authors hypothesized that innovation would influence quality but that it would be mediated through customer orientation (concern for the well-being of patients) and learning orientation (willingness to learn from mistakes), both of which were measured through perceptual surveys.

Control variables such as hospital size and the health status of the regional population were also used. The authors found that innovative activity had the expected positive and significant influence on quality for the entire sample. When they broke the entire sample into subsamples that included high and low customer orientation and high and low learning orientation, they found that innovative activity had a positive and significant effect on quality for hospitals with high customer orientation and high learning orientation, but was insignificant in explaining quality for those with low customer and learning orientation. The authors saw this as evidence that organizational culture has an impact on the ability of organizations to translate innovative activity into performance improvement. Taken together, these three studies provide some evidence that overall innovation has a positive impact on overall organizational performance. I find the Salge and Vera paper the most convincing because its measures of innovativeness are objective rather than perceptual, as was the case for Damanpour, Walker, and Avellaneda (2009) and Walker, Damanpour, and Devece (2010). The findings emerging from this stream of research are very significant because practitioners and scholars alike assume that the objective of innovation is to improve performance, and these articles have provided some empirical confirmation of this assumption.

The community of scholars engaged in statistical studies of organizational innovation is a particularly active and committed one, producing a steady stream of valuable research, much of it based in the United Kingdom. In addition to the original databases on U.K. local government, authors (Lonti and Verma 2003; Vigoda-Gadot and others 2008; Salge 2010; Salge and Vera 2012) have developed other databases and employed new conceptual models (Salge's application of Cyert and March's organizational search framework). At the same time, policymakers in several countries are demonstrating significant interest in increasing the innovativeness of public sector organizations and are using surveys such as the Innobarometer to establish at least a baseline of what is being done now, seeking to go beyond the baseline to explore how innovation could be enhanced. The OECD, European Commission, and Commonwealth of Australia (Arundel and Huber 2013) are either currently undertaking or planning to undertake additional surveys, and this holds great promise for the future of this research stream. If the data are made available, these surveys should serve as the basis for many more entries in a comparable literature survey chapter in the future.

Building on the Literature

Describing in detail multiple clusters or communities of research can produce an effect of fragmentation, and that is the negative side of the diversity this chapter details, a diversity that is a welcome sign of the vitality of the now well-established field of public sector innovation research. Key trends noted in this chapter that are of continuing importance to my own analysis in this book are the use of data from innovation award applications to learn more about the process of innovation and the statistical analysis of cross-sectional data from groups of public sector organizations to determine why some are more innovative than others. I will be making frequent reference to this growing literature, taking into account differences in methodology, of course, in particular the way samples are defined, and making every effort to indicate clearly where my own findings fit in. Diffusion of innovation studies and studies of public sector entrepreneurship are cited more occasionally, but they too clearly relate to my central question: What does the landscape of American public sector innovation look like now?

As I seek to answer that question I will also be making frequent reference to my book *Innovating with Integrity* (1998) and occasionally to my publications about public sector innovation that immediately followed it. Together they provide a stable point of comparison from which to determine what has changed in the past fifteen years, what has stayed the same, and what might happen next. I'll conclude with a return visit to the multiple communities of public sector innovation research to speculate on their futures and to discuss possible directions we might take that are suggested by my findings in this book.

3

The Class of 2010

In 2010 more than 500 applications were submitted to the Harvard Kennedy School Innovations in American Government Awards. Of these, 127 were chosen as semifinalists, 25 ranked as the top tier, and 6 as finalists, from which a single winner was selected. Collectively these applications form what I am calling "the Class of 2010," although I'll use the term most frequently to refer to the semifinalist group. What does this class look like? What are the major characteristics, or building blocks as I've referred to them elsewhere (Borins 2006), of the applicant innovations? What public management techniques or practices do they encapsulate? What are their funding sources, average duration, size in terms of budget and target population reached, organizational structure, and accountability relationships? I look for answers first in a sample of the 500 applicants who completed the awards program's short initial questionnaire, but my focus is the 127 semifinalists who went on to complete the long one (both questionnaires are reproduced in the appendix, 207–09).

This class portrait will be a comparative one, rather like those yearbook montages that bring together graduating classes of years gone by. Although the juxtaposition there highlights, often comically, the discontinuities between generations, our analysis will look as closely at what has not changed as at what has. The comparators I use are the sample of 217 semifinalists in the HKS Awards between 1990 and 1994 that I studied in *Innovating with Integrity* (Borins 1998); all 104 finalists in the HKS Awards, which included federal government programs, between 1995 and 1998 that I discussed in my article attacking the image of entrepreneurial public servants as "loose cannons and rule breakers" (Borins 2000a); and the sample of 56 applications from economically advanced countries to the 1998 and 2000 Commonwealth International Innovations Awards programs that I analyzed in two subsequent articles (Borins 2001a; Borins 2001b). The class of 2010 and its three comparator classes span most of the two decades from 1990 to 2010. The 1990–94 HKS Awards semifinalists cover the beginning, the 1995–98 HKS Awards finalists and 1998 and 2000 CAPAM Award applicants cover the middle, and the Class of 2010 covers the end of this period.

Admittedly, the composition of these comparator "classes" is not identical. I discuss at some length in this chapter, and again in chapter 6, the question of what precisely differentiates higher- and lower-ranked applications, both of which are represented here. Because I derive my samples from awards competitions, the differences are mainly in the fulfillment of the criteria of the particular awards program rather than in the characteristics of the innovations themselves. This justifies including both higher- and lower-ranked applications as comparators, given that it is characteristics we are seeking to establish. The classes were created by somewhat different processes. The HKS Awards chose 75 semifinalists annually, and out of the approximately 350 semifinalists between 1990 and 1994 (slightly fewer than five times 75 because in some years a few semifinalists had been chosen previously), I chose a sample of 217, stratified to ensure adequate representation of all policy areas. The HKS Awards chose approximately 25 finalists from the 75 semifinalists each year, and I coded all 104 finalists in the four competitions from 1995 to 1998 inclusive. The CAPAM International Innovations Awards received 119 applications in 1998 and 120 in 2000—far fewer applicants than the HKS Awards program—and used a much shorter application form. To build a data set that I could compare with the HKS Awards applicants, I sent out a questionnaire similar to the HKS semifinalist questionnaire to all 239 applicants. I received 83 responses, a response rate of 33 percent. To maintain comparability in terms of the socio-economic context of the applications, I used only the 56 applications from economically advanced Commonwealth countries (Australia, Canada, Malta, New Zealand, Singapore, the United Kingdom). As assessed by awards program judges, then, the "highest-quality" pool—those who had advanced to the highest rank in their respective competitions—were the 1995–98 U.S. finalists, followed by the 1990–94 U.S. semifinalists, and finally the initial applicants to the Commonwealth International Innovations Awards.

The comparisons to the three previous classes are based on data that I have already published rather than on additional analysis of unpublished data. This was a matter of necessity rather than choice, as it quickly became obvious during the research phase of this book that the data sets could not be reconstructed. The obsolescence of computer software was largely to blame, coupled with the (happily) developing career prospects of the talented student research assistants who performed the original data analysis. This has not proved problematic. I published results and analysis for most of the data I compiled in the previous studies. As a consequence, in almost every table in this book, at least one of the previous classes is available for comparison, and sometimes all three are.

In addition to comparisons to the two previous classes of the HKS Awards as well as the Commonwealth International Innovations Awards, I will make comparisons to the empirical innovations literature, including other innovation awards and cross-sectional surveys of innovation in public sector organizations, especially the EC Innobarometer survey (Gallup Organization 2010). The latter, by virtue of sampling from the entire population of public sector organizations in the EU and, fortuitously, asking many questions similar to those in the HKS Awards' semifinalist questionnaire, provides an important opportunity for comparison. This comparison addresses the concern raised by some scholars (Kelman 2008) about whether a sample of the strongest applications to an innovation award is representative of the entire population of innovations.

Coding and Comparing

Since so much of the analysis that follows is based on coding questionnaire responses and then comparing responses for different groups of innovations, it is important to account for the methodologies employed for both coding and comparing. The coding process used as a starting point the coding categories I had developed for *Innovating with Integrity*, modifying them as needed to reflect in as finely grained a way as possible the responses in the 2010 applications. Of course, none of the research assistants who worked with me on *Innovating with Integrity* and the studies that followed was available to repeat her work. My sole research assistant for this phase of the study, who coded both the initial and semifinalist applications between early 2011 and summer 2012, was Kaylee Chretien. Chretien was an outstanding student in my Public Management course as an undergraduate at the University of Toronto, Scarborough, receiving the course's highest grade, and I was very fortunate to secure her assistance.[1] Chretien and I both coded the applications, and our level of inter-coder reliability was an impressive .9. The coding process was essentially recursive, involving an ongoing dialogue to refine the coding categories and to categorize as sensitively as possible. (Our objective was always to minimize the number of applications falling into the "Other" category.) I deeply appreciate Kaylee Chretien's significant contribution to the research for this book, but I take full responsibility for the final result.

The HKS Awards questionnaires are self-reported, like much of the economic and social data compiled by government, for example, the census. Is self-reporting

---

1. Kaylee Chretien is now a public servant at Public Works and Government Services Canada.

likely to create biases that would affect the validity of the data? The HKS Awards make clear to applicants the four assessment criteria: novelty, significance, effectiveness, and transferability. A considerable number of the questions—for example, those asking for a developmental narrative—are not directly related to the criteria, so applicants would not know how to tweak their responses to improve their showing in terms of the criteria. The application documentation also states that expert judges will be evaluating the applications and finalists will be required to host a site visitor with expertise in the relevant policy area. Being less than truthful or candid will be problematic when the application is reviewed. I conclude that the HKS Awards program has taken appropriate steps to protect the validity of its data for both the judging process and for subsequent use in research.

To compare the 2010 semifinalists with the earlier classes, I ran simple regressions between any two distributions, for example, the characteristics of the 2010 semifinalists and those of 1990–94. If 37 percent of the 2010 semifinalists used information technology and 28 percent of the 1990–94 semifinalists did the same, those two numbers would be treated as one observation. If there were ten rows in a comparative table, there would be ten observations. If the two distributions were graphed, if each observation were identical, the relationship would be represented by a straight line on a forty-five-degree angle through the origin. Running a simple linear regression estimates that relationship statistically, where one distribution (say, the characteristics of the 2010 semifinalists) is estimated as a function of another distribution (the characteristics of the 1990–94 semifinalists) in the form $y = a + bx$. If the distributions are identical, a (the intercept term) would be 0 and b (the slope) would be 1. Simple regressions were thus used as a test for similarity between any two distributions, with ideal similarity occurring if the estimated intercept is 0, slope is 1, and the statistical goodness-of-fit measure (R^2) is strongly significant. We will be looking for how close any two distributions come to this ideal or how far they deviate from it. It is irrelevant which is designated as the dependent variable and which as the independent variable, but as a matter of convention I designate the 2010 distributions as the dependent variable and the earlier ones (1990–94 semifinalists, 1995–98 finalists, or 1998 and 2000 Commonwealth International Innovations Awards) as the independent variable. All the statistical analysis for this book was performed with great skill by Liz Lyons, a doctoral student in Strategic Management at the Rotman School of Management, University of Toronto, and I deeply appreciate her significant contribution to this book. She used the statistical analysis software Stata throughout.

Another possible method of comparison would be between individual row entries, such as the 37 percent of the semifinalist sample using information technology in 2010 and the 28 percent using it in the 1990–94 semifinalist sample.

Statistically these might be compared by testing for the difference in means of a binomial distribution. To illustrate: Assume there are two large urns each containing thousands of black and white balls in an unknown proportion. Balls are drawn from each large urn and placed in a smaller urn. Say that one small urn contains 127 balls, 37 percent of which are white, and the other small urn contains 217 balls, 28 percent of which are white. Could we say on the basis of the sizes of the samples in the two small urns that the proportions of balls in the larger urns are similar or different? Applying the binomial distribution to sample sizes of 127 and 217, it turns out that a difference in the sample proportions of more than 4 percent would be sufficient to lead us to conclude with 99 percent certainty that the population proportions are different.

I am not convinced, however, that the binomial model is appropriate for such comparisons because the tables present a *set* of possible answers to each question in the application. The answers are not independent of one another in the way that separate sets of balls taken from different urns are. In other words, this model is much better suited to comparisons of completely discrete entities. In addition, it would be possible to have two distributions with individual components that all differ by 5 percent, which the binomial model would indicate are all significant differences. But the overall pattern of the distributions, as measured by a simple regression between the two variables, could be similar. I have chosen, therefore, to be guided by both the overall pattern and the individual observation measures in comparing tables for the Class of 2010 with those for previous classes.

First Look: Consistency and Collaboration

The short questionnaire for initial applicants to the HKS Awards is intended to be quick and simple to complete and designed to encourage innovators to apply, while still providing enough information for the judges to choose semifinalists. (Semifinalists are selected by panels of two or three experts, either academics or practitioners, organized by policy areas. The process is discussed in more detail in chapter 6). The questionnaire used in 2010 asked applicants to describe their innovation, tell its story, and explain how it meets the four selection criteria of novelty, effectiveness, significance, and transferability (see the appendix for the complete initial applicant questionnaire). Applicants often found it difficult to summarize the innovation within the fifty-word limit of the first question and continued the description in their response to the second. For my purposes, the short questionnaire is valuable for its description of the innovations and for any information that could be used to predict which applicants would be selected as semifinalists. Table 3-1 shows the characteristics for initial applications for the 2010 HKS Awards and compares them to the sample of semifinalists between 1990 and 1994 used in

Table 3-1. *Innovation Characteristics for 2010 Initial Applications
(Semifinalists and Non-semifinalists) and 1990–94 Semifinalists*[a]
Percent except as indicated

Characteristic	All 2010 initial applications	2010 non-semifinalists	2010 semifinalists	1990–94 semifinalists
Collaboration within government	58	58	59	21
External collaboration	65	63	67	28
Information technology	36	35	37	28
Process improvement	29	30	28	34
Citizen empowerment	16	22	14	26
Use of volunteers	13	16	10	7
Use of market incentives	10	7	13	8
Change of public attitudes	11	12	9	13
Total characteristics	238	243	237	165
Number of Applications	234	126	108	217
Estimated slope (s.d.'s from 1)			1.08 *** (.9)	insig[b]
Estimated intercept			insig	insig
R^2 (goodness of fit)			.96***	.29 (insig)

Sources: 2010 applications coded by author and Kaylee Chretien; 1990–94 semifinalists: Borins (1998, tables 2.1 and 2.2).

*** p <.01 for slope and intercept estimates and R^2.

a. Column entries are percentages of the number of applications and add to more than 100 because most applications have several characteristics.

b. insig = insignificantly different from 0.

Innovating with Integrity. There were approximately 500 initial applications in 2010, of which roughly 150 were selected as semifinalists.[2] I wanted to code a large sample of the initial applications, with relatively equal subsamples of those selected as semifinalists and those not. I requested the HKS Awards staff to provide two-thirds of the applications not selected and one third of those selected, but with the two groups undifferentiated, so Chretien and I did not know when we were coding any particular application how it had been ranked.

What is the first impression of the Class of 2010? Even a quick glance at the table makes two observations clear. The incidence of characteristics for the Class

2. Only 127 of the 150 applicants selected as semifinalists went on to complete the much more detailed semifinalist application.

of 2010 semifinalists and non-semifinalists is very similar, usually different by no more than a percentage point or two, and this is reflected in the simple regression's estimated slope of 1.08, statistically insignificant intercept (that is, not significantly different from zero), and R^2 (goodness of fit measure) of 0.96. Both the estimated slope and R^2 are significant at 1 percent. In this and other tables I show how close the estimated slope is to 1 in terms of its standard deviations. In this case, the slope is 0.9 standard deviations from 1. A 95 percent confidence interval around the estimated slope would stretch from two standard deviations above it (1.26) to two standard deviations below it (0.90). This span includes 1, so we can say with 95 percent confidence that the estimate slope is not greater or less than 1. The strong statistical similarity between the characteristics of semifinalists and non-semifinalists suggests that the HKS Awards judges were not choosing semifinalists on the basis of the presence or absence of certain characteristics. This is explored in more detail in chapter 6, using multiple regression analysis.

Even more significant, when the 2010 and 1990–94 applicants are compared there is a dramatically higher incidence of interorganizational collaboration either inside government (58 percent) or between government and civil society (65 percent) in 2010 than in the early 1990s. The numbers then were 21 percent inside government and 28 percent between government and civil society. By interorganizational collaboration inside government, I am referring to collaboration either among organizations at the same level of government or among organizations at different levels of government. Interorganizational collaboration with civil society refers to collaboration between government agencies and the private sector or the nonprofit sector. For the other characteristics the table lists, the differences are no greater than 10 percent. As a consequence of the large differences in the collaboration variables, a regression of the 2010 semifinalists on the 1990–94 semifinalists had a statistically insignificant slope, intercept, and R^2; in effect the two were uncorrelated. (This was also the case for a regression, not shown in table 3-1, of the 2010 non-semifinalists on the 1990–94 semifinalists.)

In 1998 I noted with some surprise how much interorganizational collaboration the semifinalists I analyzed displayed (Borins 1998, 21–23). I am now more surprised at how much more interorganizational collaboration both the semifinalists and the non-semifinalists demonstrate.[3] Interorganizational collaboration has become an important topic of research in public administration, encompass-

---

3. In that section of *Innovating with Integrity* I used the category "holism" to include innovations that took a systems approach to problem solving, coordinated several organizations, and provided multiple services to program clients. The first and third of these do not necessarily engage multiple organizations, and the 29 percent of innovations coordinating multiple organizations was significantly less than the 61 percent displaying holism so defined.

ing both studies of collaboration within the public sector (Bardach 1998, 2008; Sorensen and Torfing 2011) and studies of collaboration between the public sector and civil society (Goldsmith and Eggers 2004; Ansell and Gash 2008; Donahue and Zeckhauser 2011). Most of these studies use multi-case methodologies to create typologies of initiatives, evaluate which have been more or less successful, and present advice for practitioners. On the basis of a meta-analysis of 137 cases of collaboration between the public sector and civil society, Ansell and Gash (2008) developed a model that included starting conditions (for example, a prehistory of cooperation), characteristics of the collaborative process (a commitment to trust building), and facilitative leadership (either an honest broker or a strong leader emerging from one of the stakeholders) as factors leading to successful (or, in their absence, unsuccessful) outcomes.

The complexity of the phenomena being studied—multiple-participant collaborative networks—seems to make it difficult to capture their essential characteristics in continuous variables that would lend themselves to quantitative analysis. Thomson, Perry, and Miller (2009) represent one of the initial attempts to create a quantitative multidimensional model of collaboration, which they did by asking the directors of all 1,400 organizations that participated in AmeriCorps in 2000 and 2001 about their experience in collaborations, producing a sample of 440. Kelman, Hong, and Turbitt (2013) used British data for crime rates for interagency-based Crime and Disorder Reduction Partnerships to show that when the partnerships prioritized both partnership management practices, such as building trust, and standard management practices, such as performance measurement, actual performance improved. Although the major focus of my research is innovation rather than collaboration, my findings here should prove valuable to scholars studying collaboration by providing very strong confirmation of its increased salience.

A number of the scholars discussed in the preceding chapter corroborate this finding of frequent collaboration in their own research contexts. Farah and Spink (2008, 83) noted that 80 percent of the applications to the Brazilian innovation awards reported collaboration with government agencies, the nonprofit sector, or business. Walker, Jeanes, and Rowlands (2002) observed that half the innovations undertaken by British housing associations involved partnerships. In his subsequent research, Walker (2006, 2008) found that the unhappily named "ancillary innovation," which included interorganizational collaboration, always emerged as a separate factor in his factor analysis. Although the EC Innobarometer study (Gallup Organization 2010, 43) presented its results in terms of organizations rather than innovations, it provided evidence of considerable collaboration. When asked how their service or process innovations were developed, 75 percent of the organizations sampled replied that they were developed by the organizationa themselves, but 65 percent said they developed innovations together with other public sector organizations, 45 percent together with nonprofits, and 31 percent together with business (totaling more than 100 percent because the respondents were referring to several innovations within their organizations). If these responses, which show considerable collaboration, were presented with innovations as the unit of analysis rather than organizations, they could be compared more easily to the results for the 2010 initial applicants and semifinalists.

What does this significant increase in collaboration suggest? One possible answer is that innovative public managers now are more frequently involved in developing responses to difficult and complex problems that cross organizational boundaries. For example, urban redevelopment initiatives usually involve both public and private sector organizations. Watershed management partnerships require participation of all jurisdictions touching that environment. Managers and organizations now collaborate because they must. Two decades ago managers more frequently launched initiatives to improve the effectiveness or efficiency of their own organizations. Collaboration, therefore, can fairly be taken as a feature of the innovation landscape, emergent in 1990–94 and well established, arguably even permanent, now.

Our first look at the Class of 2010 divided it only into semifinalists and non-semifinalists to consider a set of eight characteristics that emerged from the coding. Table 3-2 displays the incidence of the coded characteristics for all 127 semifinalists who completed the detailed semifinalist questionnaire, further disaggregating them according to the six policy areas by which they were classified by the HKS Awards judges and staff. The eleven coded characteristics in table 3-2 were derived from answers to parts of the first question in the semifinalist questionnaire: "Define your innovation. What problem does it address? . . . How exactly is your program or policy innovative? How has your innovation changed previous practice?" (see appendix, "Semifinalist Application Questions," question 1).[4] The incidences of characteristics for semifinalists differ between the initial applicant questionnaire and the semifinalist questionnaire. Not all semifinalists identified at the initial application stage completed the semifinalist questionnaire. Additionally, the semifinalist questionnaire was longer, permitting a more comprehensive presentation of the components and functioning of the

4. The appendix contains the 2010 initial applicant and semifinalist questionnaires. The 1990–94 semifinalist, 1995–98 semifinalist, and CAPAM applicant questionnaires are quite similar to the 2010 semifinalist questionnaire, although in some instances the order of the questions has changed. For the 1990–94 semifinalist questionnaire, see Borins (1998, 295–97). For the CAPAM applicant questionnaire see Borins (2001a, 730–31, or Borins 2006, 38–39).

innovations. Within those longer discussions, the characteristics might be found more frequently.

Looking at the incidence of characteristics for all 127 semifinalists, the third row includes any interorganizational collaboration in government, namely collaboration within one government and/or collaboration across levels of government (technically, the union of the two). Similarly, any interorganizational collaboration outside government includes collaboration with the private sector and/or the nonprofit sector. Both types of collaboration were observed in 80 percent of the sample. Collaborations ranged from formal partnerships among a number of small local governments sharing a function such as property assessment or firefighting to larger formal collaborations such as the Regional Greenhouse Gas Initiative, a carbon-trading initiative involving the public utilities of ten Eastern Seaboard states, to very large informal collaborations such as river basin management initiatives. Improving a management or production process was interpreted broadly and coded frequently. Citizen empowerment and information technology occurred approximately as frequently in the 2010 semifinalists as in the 1990–94 semifinalists, but organizational change occurred far less frequently. It was observed in only 3 percent of the 2010 semifinalists, but in 43 percent of the 1990–94 semifinalists (Borins 1998, 26). In addition, empowerment of a government workforce was coded only once for the 2010 semifinalists. This corroborates our "first look" finding that a significant shift has occurred in the focus of public sector innovation, a shift with obvious process-related implications. Fifteen years ago, innovative public managers were seeking ways to make their individual organizations work better. In 2010 the emphasis is on collaborative problem solving.

Table 3-1 shows that the incidence of all characteristics sums to 238 percent for all initial applications, and table 3-2 shows that it sums to close to 400 percent for all semifinalist applications, the latter based on the more detailed semifinalist questionnaire. Put differently, the average initial application included more than two different characteristics and the average semifinalist almost four. This result is substantially at variance with the approach taken in much of the statistical research on innovative organizations, which often began by assuming a set of mutually exclusive and collectively exhaustive categories of innovations. In my approach, I let the innovators speak for themselves, by coding what they regarded as the key characteristics of their innovations.[5] I then used exploratory factor

---

5. In a paper based on a pilot survey of Australian government middle managers about innovations introduced in their branches, Arundel and Huber (2013) also acknowledge the difficulty of creating a set of mutually exclusive categories and report that the managers they surveyed often described innovations in terms of several characteristics. They concluded, "The correct interpretation [of our results] is not that

analysis to see if some sort of intuitively plausible pattern or set of categories would emerge from the data generated by the innovators' self-descriptions. The first factor included all four types of collaborations, the use of volunteers from the public, and empowerment of the public—too many characteristics to be meaningful. The highest eigenvalue in the analysis was just 1 and the lowest uniqueness score 0.7, both indicative of weak and indistinct factors. (A factor analysis for all the initial applicants produced even weaker results.) I then calculated correlation coefficients among all the possible pairs of the four types of collaborations, for both the semifinalists and all initial applicants, and none was significant.

These results did not show a mutually exclusive and collectively exhaustive categorization of public sector innovations. Rather, I think of innovation as the creative solving of public management and policy problems, and the characteristics of the innovations as building blocks that can be used in the problem-solving process (Borins 2006). If the eleven characteristics presented in table 3-2 are considered building blocks for creative problem solving, then there are a total of 2,047 combinations of one or more such blocks that innovators can call upon. In developing their programs, innovators combine creativity, inventing unexpected combinations, with craft knowledge, experience to help in selecting the combination that is likely to be most effective.

How close do the characteristics of the 2010 semifinalists in the six policy areas defined by the HKS Awards staff compare to the characteristics of all 127 semifinalists? I have italicized instances in table 3-2 where a characteristic for a policy area differed by more than 20 percent from the full sample mean. There were none for "transportation, infrastructure, and environment"; "community and economic development"; "criminal justice and public safety"; and "health and social services"; and only one for "management and governance." The one policy area whose configuration differs most from the group as a whole is "education and training," with its relatively low incidence of collaboration within one level of government and high incidence of all other types of collaboration. Table 3-2 also shows regressions of the characteristics of each of the six policy areas on the characteristics of the entire group. The slopes are all within two standard deviations of 1, with most considerably closer. The intercepts are all statistically insignificant and the R^2 all significant at 1 percent. Of the six, "education and training" fits the least closely. In general, the uniqueness of innovations in the various policy areas depends more on the profile of their target populations and their place in the evolution of that particular policy area and on their relationship to emerging, dominant, or passing

---

40.4 percent of branches introduced a communications innovation, but that 40.4 percent of branches introduced an innovation that had the characteristics of a communications innovation" (p. 156).

Table 3-2. *Innovation Characteristics for 2010 Semifinalists*[a]

Percent except as indicated

	All semifinalists	Management and governance	Transportation, infrastructure, and environment	Community and economic development	Education and training	Criminal justice and public safety	Health and social services
Collaboration within one government	71	83	85	67	50[b]	65	69
Collaboration across levels of government	36	13	50	38	57	39	31
Any government collaboration	81	83	90	76	71	78	85
Collaboration with nonprofits	66	44	55	71	93	65	77
Collaboration with private sector	54	57	70	71	36	44	46
Any collaboration outside government	80	70	80	81	*100*	78	81
Improves a management or production process	70	70	70	52	86	87	62
Uses information technology	41	57	40	38	36	39	35
Empowerment of and consultation with public	24	35	35	29	21	13	15
Uses efforts of volunteers from the public	12	18	20	21	10	0	8
Uses market incentives in place of regulation	6	4	10	5	14	0	8
Organizational change in the public sector	3	4	0	0	0	4	8
Total characteristics	383	385	435	392	403	356	359
Number of semifinalists	127	23	20	21	14	23	26
Estimated slope (s.d.'s from 1)		.80*** (1.2)	.88*** (1)	.92*** (.6)	.71*** (1.7)	.85*** (1.7)	.97*** (.3)
Estimated intercept		insig[c]	insig	insig	insig	insig	insig
R^2 (goodness of fit)		.77***	.89***	.88***	.7***	.93***	.93***

Source: Coded by author and Kaylee Chretien.

*** p <.01 for slope and intercept estimates and R^2.

a. Percentages add up to more than 100 because characteristics are not mutually exclusive. In calculating the percentage of total characteristics, "any government collaboration" and "any collaboration outside government" were both excluded because they are both aggregates of the previous two characteristics.

b. Italics indicate when a characteristic for a policy area differed by more than 20 percent from the full sample mean.

c. insig = insignificantly different from 0.

trends in theory or practice than on the incidence of their characteristics. In chapter 7 I discuss this point in greater detail.

The increasing incidence of interorganizational collaboration can be considered from another angle by looking at the sources of funding reported by the semifinalists. Table 3-3 compares the level of government of the agency making the application with the levels of government and organizations outside government identified as having contributed to its funding. Roughly 10 percent of the applications were made by federal government programs, 40 percent by state government programs and 50 percent by local government programs. Just 10 percent of the semifinalists were federal government programs, but the federal government was recorded as having provided some funding for 45 percent of the semifinalists; state government, for 47 percent; and local government, for 47 percent. Since 52 percent of the semifinalists came from local government, this must mean that 5 percent of local government semifinalists received their funding entirely from sources other than local government. In addition, 24 percent of the semifinalists received funds from the private sector and 17 percent from nonprofits, particularly foundations. (In chapter 7 I discuss the specific foundations that appear as major funders of innovations in particular policy areas.) Finally, 13 percent of semifinalists received funding from user fees. The sum of the items in this column is 193 percent, indicating that the average semifinalist received funding from two sources.

The third column of the table shows the average percentage of the budget of the semifinalists provided by each source of funding. These range from 27 percent for nonprofits to 64 percent for local government. Clearly, the different funding sources are providing not token amounts but rather major funding for the semifinalists. In other words, interorganizational collaboration often extended beyond merely participating on steering committees, which appears to have been the case in the early 1990s, to active engagement as well as providing funding. Because the federal government was not included in the 1990–94 HKS Awards, I have not tried to compare funding sources for that period to those for the Class of 2010. Nevertheless, shared funding has now become an important characteristic of collaborative innovations. For the persistent innovator, this implies looking for a variety of sources of funding to bring an innovation to fruition. For the funder, providing partial funding represents a sharing of control, and funders must consider criteria to monitor the effectiveness, in terms of their own missions, of their contributions to a collaborative program.

Organizing for Collaboration

If consideration of funding sources provides one window into the phenomenon of collaboration and its implications, probing organizational structures and account-

Table 3-3. *Sources of Funding for 2010 Semifinalists*

Percent except as indicated

Source of funding	Level of government applying	Applications receiving funding	Average percentage of budget provided, by source[a]
Federal government	9	45	56 (48)
State government	39	47	54 (50)
Local government	52	47	64 (50)
Private sector		24	41 (25)
Nonprofits		17	27 (12)
User fees		13	51 (13)
Total	100	193	
Number of semifinalists	127	127	

Source: Coded by author and Kaylee Chretien.

a. Numbers in parentheses in column 4 indicate the number of observations used to calculate the average percentage of the budget provided by each of the funding sources.

ability relationships offers another. Here, too, there are reasonable grounds to identify an increasing institutional comfort with interorganizational collaboration, as reflected in a willingness to accommodate such collaborations within existing structures. In this instance, it is the lack of change over time—clearly indicated by the regression result—that is significant, rather than the reverse. Table 3-4 shows that about 60 percent of the innovations in both the 2010 and 1990–94 semifinalists come from line operations in one organization, line operations in several organizations, or nonprofits. These could be considered simple structures without coordination mechanisms. Conversely, approximately 40 percent of both groups of semifinalists had more formal coordinating structures. Here, too, the regression result—slope close to 1, statistically insignificant intercept, and high and statistically significant R^2—indicates little change over two decades. This lack of change is surprising, given the increased incidence of interorganizational collaboration we've charted. This might be the result of public servants' having grown increasingly familiar with interorganizational collaboration and therefore being able to effect it without having to resort to formal structures. But it must also be noted that this result might be due to measurement error. The 1990–94 semifinalist questionnaire required a description of the applicant innovation's organizational structure and accountability relationship, whereas the 2010 semifinalist questionnaire required only an organizational chart. It may be that organizational charts do not capture the existence or subtlety of coordination mechanisms.

Table 3-5 shows the accountability relationships of the semifinalist innovations as determined by the descriptions for 1990–94. It and the organizational charts

Table 3-4. *Organizational Structure of Semifinalist Innovations*
Percent except as indicated

Structure	2010 semifinalists	1990–94 semifinalists
Line operation in one organization	43	43
Several line operations	9	5
Nonprofit corporation	8	12
Program coordination from a line organization	34	25
Program coordination from a central agency	3	7
Interdepartmental committee, loose arrangement	4	7
Other	0	4
Total	101	103
Number of semifinalists	127	217
Estimated slope (s.d's from 1)		1.13 *** (.9)
Estimated intercept		insig[a]
R^2 (goodness of fit)		.93***

Sources: 2010 semifinalists coded by author and Kaylee Chretien; 1990—94 semifinalists: see Borins (1998, table 5-2).

*** $p < .01$ for slope and intercept estimates and R^2.

a. insig = insignificantly different from 0.

in 2010 show that the overall pattern has stayed relatively similar over the two decades. Approximately three-quarters of both groups reported through normal hierarchical channels. There were some changes, however: much less reporting to advisory committees in 2010 (7 percent) than in 1990–94 (27 percent), and less reporting to funding sources as well as directly to political authorities in 2010 than in 1990–94. All of these changes indicate less use of formal coordinating mechanisms for reporting, even though there was considerably more interorganizational collaboration in 2010 than in 1990–94. Consistent with the discussion of organizational structures, Table 3-5 also indicates that inter-organizational collaboration is now becoming daily practice and standard culture, with less need for formal accountability mechanisms.

Does Size Matter?

To this point I have considered the characteristics of the semifinalist innovations in terms of what they were doing. But the applications also provide information regarding the scale on which they were doing it. Table 3-6 presents two measures of scale: populations reached and budgets. The populations reached have increased slightly over two decades, from 202,000 in 1990–94 to 236,000 for the

Table 3-5. *Accountability Relationship of Semifinalist Innovations*

Percent except as indicated

Relationship	2010 semifinalists	1990–94 semifinalists
Normal channels	75	71
Direct to political authority	2	6
To board of directors	13	13
To advisory committee	9	27
To funding source	1	7
Other	1	1
Total	101	125
Number of semifinalists	127	217
Estimated slope (s.d.'s from 1)		1.07 *** (.5)
Estimated intercept		insig[a]
R^2 (goodness of fit)		.93***

Sources: 2010 semifinalists coded by author and Kaylee Chretien; 1990—94 semifinalists: see Borins (1998, table 5-3).

*** p <.01 for slope and intercept estimates and R^2.

a. insig = Insignificantly different from 0.

Class of 2010. The largest innovations are found at the state level, so the expansion of the HKS Awards to include the federal government in 1995 did not increase average population reached.

The percentage of the target population reached by the semifinalists stayed constant at slightly less than half between the early 1990s and 2010. Meanwhile, the average operating budget for the semifinalists has increased by a factor of 3.6, from $5.9 million to $ 21.5 million, and average capital budgets, by a factor of 7.6. Given the small number of instances where capital budgets were recorded, the operating budget is the more relevant comparator. Some of the increase might be accounted for by inflation—U.S. prices nearly doubled over that two-decade period. Some might also be explained by the fact that innovations in 2010 reached 18 percent more people than in 1990–94 (236,000 versus 202,000). Discounting inflation and the slight increase in scale, the average budget for the semifinalists increased by 55 percent, which is substantial. Jonathan Walters's (2008, 22–23) history of the HKS Awards makes the point that after approximately a decade of experience, judges became less likely to recognize what were colloquially referred to as "boutique innovations," small programs that were effective in a particular context but were unlikely to be scaled up. However, the data in table 3-6 do not suggest that boutique innovations accounted for a significant share of the semifinalists in the early

Table 3-6. *Measures of Size of Innovations*

Measure	All 2010 semifinalists	2010 federal	2010 state	2010 local	1990–94 state and local semifinalists
Population reached	236,000 (81)[a]	140,000	439,000	94,000	202,000 (157)
Percentage of target population reached	47 (66)	NA	NA	NA	48 (116)
Operating budget ($ million)	$21.5 (110)	$4.4	$40	$10.7	$5.9 (185)
Capital budget ($ million)	$45 (29)	NA	NA	NA	$5.9 (41)
Number of semifinalists	127	11	50	66	217

Sources: 2010 semifinalists coded by author and Kaylee Chretien; 1990–94 semifinalists: see Borins (1998, tables 5-1 and I-2).

NA = Not available

a. Numbers in parentheses indicate the number of observations used to calculate averages (for many applications data were incomplete).

1990s, and were then replaced by much larger programs in 2010. The increased scale of innovations in budgetary terms might be a result of innovators' being able to find several sources of funding or a result of greater public acceptance of public sector innovation. Whatever the reason, better funding clearly permits more extensive program development and the delivery of more services.

The Class of 2020

Up to this point I have maintained a dual focus: one eye on the past, the other on the present. But an implicit question that runs through this book is "What about the Class of 2020?" Using characteristics harvested from the semifinalist applications, the final metrics considered here relate to the effectiveness and sustainability of the HKS Awards program itself. The findings go some way to answering at least one part of the question. There seems no reason to believe there will not be such a class. And that is good news, for practitioners and scholars alike.

Data on the age of an innovation since inception were available for the applicant innovations in 2010 but not for the 1990–94 semifinalists. As shown in table 3-7, it averages 5.75 years for the entire Class of 2010—an average of 6.6 years for semifinalists and 4.9 for non-semifinalists. One of the HKS Awards program's criteria is effectiveness, and an average duration for an innovative program of almost 6 years should certainly be sufficient time to demonstrate its effectiveness. So the HKS Awards program is not being swamped by applications that are unproven because they have been in operation for only a short time. The dif-

Table 3-7. *Duration of Innovation and Previous Application Experience,*
2010 Semifinalists and Non-semifinalists

Percent except as indicated

	2010 semifinalists	2010 non-semifinalists
Average duration (years since inception)	6.6 years	4.9 years
Did not apply previously	68	76
Applied previously, not selected	21	19
Applied previously, semifinalist	7	2
Applied previously, top 50 or finalist	5	3
Number of applications	127	126

Source: Coding by author and Kaylee Chretien.

ference of 1.5 years in average duration between semifinalists and non-semifinalists would be statistically significant on its own, but when included in a multiple regression intended to explain the determinants of the selection of semifinalists, duration is not significant (as is demonstrated in chapter 6).

The data on previous applications by the Class of 2010 show that more than 70 percent of the entire class did not apply previously. From the standpoint of the sustainability of the HKS Awards program, that, too, is a heartening result, showing that the applicant pool continues to be refreshed with new applicants. If most applicants had applied previously, it would mean the program was drawing repeatedly on the same increasingly shallow pool, which would clearly be a threat to its sustainability. In its early years as the State and Local Government Awards program, it received approximately 1,500 applications every year; it now receives approximately 500 applications each year. This is partly because the organizers of the HKS Awards have discouraged repeat applications and changed their outreach approach from maximizing the number of applications to working with policy area experts to ensure that the major new trends—"the interesting things that are happening" (Farah and Spink 2008)—are well represented in the applicant pool. Even though the current level is considerably lower, it is sufficient to ensure the viability of the program.[6] In the near term several interesting things that are happening are likely to provide a considerable number of new applications, including the establishment of chief innovation officers and innovation labs in many municipal

6. Hartley and Downe's (2007) criteria for measuring the effectiveness of awards programs include having a large number of applicants from the population from which awards holders are drawn, having an increasing number of applicants, and having repeat applicants. In my view these criteria are more relevant to a threshold award intended to improve organizational performance in a small population than to a competitive award intended to identify and diffuse leading-edge ideas and practices in a large population.

Table 3-8. *Applicants' Primary Contact, 2010 Semifinalists*

Primary contact	Percentage of total
Agency head	8
Manager to whom program manager reports	23
Program manager	31
Staff person (for example, public affairs)	36
Other (for example, partner outside government)	3
Number of semifinalists	127

Source: Coding by author and Kaylee Chretien.

governments (Georges, Glynn-Burke, and McGrath 2013a, 2013b) and the use of innovation challenges by both governments and major nonprofits to stimulate new solutions to management and policy problems.

Table 3-7 shows that a slightly higher percentage of the semifinalists than of the non-semifinalists had applied previously and had been selected as semifinalists or higher. I look at this relationship in reverse in chapter 6, to ask whether it is more likely that an initial applicant who had applied previously would be selected as a semifinalist than an initial applicant who was applying for the first time. Indeed, previous semifinalists were more likely to be selected a second time than initial applicants were to be selected a first time.

The 2010 semifinalist applicants were required to designate a primary contact for the HKS Awards program. Table 3-8 shows a great diversity of primary contacts, including agency heads, managers to whom the manager of the innovative program reports, the program manager him-/herself, and, most frequently, a staff person. The questionnaire does not require applicants to indicate who actually prepared the application. Given the length of the questionnaire, it would be most reasonable to assume that it is usually completed either by the program manager or a staff person. Many of the staff people indicated as primary contacts worked in public affairs or proposal-writing functions. Given the importance of grants from other levels of government, foundations, and the private sector for funding innovations, it is reasonable to surmise that proposal writing has become an increasingly important staff role. Even though the agency head or manager to whom the program manager reports is indicated as the primary contact 31 percent of the time, it is unlikely they would actually have the time or detailed knowledge to write the application. That said, the dispersion of primary contacts can be considered a welcome sign. Applications do not come only from the program manager. Staff responsible for public affairs or proposal writing are often involved in writing the application, and agency heads or the manager to whom the innovative program manager reports are often willing to serve as the primary contact. Both indicate a widespread willingness in the organization to take ownership of the innovation as well as the importance attached to the prestige of winning the award.

Conclusion: Broadly Similar, with a Major Difference

What have we learned about the Class of 2010 so far? This chapter has sought to sketch the first outlines of a portrait, and it is clear that certain distinguishing features have already taken shape. We noted at the outset that 2010 semifinalists look quite similar to non-semifinalists. (In chapter 6 I explore this relationship more fully, providing a regression analysis of the statistical determinants of selection as a semifinalist.) Compared to an earlier comparator, the 1990–94 semifinalists, a striking difference emerges in 2010: a much greater incidence of interorganizational collaboration, whether within the public sector or between the public sector and either the nonprofit or the private sector. Other metrics reinforce this first impression. Funding data for the Class of 2010 reveals that *all* levels of government, as well as foundations and the private sector, are deeply involved in funding innovations and that the typical innovation receives funding from two sources. Despite the much greater incidence of interorganizational collaboration for 2010 semifinalists than for those from 1990–94, the incidence of other innovation characteristics—process improvement, the use of information technology, citizen empowerment, the use of citizen volunteers, and the use of market incentives—was roughly comparable. If we consider these characteristics to be the building blocks that public managers use in developing innovative solutions to policy and management problems, then one building block has become much more important: interorganizational collaboration.

When we compare the entire group of 127 semifinalists in the Class of 2010 with the six different policy areas that make up the group, it is apparent that the characteristics of the innovations in individual policy areas to a great extent mirror the characteristics of the entire group. This does not mean that there are no differences among the six policy areas. Chapter 7 discusses in detail the ways in which the semifinalists' diversity derives from the problems they tackle and their target populations, rather than the building blocks they use.

Both the 1990–94 and the 2010 semifinalists display a similar incidence of two main types of organizational structure: (1) simpler programs based in one or several organizations or nonprofit corporations and (2) more complicated structures that make greater use of explicit coordination mechanisms. In addition, normal hierarchical accountability relationships were observed for three-quarters of both groups of semifinalists. These results are surprising because of the much greater incidence of interorganizational collaboration among the 2010 semifinalists. This suggests that interorganizational collaboration is becoming common practice and complicated organizational structures and accountability relationships are no longer required to enforce or sustain collaboration.

The average sizes of both classes of semifinalists were similar in terms of target populations served, 236,000 in 2010 and 202,000 in 1990–94. The $21.5 million average operating budget for the 2010 semifinalists innovations was almost four times that of the 1990–94 semifinalists' $5.9 million average operating budget. Slightly more than half of this increase can be explained by inflation or the increase in population served, so the more recent group of semifinalists were operating at a higher scale in terms of per capita spending.

Finally, what does our initial encounter with the Class of 2010 tell us about the effectiveness of the HKS Awards program in terms of its own stated objectives and, equally important, about the prospects for a Class of 2020? A number of the characteristics this chapter has considered attest to the sustainability of the HKS Awards program's design. Initial applications, both semifinalist and finalist, have been in operation for almost six years on average since their inception, long enough to demonstrate results. More than 70 percent of initial applications are first-time rather than repeat applications, indicating a deep rather than shallow applicant pool. Perhaps most important, the applications demonstrate a wide diversity of primary contacts: the manager of the innovative program; his or her superiors, including the agency head; and agency staff, such as those in public affairs. If the primary contact is or represents the person who completes the detailed semifinalist application, it indicates widespread organizational interest in and willingness to advocate for the applicant innovations. The future looks good for the Class of 2020.

4

Present at the Creation

Innovations are not static and they are often complicated. You cannot code more than 500 descriptions of innovative initiatives over a twenty-year period of research without realizing that. A successful public sector innovation process depends on an evolving interplay of interpersonal, organizational, political, social, and economic factors. What is more, it grows out of a history of previous successful, and unsuccessful, efforts. Here I will be investigating both this history and this interplay, with a particular focus on the beginning of the innovation process—the circumstances of its creation. As in chapter 3, I approach the subject from a variety of perspectives. I look first at new data for the Class of 2010 regarding the novelty of its innovations. I then consider the organizational level and gender of the initiators who launch the innovations, as well as the triggering circumstances and the nature of the thinking and planning processes initiators employ. In addition, I delve into secondary analysis of the relationships among the circumstances of creation. Are certain types of initiators more likely to be present at the creation together? Is there a pattern of certain types of initiators being associated with certain trigger factors? Are there consistent determinants of the characteristics of the thinking and planning processes?

Some of the data regarding circumstances of creation are also available for the three antecedent innovation data sets (U.S. semifinalists, 1990–94; U.S. finalists, 1995–98; and Commonwealth International Innovations Award applicants in 1998 and 2000). The only instance where I analyzed the relationships among the circumstances of creation was for the 1990–94 innovations (Borins 1998, 37–65), primarily because the other two data sets were too small for the results of correlation analysis and regression modeling to be significant. Consequently, I compare the results of the secondary analysis of 127 semifinalists in 2010 to the

61

results of analysis for the 217 semifinalists between 1990 and 1994. I would have preferred to have a recent semifinalist data set closer to that size by including semifinalists from several other years. In a more perfect research world, that would have been possible. As it is, I felt it was more important to allocate the available resources to code initial applications to the 2010 awards, something I did not undertake in my previous work. Finally, where relevant, I provide comparisons to other data sources about public sector innovation, in particular the EC Inno-barometer's large cross-sectional sample of public sector organizations.

New or Newish?

I begin this analysis with the question of novelty because of its continuing impor-tance to the HKS Awards program itself. The program's original mandate included hastening the diffusion of good ideas throughout the public sector, and the novelty of those ideas has been one of the HKS Awards selection criteria from the outset (Walters 2008, 18). Global novelty is not intrinsic to the definition of an innovation. An initiative still constitutes an innovation if it is new to the organization in which it is being implemented. The HKS Awards program, how-ever, seeks global novelty—in effect leading-edge innovations. To determine this, the second question in the semifinalist questionnaire asks whether an innovation is an application or a replication of another innovation; if so, which program and where; and how the semifinalist adapted or improved the original innovation (see appendix, "Semifinalist Application Questions," question 2).

Table 4-1 charts the answers to that question. Forty percent of the 2010 semi-finalists replied that they hadn't heard of other programs or initiatives doing exactly the same thing, but 64 percent indicated they were replicating an original innova-tion elsewhere, and another 10 percent said that they extended the reach of an original innovation. (Multiple answers were possible.) Conceptually, there is no contradiction if a semifinalist replies that she thinks what she is doing in its total-ity is original, even if certain components of it replicate other programs. The HKS Awards judges provide a check on claims of originality. An applicant may think her program is original, but the judges, chosen for their broad-based knowledge of the state of practice nationally, may well be aware of similar programs elsewhere.

There is another way to think about and access the concept of novelty. In my 2011 article "Making Narrative Count: A Narratological Approach to Public Man-agement Innovation" (Borins 2012, 173), I used a somewhat different coding scheme for the thirty-one finalists and winners in 2008 and 2009, considering whether the innovation had a "prehistory." I was looking for some sequence of sig-nificantly related events preceding the innovation's launch, what screenwriters call a backstory. It might have involved small initial steps, such as those taken during

Table 4-1. *Semifinalists' Questionnaire Responses Concerning Novelty of Their Innovations*

Percent except as indicated

Response	Percentage making this response
We haven't heard of anyone else doing this.	40
Our innovation added features to an original innovation.	64
Our innovation extended the reach of an original innovation.	10
Number of semifinalists in database	127

Source: Applications coded by author and Kaylee Chretien.

the administration of Governor Michael Dukakis of Massachusetts in the 1980s that were precursors to the comprehensive health insurance program enacted in 2006 under Governor Mitt Romney, an HKS Awards winner in 2009. I was particularly interested in stories involving research about other programs, especially replication (with appropriate modification) of them. One such example was the Intelligence Community Civilian Joint Duty Program, an HKS Awards winner in 2008, which required senior executives in the sixteen federal intelligence agencies to serve tours of duty outside their home agency. It was modeled on a similar provision for senior military leaders included in the Goldwater-Nichols Department of Defense Reorganization Act of 1986. I found that twenty-five out of thirty-one programs had a "prehistory" defined as either small initial steps or research and replication of other programs. Revisiting the 2008 and 2009 finalists, I found that fourteen of thirty-one, or 45 percent, included some element of research and replication. This result, as well as the coding of the question about novelty for the 2010 semifinalists, indicates that innovators typically are aware of other related initiatives, either in their own jurisdiction or elsewhere, and this awareness influences their own design choices. What this perspective on novelty also makes plain is that innovations are, above all, human creations, the product of individual and collective imagination, ingenuity, and effort.

Still Local, Still Heroes

Like most academic studies, *Innovating with Integrity* came with a subtitle: *How Local Heroes Are Transforming American Government*. The reference to local heroes was intended to encapsulate one of the book's key findings: frontline public servants and middle managers were the most frequent initiators of innovations. I considered this both title-worthy and surprising in light of the traditionally top-down and politically risk-averse nature of public management at the time, and

Table 4-2. *Initiators of the Innovation*

Percent except as indicated

Initiator	2010 semifinalists	1995–98 finalists	1990–94 semifinalists	Commonwealth awards, 1998 and 2000
Political executive	27	NA	NA	NA
Politician as legislator	11	NA	NA	NA
All politicians	34	27	18	15
Agency head	44	28	23	39
Middle manager	40	43	NA	75
Frontline staff	22	27	NA	39
Middle manager or frontline staff	46	57	48	82
Interest group leader or member	11	14	13	2
Client or partner	27	5	2	5
Citizen	4	10	6	0
Other	1	10	4	9
Number of innovations	114	104	217	56
Estimated slope (s.d.'s from 1)		.77**	.88*	.41**
		(1)	(.3)	(4.4)
Estimated Intercept		insig[a]	insig	13.2**
R^2 (goodness of fit)		.60**	.56*	.58**

Sources: 2010 applications coded by author and Kaylee Chretien: 1995–98 finalists: Borins (2000a, 500); Commonwealth awards innovators: Borins (2001a, 723); 1990–94 semifinalists: Borins (1998, table 3-1).

NA = Not available

* $p <.1$, ** $p <.05$ for slope and intercept estimates and R^2.

a. insig = insignificantly different from 0.

equally in view of the popular stereotype of the cautious, rule-bound, or downright obstructionist bureaucrat—a stereotype very far removed from the individuals I was encountering in the innovation descriptions I was coding.

Innovating with Integrity's surprising finding remains true for the Class of 2010. Table 4-2 shows the pattern of answers to the semifinalist application's question about initiators: "What individuals or groups are considered the primary initiators of your program?" (see appendix, "Semifinalist Application Questions," question 3). Forty-six percent of innovations were initiated by middle managers or frontline staff. This is almost identical to the percentage for the 1990–94 semifinalists. It is slightly lower than the percentage for the 1995–98 finalists, and considerably lower than the 82 percent of innovations initiated by middle managers or frontline public servants in the 1998 and 2000 Commonwealth International Innovations Awards initial applicants. The Commonwealth sample included a much higher proportion of technology-based innovations (57 percent) than the

U.S. samples (Borins 2006, 12). At that time ministers and senior public servants were far less technologically savvy than many of their frontline staff, particularly the younger ones, so technology innovations were predominantly bottom-up in their origins (Borins 1998, 139–43). This will cease to be a factor as this technologically adept new generation rises through the ranks. Notwithstanding the general increase in levels of technological literacy, a comparable generational difference might well be found today in relation to innovations employing social media.

The 2010 semifinalists do indicate a somewhat higher incidence of initiation by politicians, agency heads, and program clients or partners than any of the three previous groups. Here, too, we may be seeing the effects of the much greater level of interorganizational collaboration displayed by the Class of 2010 than by its 1990–94 counterpart. The more frequent identification of a program's clients or collaborators as initiators in 2010 (27 percent) than in 1990–94 (2 percent) is further evidence of that trend. This is corroborated by a correlation between initiation by clients of, or participants in, a program and collaboration outside of government in 2010 of .26, significant at 1 percent. Furthermore, within the traditional vertical authority relationships that still govern public sector organizations and agencies, it is difficult for frontline staff or middle managers to initiate collaborative innovations. Collaboration usually requires agency heads or politicians to negotiate the informal interorganizational agreements or formal written protocols that govern such partnerships. The Class of 2010 data offer a limited measure of support for this latter hypothesis. The correlation between initiation by any politician and any collaboration within government was .15, almost significant at 10 percent, though the correlation between initiation by any politician and collaboration outside government was insignificant. Correlations between initiation by middle managers and frontline staff and collaboration either inside or outside government were insignificant.

The regressions of initiators in the 2010 semifinalists on the three previous classes show the pattern of slopes close to and not significantly different from 1 and intercepts not significantly different from 0 for the 1995–98 HKS Awards finalists and 1990–94 HKS Awards semifinalists. But the regression for the Commonwealth awards shows a slope significantly lower than, and more than four standard deviations below, 1 and an intercept significantly different from 0. This result occurred because the 2010 semifinalists, the dependent variable in the regression, had fewer extreme values than the Commonwealth awards applicants (for example, the latter's high incidence of technology-based innovations initiated by middle managers or frontline staff).

In 2010 for the first time I coded two types of political initiation. The first occurred through the legislative process, where the innovation is embodied in a piece of legislation ("legislative initiation"), and the second, "executive initiation," where an innovation can be launched by executive action, for example, a decision by a mayor or governor that doesn't require new legislation. Such innovations may be funded at the outset through existing budgetary lines, but if they go on to achieve significant scale it is likely they will require legislative authorization of their funding. Executive initiation was observed much more often (27 percent) than legislative (11 percent). Given the often slow and partisan nature of the legislative process in recent years at both the federal and, increasingly, state levels of government, it is not surprising that motivated politicians intent on initiating new programs would use their executive powers as much as possible.

The awards applications indicate two prototypical patterns of innovation initiation: top-down political and bottom-up frontline or middle management. In the former, the initiators were often governors or mayors. Their innovation may have been formulated as part of an election platform or while they held office. Once they conceived the informing idea they assigned it to public servants or an external group, monitoring their progress in developing plans and implementing them. Kentucky's Democratic gubernatorial candidate Steve Beshear made open government one of the key themes in his 2007 campaign. Shortly after taking office, he appointed the e-Transparency Task Force, a fourteen-member bipartisan panel with a mandate to make the state's government more open and accountable. The task force's recommendations led to a multi-agency effort by career public servants that culminated in the establishment of the Open Door Transparency Portal, a new public access website. A comparable example of persistent (or insistent) political leadership resulted in the creation of the NYC Service program. President Obama's call to public service in his first inaugural address on January 20, 2009, stirred many listeners, Mayor Michael Bloomberg among them. Bloomberg conceived of an initiative to provide opportunities for thousands of New Yorkers to volunteer to assist government in its work. He requested Deputy Mayor Patti Harris and Communications Director James Anderson to consult widely with external groups and city departments to plan the program. Anderson worked full-time, virtually round the clock, on consultation and program design, with the result that NYC Service was launched three months later, in April 2009. NYC Service recruited 55,000 volunteers who performed 600,000 hours of service in its first full year of operation and was one of the six finalists in the 2010 HKS Awards competition. Both these instances demonstrate the importance of a politician's focus on an issue and ability to assign it to the appropriate people to make it happen. Political discovery and initiative, then, coupled with a clear expectation of timely results and a keen sense of staff capacity, offer an effective route to innovation.

The bottom-up pattern of innovation necessarily looks very different. It begins when a frontline public servant or middle manager has an idea about how to improve her agency's performance, through either internal reform or new services. Successful bottom-up innovations require careful, canny positioning by their initiators with skillful canvassing for support from middle and senior management if they are to come to fruition. Allison Hamilton, a middle manager in the Office of Innovative Partnerships in the Oregon Department of Transportation, had—literally—a bright idea: use space on highway rights-of-way to install solar panels. Hamilton conceived of the idea thanks to a PBS documentary showing this practice on the German autobahns, a confirmation of our earlier observations regarding novelty.[1] Hamilton's managers were enthusiastic about the idea—if it could be done without costing the department money. Lacking funding for a site visit to Germany, she began a local process she called "pushing on open doors." She attended a presentation by the Oregon Department of Energy about its program for subsidizing public-private partnerships that produced renewable energy. Then she issued a Request for Information to the Oregon solar energy industry about how to develop a solar project on a highway right-of-way to take advantage of that subsidy. Ultimately, she found a private sector partner in the utility Portland General Electric. She also received support from the Oregon Department of Justice, which ruled that this investment could be included in the utility's rate base. It was also necessary for her to approach the Federal Highway Administration (FHWA), which regulates the Interstate Highway System. After some skepticism, the FHWA confirmed that using a right-of-way for a renewable energy project was in the public interest. The office of Governor Ted Kulongoski was informed of the initiative and was supportive. Solar panels were first put in place at an exchange near Portland, with the solar energy captured in the daytime being used to power the overhead lights in the evening. The Solar Highway was born. It has been replicated elsewhere in Oregon.

Hamilton gives full credit to her department's innovative culture, which supported her efforts, and to the equally important political and financial support she found elsewhere. (She cherishes the letter of appreciation Governor Kulongoski wrote her about the Solar Highway shortly before leaving office.) But the story of her initiative makes plain the extent of the networking, alliance building, and creative thinking required to turn those highway lights on. And this is consistent with the narratives associated with many other "local hero" innovators. Careful

1. Allison Hamilton, author interview, January 28, 2013. Hamilton mentioned Steven Latham, Larry Klein, and Evan Schwartz, producers, *Saved by the Sun,* Steven Latham Productions, broadcast on the PBS Program *Nova* on April 24, 2007. For a discussion of the origins of the German government's strong commitment to solar energy, see Cels, De Jong, and Nauta (2012, 133–53).

alliance building counts for at least as much as inspired vision. The lesson Hamilton herself drew for would-be initiators of innovations was that "reasons to reject the project were just words written on paper long ago that could be changed as circumstances changed." Or, to put it another way, organizational and structural obstacles are not insuperable: they are words, not walls.

Other research supports the finding that public sector innovations have diverse initiators. The public sector entrepreneurship literature identifies individuals in a wide variety of positions, from politicians to senior public servants to municipal chief administrative officers and "street-level policy entrepreneurs" (see Petchey, Williams, and Carter 2008). The EC Innobarometer study (Gallup Organization 2010, 34) asked about the relative importance of a variety of information sources to the development of an organization's innovations. Being the source of information, or even of an idea, is much less arduous than making the idea a reality, but this question is as close as the survey comes to asking respondents to identify the initiator(s) of innovations. Possible answers were "very important," "somewhat important," and "not important," to which I assigned values of 2, 1, and 0, respectively. Using these values and the percentage distribution of responses by each source, the following scores represent the significance of each source (the maximum score being 2 X 100 percent = 2): ideas from staff, 1.36; ideas from management, 1.36; citizens as clients or users, 1.29; best practices in another government organization, 1.1; conferences, .89; professional organizations, .75; enterprises as clients or users, .79; and enterprises as suppliers, .66. It is noteworthy that bottom-up ideas from staff were cited as frequently as top-down ideas from management. The implications of this for organizations is clear: "Cast your net wide." Encourage and empower all staff to speak. You never know where the next innovative idea will come from.

It was possible from reading the applications to establish the gender of the initiators in roughly half the 2010 semifinalist applications (see table 4-3). Ninety percent of the initiators we could identify at the political level were male, with the percentage of female initiators of innovations increasing at lower organizational levels. Forty-three percent of the middle management initiators were female. To determine whether initiating an innovation—an atypical activity—was something males and females would be equally likely to do, this table could be compared to data for the overall distribution of the public service by rank and gender. Given the number of jurisdictions involved, attempting to construct a database at the state and local levels would be exceedingly time-consuming. I used the distribution of federal politicians and public servants by rank and gender, which was readily available, as a proxy.

Table 4-4 uses the recent gender distribution at the Senior Executive Service (SES) level, and gender distributions by General Schedule (GS) pay scale levels

Table 4-3. *Initiators, by Gender, as a Percentage of Total Where Gender Was Identified among 2010 Semifinalists*

Percent except as indicated

Initiator	Male	Female	Number where gender was identified	Number where gender was not identified
Politician	91	9	33	22
Agency head	77	23	40	12
Middle manager	57	43	30	17
Frontline staff	40	60	5	20
Interest group leader or member	100	0	1	12
Client of or participant in program	55	45	9	24
Citizen	100	0	4	1

Source: Applications coded by author and Kaylee Chretien.

for the middle years of the previous decade, the latest that are available. Given that the average semifinalist innovation in the class of 2010 was initiated six years previously, the gender distribution at the time would most closely match that of the GS levels. Our results are similar if we compare innovations initiated by politicians with the gender distribution of the 109th Congress (2005–06), innovations initiated by agency heads with the gender distribution of the SES in fiscal year 2010, and innovations initiated by middle managers with the gender

Table 4-4. *Gender of U.S. Government Politicians and Public Servants, as Percentage of Total by Occupational Level*

Percent

	Male	Female
Politicians (109th Congress, 2005–06)	85	15
Senior Executive Service, FY 2010	68	32
GS 14–15, FY 2006	68	32
GS 9–13, FY 2006	56	44
GS 1–8, FY 2006	34	66

Sources: Donald R. Wolfensberger, "Information on the 109th Congress," Woodrow Wilson Center, Congress Project (www.wilsoncenter.org/sites/default/files/profile109.pdf); David Wiesman, "Senior Executive Service, Fiscal Year 2010," table 6 (http://beta.opm.gov/policy-data-oversight/data-analysis-documentation/federal-employment-reports/reports-publications/ses-summary-2010.pdf); GS data: Office of Personnel Management, Central Personnel Data File, 2006, tables 1-6 and 1-7 (http://opm.gov.feddata/index.asp).

distribution of the GS 9–15 groups. In each of the three cases the distributions of initiators of innovations by gender and of the entire public service by gender are reasonably close—within about 10 percent of one another. This suggests that the impetus to innovate is not stronger for either males or females than their share of the overall population of public servants would lead us to expect. Initiating an innovation is an equal-opportunity exceptionality: neither a male preserve nor a female ghetto. This is a welcome finding as it effectively contradicts two essentialist stereotypes that might otherwise inform assumptions about who initiates innovations: that women are less likely to be risk-takers (innovations do not come with guarantees of success) and are less comfortable articulating and pursuing their own vision, preferring to work by consensus and team building (necessary components of implementation, as we'll see, but less useful in the initiation phase).

Why Innovate?

We now have a clearer picture of who the initiators of innovations are likely to be. But why do they do it? To put it another way, what is the rationale for the innovation? Like the identity of the initiator, this too was coded from part of the third question in the semifinalist questionnaire: "How was the program or initiative embodying your innovative idea designed and launched?" (see appendix, "Semifinalist Application Questions," question 3). Since an innovation could have several inciting factors or catalysts, categories were not mutually exclusive, and the average 2010 semifinalist had slightly fewer than two.

Table 4-5, which charts the data on inciting factors, contains five broad categories (some categories had several components):

1. A crisis
2. A problem
3. Political influence
4. New leadership (for the innovating organization)
5. New opportunities.

The most important result was consistent across all four data sets: the contrast between crises and problems as inciting factors. In every case, problems appear more frequently than crises, and in the 2010 semifinalist and Commonwealth awards data sets, problems appear five times as frequently. In the 2010 coding, as in the three previous data sets, a crisis was defined as a current or anticipated publicly visible governmental performance failure. Including an anticipated failure in the definition of crisis broadened the definition and so increased the frequency of this factor (Borins 1998, 44–45). In the three previous data sets, greater efforts were made to identify specific internal problems, such as the need to keep up with

Table 4-5. *Conditions Leading to Innovations*

Percent except as indicated

Condition	2010 semifinalists	1995–98 finalists	1990–94 semifinalists	Commonwealth awards, 1998 and 2000
Crisis	14	25	30	14
Solves a noncrisis problem	74	64	49	73
Environment changing	8	23	8	14
Unable to reach targets	1	29	27	16
Unable to meet demand	2	14	11	18
Resource constraints	5	15	10	21
All political influence	41	40	19	36
New legislation or regulation	28	18	11	9
Lobbying	13	22	6	25
Election mandate	6	5	2	2
Any new leadership	6	16	9	4
Inside new leadership	4	2	4	2
Outside new leadership	2	14	6	2
Any new opportunities	20	15	33	48
New technological opportunities	7	8	18	41
New resources opportunities	7	NA	NA	NA
Other new opportunities	6	9	16	13
Research supports idea	9	NA	NA	NA
Number of innovations	127	104	217	56
Estimated slope (s.d.'s from 1)		1.06***	1.08***	.79***
		(.3)	(.3)	(1.1)
Estimated intercept		insig[a]	insig	insig
R^2 (goodness of fit)		.60***	.53***	.61***

Sources: 2010 applications coded by author and Kaylee Chretien; 1995–98 finalists: Borins (2000a, table 3, 503); 1990–94 semifinalists: Borins (1998, table 3-2): Commonwealth awards: Borins (2001a, 726).

NA = Not available

*** $p < .01$ for slope and intercept estimates and R^2.

a. insig = insignificantly different from 0.

a changing environment, inability to reach the program's target population, inability to meet demand for a program, and resource constraints. In these data sets, these specific issues were gathered under the overall rubric "problem."

The greater frequency of problems than crises in our data has important implications. A cynical view of the public sector, such as public choice theory, maintains that public sector organizations, which are often monopolies, are slow to respond to signals of public dissatisfaction with problems of performance until the organization breaks down and experiences a publicly visible crisis (Borins

1988).[2] A more optimistic view of the public sector is that public servants are aware of the performance of their organizations through their own formal and informal monitoring systems, and have the desire and the energy to solve these problems *before* they become crises. These data surely are consistent with the more optimistic view. It is worth noting that channels for public response have proliferated in the past decade—every agency has its portal—and this offers multiple means to "meter" dissatisfaction with services. It is, in fact, increasingly difficult to avoid being aware.

Farah and Spink's (2008, 84) study of the Brazilian innovation award supports this view. They coded answers to the open-ended question of why the applicant's program was innovative. The answer most frequently given (58 percent) was that applicants were "assuming the initiative in the search for new solutions to existing problems." The second most frequent answer (21 percent) was "changing or broadening the frame for thinking about action." Immediate response to a crisis was not mentioned. Cels, De Jong, and Nauta (2012, 35–38) also found that many of the innovations they studied were initiated in response to problems rather than widely acknowledged, visible crises.

Table 4-5 divides the category of political influence as the catalyst for innovation into three subcategories: (1) new legislation or regulations, (2) lobbying, and (3) an election mandate to undertake an innovation that had been part of the winning candidate's platform. New legislation could mean either that the innovation itself required new legislation or regulations or that it was a response to new legislation. Lobbying indicates that either politicians or interest groups were advocating on behalf of the innovation. An election mandate is consistently the least frequently observed of the three categories of political influence. The 1990–94 semifinalists demonstrated considerably less political influence (19 percent) than any of the three other data sets, which average close to 40 percent. This would appear consistent with the lower frequency of politicians as initiators in the 1990–94 semifinalists than in the 2010 semifinalists. This might be due to the necessity of political involvement to facilitate interorganizational collaboration, or it may be the case that politicians increasingly believe that championing innovation is a good electoral strategy.

"New leadership," from either inside or outside the organization, very infrequently appears as a factor leading to innovation and in every case but one is in the single digits. The cynical view of public sector organizations is that they are resistant to change, requiring new leaders—new brooms—for change to occur. The experience embodied in these innovations contradicts this view, for the vast

---

2. The noted economist Paul Romer's adage "A crisis is a terrible thing to waste" can be interpreted to mean that crises can be used by advocates of change to provide an impetus for the changes they seek to implement, but that does not mean change cannot occur without a crisis.

majority of innovations were put in place by current leaders or staff. Teodoro (2011, 17) argues that public servants who attempt to advance their careers by moving from agency to agency are likely to adopt professional innovations. The consistent and marked infrequency of new leadership being associated with applications to innovation awards in the United States and the Commonwealth countries is at odds with this explanation of public sector innovation as primarily self-serving careerism.

"New opportunities" is the fifth causal factor. For the 2010 semifinalists it was divided into new opportunities created by the availability of a new technology, by the availability of new resources, and other new opportunities. The incidence of new opportunities varied from 15 percent for the 1995–98 finalists to 48 percent of the Commonwealth awards applications. Our data have already suggested an ongoing professional commitment to innovation among public servants, and here, too, we find many innovations initiated by individuals grasping new opportunities, having had the vision and inclination to recognize them. Were it simply a matter of careerism, there would be a strong inducement not to disrupt the status quo in this way. Technological opportunities were cited in 41 percent of the Commonwealth awards applications and 18 percent of the 1990–94 semifinalists, both significantly higher than the 7 percent observed in the 2010 semifinalists. We have already discussed the unusually heavy representation of technology in the Commonwealth awards applications. The 1990–94 semifinalist applications reflect a time when the use of information technology in government was picking up speed. Now, IT is both more pervasive and more mature in a public sector context, which would lead us to expect fewer new technological opportunities to appear as sources of innovation (discussed in more detail in chapter 7). We might construe this as people driving innovation without the external stimulus of new tools. It is a point worth repeating: new opportunities lead to new initiatives only if there are individuals capable of recognizing them.

Looking at table 4-5 as a whole, the regressions of the Class of 2010 on the three previous groups of innovators show slopes that are statistically significant and close to one, intercepts that are not significantly different from zero, and statistically significant R^2 a pattern indicative of a relatively constant set of causal factors explaining innovation.

Planning? Groping Along? or Both?

The literature review in chapter 2 discussed in some detail Robert Behn's important formulation of "management by groping along" as opposed to "management by planning" and the scholarly debate it sparked. It noted, too, that that particular spark had effectively burned out within the field of public management innovation scholarship. But the issues informing Behn's formulation of "management by groping along" versus "management by planning"—which can be reformulated as an opposition between adaptive incrementalism and strategic planning—continue to be very much alive in management research more generally. Henry Mintzberg's long-standing advocacy of emergent strategy and strategy as learning (Mintzberg, Ahlstrand, and Lampel 2009) is one excellent example. I have already emphasized the importance of understanding public sector innovation as an evolving process. It seems highly pertinent, therefore, to look more closely at the modes of analysis that shape that process. *Innovating with Integrity* paid considerable attention to the debate over planning and groping along for this very reason. Since the present study is designed to replicate the research that produced the earlier book, consistency, no less than its own intrinsic importance, dictates a return to the question for the Class of 2010.

Examining the semifinalist applications for evidence of either incrementalism or strategic planning involved considerable interpretation. I was looking for indications that the initiator of the innovation had only an approximate idea of the shape the innovation should take and refined that idea on the basis of learning and experience ("groping along"), or that the innovator had a comprehensive view of the innovation and proceeded to implement it relatively quickly and without a great deal of modification ("planning"). Table 4-6 shows that all three data sets prior to the Class of 2010 displayed more planning than groping along. In the Commonwealth awards innovations survey, I had included a question on planning and groping along that briefly defined each approach and asked each innovator whether the process could better be described as planning, groping along, or a mix of the two (Borins 2001a, 730, question 6). In other data sets, this question was not asked explicitly, but the answer was inferred from the application cumulatively, in particular the answers to question 3, which asked how the program was designed and launched, and question 4, which asked "How [has] the implementation strategy of your program or policy initiative evolved over time?" and also requested an outline of the chronology of the innovation (see appendix, "Semifinalist Application Questions," question 4).[3] In all four data sets, planning was observed much more frequently than groping along.

The Class of 2010 showed much more planning (70 percent of the semifinalists) than either groping along (17 percent) or groping along and planning

---

3. *Innovating with Integrity* (Borins 1998, 51–52) used as an example of groping along a patient record system that started in one clinic in 1970, was in place in ten Indianapolis hospitals by 1992, and had milestones stretching over twenty-two years. An example of planning was Chicago's Parking Enforcement Program, which Mayor Richard M. Daley made a priority when he took office in 1989. His creation of the senior position of city parking administrator and the development of a strategic plan made the program operational in little more than a year.

Table 4-6. *Mode of Analysis for Innovations*

Percent except as indicated

Mode of analysis	2010 semifinalists	1995–98 finalists	1990–94 semifinalists	Commonwealth awards, 1998 and 2000
Comprehensive plan	70	55	59	43
"Groping along"	17	24	30	17
Planning and groping along	11	NA	NA	36
Pilot study or project	41	38	35	20
Public consultation	35	7	11	16
Legislative process	27	0	8	2
Task force	26	0	0	0
Consultant	17	0	7	0
Organizational strategic plan	13	5	7	7
Replicate public sector	0	0	12	14
Replicate private sector	8	0	0	0
Replicate nonprofit sector	0	0	4	0
Client survey	2	4	4	16
Number of innovations	127	104	217	56
Estimated slope (s.d.'s from 1)		.92*** (.4)	.93*** (.3)	.78** (.6)
Estimated intercept		11.6**	insig[a]	insig
R^2 (goodness of fit)		.68***	.65***	.31**

Sources: 2010 applications coded by author and Kaylee Chretien; 1995–98 finalists: Borins (2001b, 17); 1990–94 semifinalists: Borins (1998, table 3-5); Commonwealth awards: Borins (2001a, 727).

NA = Not available

** $p <.05$; *** $p <.01$ for slope and intercept estimates and R^2.

a. insig - insignificantly different from 0.

together (11 percent). There were a number of other information gathering or decisionmaking approaches that were also popular in 2010. These include the use of a pilot study (41 percent), public consultation (35 percent), the legislative process (27 percent), task forces (26 percent), and consultants (17 percent). The regressions of the 2010 semifinalists on the three other data sets all had slopes that were close to, and not significantly different from, 1, had statistically significant R^2s and in two of three instances had an intercept that was not significantly different from 0. All told, the results were reasonably constant over the four data sets. But the greater incidence of, or preference for, planning over groping raises further questions. Who prefers one method over the other? Are there particular internal or external circumstances that make one approach preferable? Secondary analysis of the data explored here can offer some answers.

Innovators, Triggers, and Modes of Analysis: A Secondary Analysis

I use the term "secondary analysis" with some reluctance, since it carries unfortunate connotations of both afterthought and less-than-first-rank significance. But this analysis of possible interrelationships and connections between this chapter's various findings is anything but secondary. It has been driven by my understanding of the dynamic nature of innovation and the value of probing the various possible confluences of people, triggers, and modes of analysis that can produce it. My first focus was the four main initiators of innovations—politicians, agency heads, middle managers, and frontline staff—to determine if any of them appear together. If the question were coded on a mutually exclusive basis, then correlations among the groups would necessarily be negative, but because more than one initiator could be coded, it was possible for some correlations among the four groups to be positive. Table 4-7 presents a matrix of correlation coefficients among the four groups. The only positive correlation coefficient, (.35), is between middle managers and frontline staff, meaning that these two groups tend to work together in initiating innovations. The negative correlations between politicians and both middle managers (–.32) and frontline staff (–.20), and between agency heads and both middle managers (–.28) and frontline staff (–.30), mean that politicians and agency heads don't tend to initiate innovations jointly with either middle managers or frontline staff. We will explore the implications of this once we have considered two other sets of possible relationships.

I then looked at the relationships among the five main factors leading to innovations (see table 4-8). Both any opportunity and any new leadership are uncorrelated with the others. Crisis is positively correlated with all political influence (.21), problem is negatively correlated with political influence (–.20), and crisis and problem are also strongly negatively correlated with one another (–.53). Crisis and problem are very unlikely to occur together and can be seen as distinct alternatives. Political influence is likely to be present when there is a crisis but absent when the innovation involves a problem.

The next step was to examine the relationship between initiators of innovations and the five main factors leading to innovations (see table 4-9). Politicians as initiators, unsurprisingly, are positively correlated with all political influence (.24). Politicians as initiators are also correlated with any new leader (.24), suggesting that there is a tendency for newly elected politicians to introduce innovations. Agency heads are positively and significantly correlated with crisis (.23) and politicians are positively, but not significantly, correlated with crisis (.11). Both middle managers (–.19) and frontline staff (–.22) are negatively correlated with a crisis. Politicians (–.07) and agency heads (–.07) are negatively, but not significantly, correlated with

Table 4-7. *Correlation Matrix, Initiators of Innovations, 2010 Semifinalists*

Correlation coefficients

	Politician	*Agency head*	*Middle manager*	*Frontline staff*
Politician[a]	1	.00	−.32*	−.20*
Agency head		1	−.28*	−.30*
Middle manager			1	.35*
Frontline staff				1

Source: Statistical analysis by author and Elizabeth Lyons.
* Significance > .05.
a. Politician in executive or legislative capacity.

Table 4-8. *Correlation Matrix, Conditions Leading to Innovations, 2010 Semifinalists*

Correlation coefficients

Factor leading to innovation	*All political influence*	*Crisis*	*Problem*	*Any opportunity*	*Any new leader*
All political influence	1	.21*	−.20*	−.09	.11
Crisis		1	−.53*	−.03	−.01
Problem			1	−.02	−.07
Any opportunity				1	−.05
Any new leader					1

Source: Statistical analysis by author and Elizabeth Lyons.
* Significance > .05.

Table 4-9. *Correlation Matrix, Conditions Leading to Innovations with Initiators, 2010 Semifinalists*

Correlation coefficients

	Initiators			
Condition	*Politician*	*Agency head*	*Middle manager*	*Frontline staff*
All political influence	.24*	.03	−.04	−.21*
Crisis	.11	.23*	−.19*	−.22*
Problem	−.07	−.07	.08	.12
Any new leader	.24*	−.04	−.08	−.15
Any opportunity	.01	.13	.00	.00

Source: Statistical analysis by author and Elizabeth Lyons.
* Significance > .05.

a problem and middle managers (.08) and frontline staff (.12) positively, but not significantly, correlated with a problem.

What do these findings suggest? Putting tables 4-7, 4-8, and 4-9 together, it appears that there are two distinct paths to innovation. Politicians or agency heads are associated with innovations in response to crises.[4] Middle managers and frontline staff tend to initiate innovations together and are more likely to be the initiators when there is a problem than when there is a crisis. The negative correlation between problem and crisis reinforces the distinctiveness of the two approaches. *Innovating with Integrity* found similar patterns for the 1990–94 semifinalists (Borins 1998, 49). The replication is important. It indicates that middle managers and frontline civil servants can be proactive problem solvers, but when there has been no proactive problem solving and a problem has escalated to a crisis, then politicians or agency heads take over the role of developing and leading an innovative response to the crisis. Being closer to the day-to-day workings of a program makes preemptive diagnosis easier. Warning signs can be noted and targeted action envisioned, implemented, and adjusted as needed. A crisis by definition implies dysfunction on a different scale, and addressing it in its totality likely requires both a larger view and a wider authority.

Levin and Sanger (1994, 164), in their more impressionistic analysis of a small sample of thirty-five winners of the State and Local Government Innovation Awards seem to recognize this duality and note another implication—the freedom that comes from relative organizational obscurity:

> "In some instances—in crises or for large programs—the relationship [between top political executives and program managers] was close and supportive at the outset. In others—indeed most of them—the relationship with a top political executive proved important only in sustaining an already successful enterprise. These smaller programs, not facing crises, seemed to benefit from the initial freedom to experiment that came from distance from top political executives."

A different way of demonstrating the distinctiveness of the two paths to innovation is to correlate the initiator of the innovation with the strongest supporters, one element of the response to question 10 in the semifinalist questionnaire, "What individuals or organizations are the strongest supporters of the program or policy initiative and why?" (see table 4-10). When politicians initiate an innovation, they are most likely to acknowledge support from the political leader of the jurisdiction—the mayor, governor, or president—(a .21 correlation), from

---

4. Politicians and agency heads are not correlated with one another as initiators of innovations, as indicated by the .00 correlation coefficient in the second column of table 4-7, and so are as likely as not to launch innovations together.

Table 4-10. *Correlation Matrix, Initiators of Innovations with Strongest Supporters, 2010 Semifinalists*

Correlation coefficients

Strongest source of support	Initiators			
	Politician	*Agency head*	*Middle manager*	*Frontline staff*
Supervisor of initiator	−.12	−.03	.09	.18*
Middle manager(s)	−.13	−.19*	.19*	.10
Political head of agency	.05	.15	−.11	−.07
Mayor, governor, president	.21*	−.08	−.06	−.10
Any political support	.21*	−.06	−.03	−.12
Business lobby	.27*	−.08	−.05	.08
Media	.23*	−.15	−.02	−.09
General public	.30*	−.09	−.06	−.09

Source: Statistical analysis by author and Elizabeth Lyons.
* Significance > .05.

other politicians (.21), from the business lobby (.27), from the media (.23), and from the general public (.30). They seek support from both the political and public milieus. For middle managers, the strongest supporters are other middle managers (.19), and for frontline staff, their supervisors (.18). The result for agency head is equivocal, showing only that middle managers tend not to be the strongest supporters of their initiatives. Again, we find politicians looking to the political system and to public support, and middle managers and frontline public servants looking to their own organizational milieus. This is identical to my conclusion after conducting a similar analysis of the 1995–98 finalist data (Borins 2000a, 504): "Public servants worked through bureaucratic channels, rather than going over the heads of their colleagues to appeal directly for political support, and politicians went through political channels and mobilized public support. Working through appropriate channels is the hallmark of a responsible public servant whose commitment to desired ends does not negate respect for due process."

The final relationships involved in the evolution of an innovation we'll consider here return us to the question of conceptualization. Olivia Golden's 1990 article "Innovation in Public Sector Human Services Programs: The Implications of Innovation by 'Groping Along'" proposed a number of useful hypotheses. She found that planning is more likely to occur, and groping along less likely, when chains of cause and effect are well understood, when large capital budgets are required at the outset, and when a program is part of a complex intergovernmental system, for example, one involving conditional grants from the federal government. *Innovating with Integrity* tested a number of Golden's hypotheses, as well as the impact of different initiators: politicians, middle managers or frontline public servants (who were not differentiated from one another in the 1990–94 semifinalist data set), and new leaders. It found that planning was positively and statistically significantly associated with large capital budgets, with operationalization of a theory (the variable I used to represent Golden's idea of chains of cause and effect being well understood), and with innovations involving intergovernmental collaboration. Planning was negatively and statistically significantly associated with new leadership and initiation by a middle manager or frontline staff. Groping along was positively and statistically significantly associated with initiation by a public servant and with a new program, and negatively and significantly associated with political influence (Borins 1998, 61). Because there was a strong negative correlation between planning and groping along, the signs of the estimated coefficients for any independent variable were usually reversed for planning and for groping along.

In repeating the analysis for the Class of 2010, in addition to coding planning and groping along separately, we coded planning and groping along together, which can be regarded as occupying a central location between the two polar opposites (see table 4-11). Before doing a regression analysis on the determinants of planning and groping along, I investigated the correlation coefficients between possible independent variables and planning, planning and groping along, and groping along.

As initiators of innovations, politicians and middle managers appear more likely to be associated with planning and frontline staff with groping along. Neither crises nor problems appear to have any impact on whether to plan or to grope. Innovations that involved opportunities created by new technology had a strong positive association with groping along (correlation of .23) and a strong negative association with planning (–.41). Innovations in which the applicants said their most important achievement was enabling inter-organizational collaboration (a possible response to question 6 in the semifinalist questionnaire discussed further in chapter 6) were strongly associated with planning (.19). Operationalizing a theory, another possible response to question 6, appeared to be slightly associated with planning, as had been hypothesized by Golden. Because of the scarce capital budget data (only 29 of 127 semifinalists showed a capital budget), I used the size of operating budget as a measure of the scale of the innovations, and here found a slight association with planning.

I was curious whether these bivariate relationships would hold in a multivariate context. I estimated the determinants of planning and groping along in two ways, by an ordered logit and by ordinary least squares (see table 4-12). For the ordered logit, which is the more appropriate of the two, the three settings of the dependent variable are, in order, planning, planning and groping along, then

Table 4-11. *Correlations with Planning or Groping Along, 2010 Semifinalists*
Correlation coefficients

	Planning	Planning and groping along	Groping along
Any political initiator	.07	.01	−.03
Agency head initiator	−.03	−.17	−.10
Middle manager initiator	.12	.14	−.01
Front-line staff initiator	−.16	.06	.15
Crisis	.02	.01	.00
Problem	.03	.03	.01
New technology opportunity	−.41*	−.10	.23*
Most important achievement enabling collaboration	.19*	.20*	.00
Most important achievement operationalizing theory	.04	.00	−.06
Current operating budget	.06	−.05	−.11

Source: Statistical analysis by author and Elizabeth Lyons.
* Significance > .05.

groping along.[5] For the dependent variable in ordinary least squares, planning had a value of 1, groping along and planning, .5, and groping along, 0. The OLS results, if similar to the ordered logit, can be seen as confirmation. Given the way the dependent variable was defined, if an independent variable had a positive sign, it exerted an influence to plan. An independent variable with a negative sign exerted an influence to grope along. In addition to using enabled individuals or groups to collaborate as an independent variable, I also used two direct measures of collaboration, namely collaborations within government and collaborations outside government, as independent variables.

This produced four equations, the first two including the two types of collaborations—one using OLS and the other using the ordered logit—and the second two excluding the two types of collaborations, with one again using OLS and the other again using the ordered logit. In each equation there were 99 observations, rather than the full data set of 127 semifinalists, because a semifinalist application had to be deleted if it did not have an observation for any independent variable.

5. The problem with a linear model in which the dependent variable is a probability between zero and 1 is that predicted values of the dependent variable could be either less than zero or greater than 1, which would be meaningless. A logit uses the logarithm of the odds associated with the probability as the dependent variable, transforming it to vary from negative to positive infinity, eliminating the problem of meaningless predictions (Borins 1998, 60).

Table 4-12. *Determinants of Planning and Groping Along, 2010 Semifinalists*[a]

	Regression format			
Variable	OLS	Ordered logit	OLS	Ordered logit
Collaboration in government	−.05 (.45)	−.23 (.31)		
Collaboration outside government	−.04 (.40)	.37 (.59)		
Political executive	.02 (.25)	.15 (.25)	.01 (.11)	.09 (.16)
Agency head	.02 (.25)	.27 (.49)	.02 (.25)	.26 (.48)
Middle manager	.11 (1.2)	.55 (1.1)	.12 (1.3)	.54 (1.0)
Front-line staff	−.28 (2.5)**	−1.44 (2.29)**	−.29 (2.6)**	−1.5 (2.4)**
New leadership	−.04 (.30)	−.67 (.77)	−.03 (.21)	−.56 (.69)
New technology	−.49 (3.2)***	−2.7 (2.7)***	−.51 (3.4)***	−2.8 (2.8)***
Enabled collaboration	.06 (.66)	.24 (.55)	.05 (.63)	.11 (.22)
Operationalized theory	.05 (.55)	.32 (.58)	.05 (.63)	.28 (.52)
Operating budget	.00 (0)	.03 (0)	.00 (0)	.03 (0)
Constant	.82 (6.3)***		.76 (8.4)***	
Cut 1		−2.2 (2.4)		−1.8 (3.1)
Cut 2		−1.3 (1.4)		−.90 (1.58)
Mean VIF	1.19	1.19	1.17	1.17
Number of observations	99	99	99	99
Pseudo R^2		.1199		.1171
R^2	.2154		.2121	

Source: statistical analysis by author and Elizabeth Lyons.
** $p <.05$; *** $p <.01$.
a. *t*-ratios are in parentheses.

For each set of independent variables, the variance inflation factors (VIFs) were also included.[6] The variance inflation factors were close to 1, indicating that correlation among the independent variables is not a problem. The different regressions, whether using a slightly different set of independent variables, or differing in the choice of OLS or ordered logit, yielded similar estimates. The regressions were disappointing in that only two variables were found to be statistically significant: initiation by frontline staff and opportunity created by new technologies. Both are negative, indicating that both exert an influence to groping along rather than planning. The correlations between both these independent variables and the planning–groping along continuum shown in table 4-11 were also negative, which is consistent with these multiple regressions. None of the other indepen-

6. Variance inflation factors (VIFs) measure the extent of correlation among independent variables, a problem known as multicollinearity. The higher the VIFs, the greater the problem. VIFs of 1 for all independent variables would indicate the desirable state of a complete absence of multicollinearity.

dent variables that I had hypothesized to have an impact on the planning–groping along continuum—political initiation, facilitation of interorganization collaboration, a large financial commitment—were close to significant. Comparing these results to the more definitive results in *Innovating with Integrity* for the 1990–94 semifinalists, the reason for the difference might be the difference in specifications or the fewer observations for the 2010 semifinalists (99) than for the 1990–94 semifinalists (217). Having fewer observations reduces the likelihood of finding significant coefficients for independent variables.

The Who, Why, and How of Innovation in Government

We have been considering in depth the initiation or creation phase of public sector innovation, scrutinizing new data for the Class of 2010 while building on previous evidence from the 1990–94 HKS Awards semifinalists, the 1995–98 finalists, and the 1998 and 2000 applicants to the Commonwealth International Innovation Awards. We began by probing discrete aspects or questions (novelty, identity of initiators, triggers, and conceptual methods), and also looked at possible relationships among them. The results of the exercise were less definitive than I'd hoped, likely because of the relatively small database used, but that does not negate its value. Considering possible connections and relationships is an important reminder of the multiple factors at work in any public sector innovation.

Although the HKS Awards are designed to recognize novelty, many of the Class of 2010 acknowledge that they did research about leading-edge practice within their policy area and replicated aspects of previous innovations in developing their own initiatives. This suggests very strongly that innovative public sector initiatives evolve within a context of innovation, and this in turn underscores the importance of awards competitions such as the HKS. As a showcase for the strongest examples of current innovative practice, they offer some practitioners a means of publicizing their efforts, other practitioners an opportunity to learn about leading-edge practice, and still other practitioners a chance to do both.

The Class of 2010 demonstrated an increased frequency of initiation by politicians, agency heads, and clients or participants in collaborative efforts compared to previous years. There is some evidence that this may be due to the greater incidence of collaborative innovation now than previously. But local heroes, defined as middle managers or front-line workers, were also present in the Class of 2010 to approximately the same extent as in the three previous classes. It was possible to determine the gender of approximately half of the Class of 2010 initiators and compare this information to data about gender and organizational rank (SES and GS levels) for federal government legislators and public servants. The distribution of initiators of innovations by gender was similar to the gender distribution of the federal government overall, suggesting that innovation is not the preserve of either gender. This evidence contradicts essentialist stereotypes that would predict less female involvement in innovation.

Moving from who innovates to why, we explored the causal factors explaining innovation. Problems, we found, remain much more significant than crises. This is consistent with a view of public servants as being attuned to results and outcomes and dealing with problems before they escalate to crises. Approximately a fifth of innovations were sparked by opportunities, implying that public servants are frequently entrepreneurial enough in their thinking to both recognize and exploit them. This is far from the cynical view of careerists wedded to the status quo and prompted to innovate out of self-interest alone. Political impetus to innovate has increased somewhat, but the reasons for this are elusive. We could speculate that in this era of global crises and apparent political dysfunction, there is capital to be gained from positioning oneself as offering new ideas and new methods, distancing oneself from an inadequate and unloved status quo. Finally, new leadership, from either within or outside the innovating organization, was rarely associated with innovation, and this reinforces the view that political incumbents or career public servants can innovate in response to changing circumstances or ongoing problems and that new leadership is not a necessity to spark innovation. Old brooms can sweep just as well as new.

Regarding the question of how innovations are conceptualized, the data for the Class of 2010 were consistent with the data for three previous groups of innovators. Framed as a choice between incrementalism and strategic planning ("groping along" or "planning"), planning proved to be favored by a large margin. Considering these two findings together—the predominance of proactive problem solving and planning—it would seem obvious that innovating when not facing the heat of a crisis allows the time and energy for more careful preparation and groundwork. It is also possible that the inclusion of a comprehensive strategic plan makes an innovative proposal appear more persuasive and therefore more likely to attract the patrons and partisans it needs to succeed.

We probed further by testing the interrelationships among the findings about initiators of and causal factors for innovations. Middle managers and frontline staff tended to collaborate on initiating innovations, but other groups tended to initiate innovations on their own. Politicians and agency heads tended to initiate innovations undertaken in response to crises, while middle managers and frontline public servants were more likely to initiate innovations intended to solve problems before they escalated to crises. When politicians initiated innovations, they reported that their strongest supporters were in the political sphere (chief executives or other politicians) or in the public realm (the business lobby, the media, or the general public); middle managers reported that their strongest supporters were other middle managers; and frontline public servants, that their strongest support came from their immediate supervisors. Taken together these data show relatively separate paths for politically initiated innovations and for "local hero innovations," the former being more crisis-driven and externally oriented in terms of building support and the latter, more problem-driven and internally oriented.

A final exploration concerned the determinants of whether the initiator of an innovation would choose to plan, to grope along, or to combine the two approaches. Although a number of hypotheses confirmed in *Innovating with Integrity* were more or less strongly supported by bivariate correlations (such as political initiators tending to plan, and collaborative, theory-driven, and large budget innovations tending to be characterized by planning rather than groping along), the only relationships supported in multivariate regressions were that innovations launched by frontline staff and innovations stemming from opportunities created by new technology both exerted an influence to grope along rather than to use a planning process.

In the previous chapter I concluded that the 2010 HKS Awards semifinalists were broadly similar to those of 1990–94, the major difference being that the more recent semifinalists displayed a much greater incidence of interorganizational collaboration. At the end of this chapter I conclude that with respect to the questions of who initiates innovations, what conditions lead to innovation, and what is the innovation's analytical process, the recent semifinalists are also broadly similar to those of two decades ago. The greater incidence of interorganizational collaboration in 2010 did not appear to affect most of these results. The one result it may explain is the greater incidence of politicians and agency heads as initiators in 2010, given that it is difficult for frontline public servants, or even middle managers, to initiate innovations involving collaboration with other organizations. However, the evidence for this hypothesis is debatable. The next chapter continues this search for similarities and differences between the 2010 semifinalists and those of 1990–94, but at a different stage in the life cycle of innovations: after they have been put in place and have begun to generate reactions, either supportive or critical.

5

Innovation Stories: Real People, Real Challenges, Real Outcomes

The previous chapter dealt with the launch of an innovation. This one deals with the life of an innovation up to its appearance in the HKS Awards data set. For our 2010 semifinalists that is an average span of more than six years (see table 3-8), a considerable period of time in the life of a government program. In this chapter I examine the life stories of the Class of 2010 as recounted in the HKS Awards applications. You will be reading narratives of innovative initiatives written by either an originator or someone closely associated with the innovation. Participants are notoriously unreliable narrators, but the HKS Awards judging process should constrain applicants to keep their stories within the realm of nonfiction.

It is not hard to imagine the sort of story applicants would like to tell, a tale of ingenuity triumphant and public interest well served. The narrative might run like this: The originality and effectiveness of the proposed innovation were quickly recognized. The initiative was promptly adopted by the organization or group of collaborating organizations to which it was proposed. The program or initiative rapidly grew. It created significant and widely appreciated public value, leading to widespread transfer and, perhaps, the public recognition of a prestigious award. That would be what Hollywood calls a feel-good story, and champions of the public sector (generally but not exclusively liberals) seize on instances of actual feel-good accounts eagerly when they can be found.

But there is also an innovation failure story: An innovation is launched and begins to scale up, but it encounters so many problems, perhaps poor organizational design or perverse incentives, that it sinks under their weight and is terminated.[1] This failed innovation story holds a particular appeal to those who equate innova-

---

1. The recent Australian Public Service Innovation Index (APSII) pilot survey asked public servants to provide information about failed innovations with which they were associated. This question received so little response that the researchers dropped it. See Arundel and Huber (2013).

tion with government activism and for whom such activism is anathema. They seek such stories out and publicize them wherever they can.[2]

For most innovations, the truth lies somewhere between triumphant success and abject collapse. Innovations meet obstacles: some can be overcome, others must be lived with. Innovations encounter critics, whom their initiators or champions attempt to answer. Sometimes the critics are silenced, but not always. Innovations may grow as a result of increasing demand or may take advantage of new opportunities, but it may also be necessary to modify, redesign, or even reinvent the innovation. Some of the initiative's target population embrace it, others object on grounds of principle or oppose the use of resources. Still others feel the program fails to reach far enough. More rethinking and repositioning may be necessary. And this is what I consider here: the real stories of obstacles, criticism, and evolution that can be read in the 2010 semifinalist applications—sometimes between the lines.

To begin with the obvious, the author of the award application is an initiator or champion, a partisan. He or she is asked to respond to a series of sixteen questions, some of them multipart, designed to elicit as comprehensive an account as possible of the innovation. Six of the questions (questions 1, 2, 4, 6, 7, 12) offer significant latitude to the author to frame the innovation's story as positively as possible. Five of them (3, 8, 10, 13, 16) deal largely with factual, process-related, or organizational issues such as personnel, oversight, and budget. Three questions (11, 14, 15) ask for information concerning various forms of outside response, media coverage, formal evaluation, awards and recognition, information that would be largely a matter of public record and quite easily confirmed.

But there are two questions (5 and the latter part of 10) that require the applicant to tell another side to the story, asking for details of the obstacles and criticism the innovation encountered. Thus, part of completing the application requires the innovation's initiator or champion to speak on behalf of its opponents or critics. Do the applicants do so fully and fairly? There are reasons to trust their accounts. The application documentation makes clear that expert judges will be evaluating the applications, and finalists will be required to host a site visitor with expertise in the relevant policy area. Less than full candor will be problematic when the application is reviewed. We might predict a strong temptation to understate both obstacles and criticism to avoid any suggestion that an innovation might not be sustainable. But the sanction for understating opposition would be loss of credibility in the judging process.

2. There have been numerous studies of high-profile public sector management failures—some of them involving innovation—by internal inquiries, journalists, or academics. One can anticipate that such studies of the problems attendant on the launch of the healthcare.gov website in late 2013 will soon appear. Quiet innovation failures, however, are more likely to escape public notice or academic inquiry.

The ultimate purpose of this chapter is to frame a representative innovation story and draw out is implications, which is accomplished by identifying and analyzing that story's constituent parts. I look first at the different obstacles to innovation as identified by the applicants, as well as the means by which and frequency with which these were reported to be overcome. I then consider the criticisms and critics of the innovations and the relationship between the two, looking, as always, for significant patterns of association. The questionnaire asks applicants to identify what they themselves feel to be major obstacles, so both internal and external criticism are encountered. Finally, I look at patterns of response: how applicants represent the evolution of their initiatives over time in the face of obstacles and criticisms they encountered, as well as the unexpected opportunities that arose once their initiatives were in operation.

If You Can't Go over It . . . Obstacles and Tactics

Question 5 of the semifinalist questionnaire asked applicants a three-part question concerning obstacles: "Please describe the most significant obstacle(s) encountered thus far by your program. How have they been dealt with? Which ones remain?" (see appendix, "Semifinalist Application Questions" for all references to questions on the HKS Awards semifinalists questionnaire). Table 5-1 summarizes the answers to the first part. Sixteen obstacles were coded for all four groups of innovations: 2010 HKS Awards semifinalists, 1995–98 HKS Awards finalists, 1990–94 HKS Awards semifinalists (this included state and local government applicants only), and 1998 and 2000 Commonwealth International Innovations Awards applicants. The table's fourth last line shows the average number of obstacles per applicant for each of the four groups, which varies between two and three. Applicants may have preferred to underreport the number of obstacles faced by their initiative, but the question's use of the adjective "significant" builds in something of a safeguard, significance being a highly subjective criterion. Had the questionnaire asked for all obstacles rather than just the most significant, the average number of obstacles might have been higher, but there might also have been a greater pressure for applicants to be less than accurate to avoid undermining the application's overall positive impact.

The obstacles fall into three main groups: internal barriers arising primarily within the bureaucracy, lack of resources, and obstacles coming from an organization's external environment. Together they offer a cogent reminder of just what a complex enterprise innovating is, how many competing organizational and personal interests must be balanced, how many logistical pitfalls avoided to achieve a successful outcome. Internal barriers arising primarily within the bureaucracy included forms of resistance such as hostile or skeptical attitudes or turf fights, dif-

Table 5-1. *Types of Obstacles to Innovation as Percentage of Total Obstacles*
Percent except as indicated

Obstacle	2010 semifinalists	1995–98 finalists	1990–94 semifinalists	1998 and 2000 Commonwealth awards
Internal barriers				
Bureaucratic resistance	15	17	18	19
Coordination	5	7	10	11
Logistical	21	7	10	15
Burnout	4	2	6	1
Technology	6	4	6	9
Unions	0	3	1	3
Middle managers	0	2	1	2
Oppose public entrepreneurs	0	1	1	2
Total internal barriers	51	43	55	62
Lack of resources	18	12	17	19
External obstacles				
Laws, regulations	3	7	7	4
Political opposition	2	6	2	4
Political transition	3	NA	NA	NA
Public doubt	8	14	10	7
Reaching target group	8	9	6	1
Affected interests	4	7	3	1
Competitors	1	3	1	1
Total external obstacles	29	46	29	18
Total number of obstacles	284	207	512	166
Obstacles per applicant	2.2	2	2.4	3
Estimated slope (s.d.'s from 1)		.96*** (.1)	1.0*** (0)	.87*** (.9)
Estimated intercept		insig[a]	insig	insig
R^2 (goodness of fit)		.45***	.70***	.72***

Sources: 2010 applications coded by author and Kaylee Chretien; 1995–98 finalists: Borins (2000a, table 5); 1990–94 semifinalists: Borins (1998, table 4-1); Commonwealth awards: Borins (2006, table 2).
NA = Not available
*** $p < .01$, for slope and intercept estimates and R^2.
a. insig = insignificantly different from 0.

ficulty coordinating organizations, logistical problems, difficulty maintaining the enthusiasm of program staff (burnout), difficulty implementing a new technology, opposition by unions, opposition by middle management, and opposition to entrepreneurial action within the public sector.

Lack of resources was classified separately because it might be due to constraints at either the political or bureaucratic levels. Obstacles arising from the organization's external environment include legislative or regulatory constraints, political opposition, the concern that an innovation will not survive the transition to new political leadership (an obstacle introduced into our codebook for the first time for the 2010 semifinalists), public doubts about the effectiveness of the program, difficulty reaching the program's target group, opposition by affected private sector interests, and opposition from private sector entities that would be forced to compete with the innovative program.

The sixteen obstacles appear with similar frequencies in all four groups of innovations over two decades, and the regressions of the 2010 semifinalists' obstacles on those of the other three groups all show slopes close to and not significantly different from 1, insignificant intercept terms, and statistically significant R^2. The largest percentage of obstacles were internal to the bureaucracy, encompassing more than 50 percent of all obstacles for three of the four groups. The obstacles encountered reflect the tendency of these innovations to challenge occupational patterns, standard operating procedures, and power structures. It is surprising that the Class of 2010, despite its very high level of interorganizational collaboration (see table 3-1), reports coordination problems as an obstacle slightly less frequently (5 percent) than any of the three previous groups (between 7 and 11 percent).[3] The good news this finding might herald is that the American public sector has become more proficient at managing interorganizational collaboration, drawing on an accumulating body of research and experience. Studies based on comparative case analysis, such as Bardach's (1998) on interorganizational collaboration, Donahue and Zeckhauser's (2011) on collaboration between the public and private sectors, and Ansell and Gash's (2008) meta-analysis of studies of public sector collaboration with civil society all contain strong normative components for practitioners to apply to the challenges posed by their own contexts.

Consider, now, the obstacles under the rubric external. Legislative or regulatory constraints occurred when an innovator was hampered by legislation or regulations that had been enacted previously for other reasons—what Allison Hamilton, of Oregon's Solar Highway, called "words written on paper long ago" (see chapter 4, p. 68). Other obstacles based in the political system were outright political opposition and the concern that an innovation will not survive the transition to new political leadership. Total opposition based in the political system—the sum of the three—only once exceeded 10 percent of total obstacles (the 1995–98 finalists). The infrequency of political obstacles may mean that bureaucratic innovators were

---

3. As discussed at the beginning of chapter 3, the threshold for a statistically significant difference between individual variables in two groups of innovations is approximately 4 percent, so the frequency of coordination problems as an obstacle to innovation for the 2010 semifinalists was at the threshold of being significantly lower from the 1990–94 semifinalists and Commonwealth awards applications. What is surprising is that it was not significantly *higher*.

working far enough from the political arena that they largely escaped notice by politicians. But if their innovations did register at the political level, the innovators may have understood what was and was not politically feasible and gauged their actions accordingly, forestalling political intervention or obstruction. I shall return to this point, but it is worth exploring briefly here. There may be no single "innovator" personality type, but the application stories make it clear that a certain interpersonal skill set is essential for successful innovators: a combination of persistence, flexibility, political sensitivity, and highly developed strategic instincts—a list that makes plain why innovating remains an atypical activity. Other external obstacles reported included public doubts about a program, difficulties reaching the program's target population, and opposition by affected interests and competitors.

The EC Innobarometer survey (Gallup Organization 2010, 41) also asked about obstacles to innovation. Despite having a predefined set of obstacles and being addressed to a far larger sample, its results display considerable similarities to the obstacles recounted by HKS Awards semifinalists. The possible responses for the Innobarometer survey, and points I accorded them, were as follows: an obstacle was of high importance (3 points), of medium importance (2), of low importance (1), or of no importance (0). The following were the point values for the different obstacles for which reactions were asked, based on the distributions of answers: lack of sufficient human or financial resources, 2.15; regulatory requirements, 1.78; lack of incentives for staff, 1.45; lack of management support, 1.4; staff resistance, 1.34; risk-averse organizational culture, 1.38; uncertain acceptance by users of the services, 1.35. These categories and their distribution align fairly closely with the HKS semifinalists' accounts. For the latter, lack of resources is the most frequent obstacle; internal obstacles are comparable to the Innobarometer survey's lack of incentives, lack of managerial support, staff resistance and risk aversion; regulations and political opposition are comparable to the survey's regulatory requirements; and, finally, difficulty reaching the target group and public doubt are comparable to the Innobarometer's uncertain acceptance by users.

In the face of such extensive evidence of obstacles to innovation, it is heartening to note the equally extensive array of responses the applications chronicled. Table 5-2 shows eighteen tactics that were used to deal with the obstacles and records the number of times each was cited for all four groups of innovations. The average number of tactics per applicant is quite close to the average number of obstacles (between two and three), which indicates that applicants were actively trying to overcome obstacles rather than passively accepting them. As with the obstacles, the tactics appear with reasonably similar frequencies for all four groups of innovations over two decades. Regressing the tactics used by the 2010 semifinalists on those used by the 1995–98 HKS Awards finalists and the 1990–94

Table 5-2. *Tactics Used to Respond to Obstacles as Percentage of Total Times Tactics Used by Each Group*

Percent except as indicated

Tactic	2010 semifinalists	1995–98 finalists	1990–94 semifinalists	1998 and 2000 Commonwealth awards
Show benefits	10	8	11	17
Social marketing	6	10	5	2
Demonstration project	4	6	5	1
Consultation	11	11	9	5
Co-optation	7	9	8	9
Provide training	6	11	10	8
Make program culturally sensitive	0	1	3	1
Compensation	1	3	1	1
Find resources	12	8	10	9
Solve logistical problems	14	5	8	5
Build political support	6	5	5	2
Modify technology	4	3	4	10
Change laws	2	4	2	3
Find support elsewhere in the bureaucracy	3	NA	NA	NA
Be persistent	8	9	9	4
Focus, maintain clear vision	6	3	4	3
Provide recognition	0	1	1	0
Change managers	0	2	1	1
Number of tactics	302	224	533	202
Tactics per applicant	2.4	2.2	2.5	3.6
Estimated slope (s.d.'s from 1)		.83*** (.7)	1.08*** (.5)	.54** (2.2)
Estimated intercept		insig[a]	insig	3.1**
R^2 (goodness of fit)		.44***	.74***	.32**

Sources: 2010 applications coded by author and Kaylee Chretien; 1995–98 finalists: Borins (2000a, table 6); 1990–94 semifinalists: Borins (1998, table 4-2); Commonwealth awards: Borins (2006, table 3).

NA = Not available

** $p < .05$, *** $p < .01$ for slope and intercept estimates and R^2.

a. insig = insignificantly different from 0.

semifinalists yielded the now-familiar pattern of a slope estimate close to and not significantly different from 1, an insignificant intercept term, and a statistically significant R^2. The regression of the 2010 semifinalists on the Commonwealth awards applicants didn't yield quite as close a fit, with a slope significantly lower than 1, a small but significant intercept term, and a smaller, but still statistically significant, R^2.

The first three tactics—showing the benefits of an innovation, social marketing, and establishing a demonstration project—can be seen as varieties of persuasion. They represent approximately 20 percent of the total number of tactics for all four groups. Social marketing and demonstration projects—rarely present in the Commonwealth awards group but robustly present in the three U.S. groups—might be particularly American forms of persuasion.[4] The U.S. government frequently uses demonstration projects to test the feasibility of innovations before implementing them widely. This may be the result of a stronger faith in the value of evaluation, or it may be due to the American legislative system—at least in comparison to the parliamentary democracies of the Commonwealth—in which legislators operate as free agents who lobby for demonstration projects in their own constituencies or who want to see the outcomes of demonstration projects before agreeing to programs at a national level. The next five tactics—consultation with affected parties; co-optation of affected parties by involving them in the governance of the innovation; providing training for those whose work would be affected by the innovation; increasing a program's cultural or linguistic sensitivity; and compensating those whose interests would be adversely affected by an innovation (such as workers made redundant by information technology or middle managers made redundant by organizational restructuring)—were all ways of accommodating people who saw themselves as adversely affected by the innovation. These tactics represented 24 to 35 percent of the total number of tactics for the four groups. The salience of persuasion and accommodation as tactics—almost half of all instances of tactics used to overcome opposition—makes clear that the innovators took objections seriously and attempted either to change the minds of opponents or skeptics or to modify the innovation so that opponents or skeptics would be more comfortable with it. Again, this speaks to the difficult balance a successful innovator must strike between singleness of purpose and adaptability of process.

Tactics that appear to have been targeted to particular problems include finding resources, solving logistical problems, building political support, modifying a technology to make it more user-friendly to staff or users, and changing previously enacted laws or regulations that constrain an innovation. Finding support elsewhere in the bureaucracy than the unit where an initiative was originally introduced was coded for the first time for the 2010 semifinalists. Two tactics appear applicable to virtually any obstacle: being persistent and having a clear and focused vision of the innovation. It is instructive that the second-least frequently used tactic for all four innovation groups was a "power politics" approach—

---

4. Cels, de Jong, and Nauta (2012, 28) did present instances of Japanese, Canadian, and German innovators using pilot projects as a tactic to win support for their programs.

changing managers responsible for program implementation. The innovators usually attempted to persuade or accommodate their opponents, rather than to appeal to the authority of superiors to remove them. These successful change agents overwhelmingly employed consensus-building rather than strong-arm tactics. I previously argued (Borins 1998, 75) that this behavior was evidence of innovating with integrity and that it effectively countered the claim made by the critics of New Public Management that innovative public servants were loose cannons, rule breakers, self-promoters, and power politicians (Borins 2000a, 505–06). What the present data increasingly suggest is that the trajectory of an innovation might best be described as a careful progress through recursive steps of refining, responding, and reframing, with innovators deploying both adaptability and persuasion, so that public sector innovation, even within a single agency, is always collaborative, because it always requires bringing people on board.

But did these tactics work? Table 5-3 charts the outcome of the innovators' efforts to deal with the obstacles they faced. Question 5 on the semifinalist questionnaire asks applicants which of the obstacles they have identified still remain. Those that were not listed as remaining were coded as having been overcome. The percentage of obstacles successfully dealt with was substantial and increased from 58 percent for the 1990–94 semifinalists to 77 percent for the Class of 2010. The most dramatic change was the increase in the frequency with which a shortage of resources was overcome, from only 19 percent for the 1990–94 semifinalists to 58 percent for 2010. The growing incidence of multiple funding sources for innovation, both within and outside the public sector (see table 3-3) surely provides an explanation for this improvement. This in turn speaks to an increasing realism among innovators regarding the scarcity of government resources and the need to look elsewhere. We might also link this increasing success rate to an increasing comfort among other funding sources with shared stewardship and the role of contributing partner. Here again we may be seeing signs that the increasing incidence of and experience with interorganizational collaboration may be creating a new culture within the public sector. The regression of the frequency obstacles were overcome by the 2010 semifinalists on the frequency they were overcome by the 1990–94 semifinalists yielded an insignificant slope, a large and significant intercept, and a statistically insignificant R^2—there was no significant relationship between the two. The key factor contributing to this result was the increase in the frequency with which resource issues were overcome by the 2010 semifinalists. This is the only instance in this chapter where the pattern of responses for a variable in 2010 was not close to that of its precursors.

Table 5-4 builds on the previous two tables by showing the tactics that were most frequently used to address each obstacle. Sixteen obstacles and eighteen tactics would have produced a full matrix of 288 cells. I simplified this considerably

Table 5-3. *Frequency of Overcoming an Obstacle as Percentage of Total Times Obstacle Encountered*

Percent except as indicated

Obstacle	2010 semifinalists	1990–94 semifinalists
Bureaucratic resistance	70	71
Coordination	79	65
Logistical	45	55
Burnout	55	45
Technology	56	70
Unions	NA	71
Middle managers	NA	71
Oppose public entrepreneurs	NA	NA
Lack of resources	58	19
Laws, regulations	38	53
Political opposition	83	63
Political transition	62	NA
Public doubt	65	90
Reaching target group	59	60
Affected interests	82	64
Competitors	NA	50
Total[a]	77	58
Estimated slope (s.d.'s from 1)	insig[b]	
Estimated intercept	46.2**	
R^2 (goodness of fit)	.11	

Sources: 2010 applications coded by author and Kaylee Chretien; 1990–94 semifinalists: Borins (1998, table 4-1).

NA = Not available

** $p < .05$ for slope and intercept estimate.

a. Frequency with which all obstacles were overcome.

b. insig = insignificantly different from 0.

by listing only the four most frequently used tactics for the eleven most frequently observed obstacles. The table compares the most frequently used tactics for the 2010 and 1990–94 semifinalists by placing the two groups in alternating rows and using italics to indicate instances where the same tactic appeared in the top four for *both* groups of semifinalists. Glancing at the table, the visual impression is of a great deal of italics. I confirmed this impression by counting the number of instances where there was a match—a tactic appearing in the top four for both groups of semifinalists—and the number of instances where there was not. The total number of possible matches for the table was 44. There were 26 matches, constituting 59 percent.

Table 5-4. *Four Tactics Used Most Frequently by 2010 and 1990–94 Semifinalists to Respond to Obstacles, as Percentage of Number of Occurrences of each Obstacle*[a]

Percent except as indicated

Obstacle	Number[b]	Tactic 1	Tactic 2	Tactic 3	Tactic 4
Logistical, 2010	60	Solve logistics, 50	Get resources, 20	Consultation, 12	Training, 10
Logistical, 1990s	51	Solve logistics, 86	Training, 7	Persistence, 7	
Bureaucratic, 2010	44	Consultation, 30	Show benefits, 27	Training, 27	Co-optation, 18
Bureaucratic, 1990s	92	Training, 24	Show benefits, 23	Consultation, 20	Persistence, 15
Technology, 2010	16	Modify tech, 50	Persistence, 38	Consultation, 6	Focus, 6
Technology, 1990s	30	Modify tech, 52	Training, 31	Social marketing, 7	Get resources, 7
Coordination, 2010	14	Consultation, 21	Co-optation, 14	Clear vision, 14	Persistence, 14
Coordination, 1990s	52	Consultation, 31	Co-optation, 27	Clear vision, 19	Persistence, 15
Burnout, 2010	11	Consultation, 45	Show benefits, 18	Training, 18	Clear vision, 18
Burnout, 1990s	33	Show benefits, 41	Persistence, 26	Marketing, 11	Consultation, 11
Resources, 2010	52	Get resources, 50	Persistence, 17	Logistics, 13	Political support, 10
Resources, 1990s	89	Get resources, 71	Persistence, 8	Political support, 3	
Laws, regulations, 2010	8	Persistence, 38	Consultation, 25	Focus, 25	Political support, 13
Laws, regulations, 1990s	34	Change laws, 27	Political support 23	Persistence, 20	Show benefits, 9

Political transition, 2010[c]	8	Show benefits, 50	Persistence, 25	Political support, 25	Bureaucratic support, 25
Political opposition, 2010	6	*Show benefits, 50*	*Political support, 33*	Change laws, 16	Change manager, 16
Political opposition, 1990s	8	*Political support, 25*	*Show benefits, 25*	Persistence, 25	Training, 13
Public doubts, 2010	23	*Show benefits, 26*	Social marketing, 26	*Demonstration project, 13*	Consultation, 13
Public doubts, 1990s	48	Show benefits, 31	Consultation, 23	*Demonstration project, 21*	Co-optation, 19
Hard-to-reach target group, 2010	22	Social marketing, 36	Get resources, 23	Logistics, 18	Demonstration project 9
Hard-to-reach target group, 1990s	30	Social marketing, 32	Culturally sensitive, 20	Persistence, 20	Training, 12
Opposition by affected interests, 2010	11	Show benefits, 27	Focus, 27	*Consultation, 27*	Co-optation, 18
Opposition by affected interests, 1990s	14	*Show benefits, 62*	Training, 15	Social marketing, 8	*Consultation, 8*

Sources: 2010 applications coded by author and Kaylee Chretien; 1990–94 semifinalists: Borins (1998, table 4-3).

a. italics indicate top four tactics for both 2010 and 1990–94 semifinalists.

b. Number of times an obstacle occurs.

c. "Political transition" was coded only in 2010. This phrase refers to "difficulty maintaining an innovation during the transition to new political leadership."

Some of the sets of tactics used to respond to certain obstacles are particularly noteworthy. For both groups of semifinalists, common responses to bureaucratic resistance combined persuasion (showing the benefits of the innovation) with accommodation (consultation about implementation and training when necessary). Accommodation (consultation and co-optation) also played an important role in the two groups' common responses to coordination problems, as did the development of a clear vision of the innovation so that all collaborators could focus on it, and persistence. Their responses to burnout on the part of participants in the innovation also included persuasion (showing the benefits of the innovation) and accommodation (in the form of consultation). Although the predominant response to inadequate resources was finding additional resources, both groups of semifinalists cited the importance of persistence and occasionally seeking political support.

Moving to the more explicitly political obstacles, the common responses to existing laws and regulations that hindered innovations were seeking political support and persistence. Common responses to political opposition included persuasion (showing the benefits of the innovation) and seeking political support. The preferred responses to the obstacle of keeping an innovation in operation despite a change in political leadership, coded only for the 2010 semifinalists, resemble responses to the other political obstacles: showing the benefits of the innovation, seeking political support, and persistence. The common responses to public doubts about innovations included persuasion (showing the benefits of the innovation, demonstration projects) and accommodation (in the form of public consultation). Similarly, the common responses to opposition by interests affected by innovations included persuasion (showing benefits) and accommodation (public consultation). Finally, the common response to difficulty reaching target groups was social marketing.

A number of common threads emerge in these patterns of responses. Tactics involving persuasion were often combined with tactics involving accommodation. The responses to obstacles within the bureaucracy involved action within the bureaucracy, whereas responses to political obstacles included the mobilization of political support. The previous chapter showed that there were separate bureaucratic and political paths to initiate innovations, which is consistent with this chapter's demonstration of separate bureaucratic and political paths to respond to obstacles. When the obstacles to innovation were in the public arena (public doubts, difficulty reaching target groups, opposition by affected interests), innovators resorted to both persuasion, including the use of social marketing, and accommodation. Finally, the tactic of persistence appears in numerous places, reminding us that innovation often comes about because innovators are people who are less willing than most to take no for an answer. What this analysis also makes clear, however, is that persistence alone—understood in the sense of perseverance, sticking to one's guns—is not enough.

The Critics Speak

Reading the awards applications, it is difficult not to be impressed by the evidence of individual vision, ingenuity, resourcefulness, and tenacity they contain, even to derive a certain "happy ending" satisfaction from learning of an innovation's ultimate success. But there are two sides to every story. and the HKS Awards questionnaire explicitly seeks to ensure that the other side is represented too. Question 10 on the semifinalist questionnaire asks both "What individuals or organizations are the strongest critics of the program or policy initiative and why?" and "What is the nature of their criticism?" Putting the question this way rather than asking for *all* critics limits the number of responses. Like the request for the most "significant" obstacles, this phrasing may also actually increase the incentive to report fully. Table 5-5 shows the identity of the critics, where it could be determined, and table 5-6 the nature of their criticisms. Table 5-5 indicates the range and number of critics reported, including participants in the innovative program, professionals in its policy area, public interest groups, politicians, governmental or nonprofit organizations affected by the program, competing businesses (in situations where the innovative program provides a service that competes with something already being offered privately), clients of the program, individuals affected by the program, media, and public sector unions. Twenty-five percent of the 1990–94 semifinalists and 15 percent of the 2010 semifinalists claimed they had no critics. For the majorities that reported having critics, there was an average of 1.3 critics per semifinalist in both 2010 and 1990–94. The regression of critics of the 2010 semifinalists on critics of the 1990–94 semifinalists showed a slope close to and not significantly different from 1, an intercept that was insignificant, and a statistically significant R^2.

What were the nature and extent of the criticisms these innovations encountered? Table 5-6 shows that where there were critics, the average number of criticisms for both the 2010 and 1990–94 semifinalists was 1.4. For both groups of semifinalists, by far the most frequently heard criticism was of the program's "philosophy"—its informing theoretical concept, model, or approach, a criticism often voiced by those advocating an alternative course. For example, a charter school's use of project-based learning might be opposed by proponents of an educational model emphasizing performance on standardized exams. Several criticisms (economic loss inflicted on the critic, other negative impact, and effect on working conditions) involved the program's direct impact on the critic. Finally, there were criticisms calling for an expansion of the program as well as criticisms

Table 5-5. *Sources of Criticism as Percentage of 1990–94 and 2010 Semifinalists*
Percent except as indicated

Source of criticism	2010 semifinalists	1990–94 semifinalists
Unspecified	28	17
Program participants	22	10
Professionals	13	17
Public interest groups	8	8
Politicians	7	10
Organizations affected by program	6	13
Competing businesses	6	5
Clients of program	5	8
Individuals affected by program	4	4
Media	2	NA
Other	2	0
Unions	1	9
Program has no critics	15	25
No response to question	7	0
Total number of critics	134	210
Critics per semifinalist	1.3	1.3
Estimated slope (s.d.'s from 1)		.72** (1)
Estimated intercept		insig[a]
R^2 (goodness of fit)		.38**

Sources: 2010 applications coded by author and Kaylee Chretien; 1990–94 semifinalists: Borins (1998, table 4-4).
NA = Not available
** $p < .05$ for slope and intercept estimates and R^2.
a. insig = insignificantly different from 0.

asking that it be curtailed (inappropriate use of public money, public money should be spent differently). The surprising finding here is that criticism about the program's philosophy made up about half of the total. Many innovators based their innovations on recognized philosophies and conceptual approaches within their policy area (discussed at greater length in the next chapter), and their philosophies and approaches were often the subject of informed criticism by people with specific, program-related objections. Dispute about an innovation's philosophy strikes me as healthy public dialogue, motivated not by calculations of self-interest but a genuine concern for both what government is doing to meet citizens' needs and how it is doing it. The regression of the pattern of criticisms for the 2010 semifinalists on the pattern of criticism for the 1990–94 semifinalists yielded a slope close to and not significantly different from 1, an insignificant intercept, and a very high and statistically significant R^2.

Table 5-6. *Types of Criticism as a Percentages of Total Criticisms, 1990–94 and 2010 Semifinalists*
Percent except as indicated

Criticism	2010 semifinalists	1990–94 semifinalists
Don't like program philosophy	49	45
Economic loss inflicted	12	10
Other negative impact on critic	14	9
Hurts work conditions	5	7
Inappropriate use of public money	5	7
Public money should be spent differently	5	6
Program should be expanded	6	8
Other	5	7
Total number of criticisms	154	234
Criticisms per semifinalist	1.4	1.4
Estimated slope (s.d.'s from 1)		1.13*** (1.7)
Estimated intercept		insig[a]
R^2 (goodness of fit)		.97***

Sources: 2010 applications coded by author and Kaylee Chretien; 1990–94 semifinalists: Borins (1998, table 4-4).
*** p <.01 for slope and intercept estimates and R^2.
a. insig = insignificantly different from 0.

In table 5-7 I link criticisms with the critics who voice them, for both the 2010 semifinalists and the 1990–94 semifinalists. Criticisms made by each type of critic are shown for the 2010 semifinalists and 1990–94 semifinalists in alternating lines. Italics indicate instances where the percentages of a given type of critic making a given type of criticism were within 10 percent of one another for both groups of semifinalists. There were fifty-six possible pairs (eight types of critics making seven types of criticisms), and I found that in thirty-five of the fifty-six possible pairs (62 percent) the percentages making the criticism were within 10 percent of one another for both groups of semifinalists. Consider the results for the different types of critics. Professionals and unspecified critics (not known) were most likely to dispute a program's philosophy. Public interest groups criticized the innovation's philosophy approximately half the time, but they were also the most likely to call for the program to be expanded. Clients of programs displayed a similar pattern of criticisms. Participants in the program criticized the innovation's philosophy half the time but were also the most frequent critics of its effect on conditions at work. Politicians criticized the innovation's philosophy approximately half the time and frequently called for innovations to be curtailed. Businesses affected by innovations focused most frequently on their economic

Table 5-7. *Type of Criticism as a Percentage of Criticisms by Each Source, 2010 and 1990–94 Semifinalists*[a]

Percent except as indicated

Source of criticism	Number of criticisms by source	Philosophy behind innovation	Negative impact	Economic loss	Expand program	Inappropriate use of money	Spend differently	Working conditions
Source of criticism unknown, 2010	35	63	14	6	11	6	9	0
Not known, 1990s	35	69	0	0	14	0	17	0
Participant, 2010	29	45	21	14	7	3	0	24
Participant, 1990s	22	55	0	0	18	0	5	23
Professionals, 2010	17	76	18	12	0	6	6	0
Professionals, 1990s	35	75	3	3	9	11	3	9
Public interest group, 2010	11	55	18	0	18	9	0	0
Public interest group, 1990s	17	53	0	0	18	6	6	0
Politicians 2010	9	56	11	22	11	11	22	0
Politicians, 1990s	21	43	0	5	5	33	5	5
Businesses, 2010	8	38	0	50	0	0	13	5
Businesses, 1990s	36	6	50	44	0	0	0	5
Organizations affected by innovation, 2010	8	38	25	38	0	13	0	0
Clients, 2010	7	71	0	14	0	0	0	0
Clients, 1990s	16	56	0	0	25	13	0	6
Individuals, 2010	5	60	40	20	0	0	0	0
Individuals, 1990s	8	63	0	0	0	38	0	0
Number, 2010[b]		75	21	19	9	17	7	7
Number, 1990s[b]		106	21	24	19	17	13	17

Sources: 2010 applications coded by author and Kaylee Chretien; 1990–94 semifinalists: Borins (1998, table 4-4).

a. In the 1990–94 data there were two categories of business: those affected (27 cases) and competitors (9 cases). They were aggregated to be comparable to the 2010 data. The category of affected organizations used in 2010 was not used for the 1990–94 semifinalists. Percentages across a row sometimes add up to more than 100 because some critics make more than one criticism. Italicized numbers indicate instances where the percentages of the criticisms by a given source for both 2010 and 1990–94 semifinalists were within 10 percent of one another.

b. Number of instances of the criticisms.

Table 5-8. *Most Significant Remaining Shortcomings of Innovations as Percentage of Semifinalists*

Percent except as indicated

Shortcoming	2010 semifinalists	1990–94 semifinalists
Needs fine-tuning	41	29
Lacks resources	33	39
Hasn't spread as much as hoped	20	12
Difficulty maintaining continuity	10	NA
Logistical issue	7	NA
Difficulty maintaining collaboration	5	5
Coping with growth	1	4
Related programs holding innovation back	1	7
Other	3	15
Total number of shortcomings	154	240
Shortcomings per semifinalist	1.2	1.1
Estimated slope (s.d.'s from 1)		1.08** (.3)
Estimated intercept		insig[a]
R^2 (goodness of fit)		.75**

Sources: 2010 applications coded by author and Kaylee Chretien; 1990–94 semifinalists: Borins (1998, Table 4-5).

NA = Not available

** $p < .05$ for slope and intercept estimates and R^2.

a. insig = insignificantly different from 0.

impact rather than their philosophy. Looking at this table in its totality, it is noteworthy that all types of critics, with the exceptions of businesses and affected organizations for the 2010 semifinalists, engaged in dialogue about an innovation's philosophy much more often than they discussed its impact on their self-interest. This makes the innovator's ability to respond, persuade, accommodate, and adapt all the more important and suggests, further, that an ability to educate might be an important addition to that skill list.

The semifinalist questionnaire sought to determine internal as well as external criticisms of the innovations, asking applicants in question 9 to identify their program's "most significant remaining shortcoming." Table 5-8 shows the results for the 2010 and 1990–94 semifinalists. On average, semifinalists indicated slightly more than one shortcoming, the wording of the question relieving them of the need to be exhaustive. The two most frequent shortcomings identified were that the innovation lacked resources and that it needed fine-tuning, with the former given more frequently in 1990–94 and the latter more frequently in 2010. The 6 percent decline in the frequency with which a lack of resources was cited from

1990–94 to 2010 is likely a result of the recent increase in the diversity of available funding sources. Other shortcomings cited were that the innovation hadn't spread as much as envisaged, that there was difficulty maintaining the continuity of the program (especially in the event of a change in political leadership), and difficulty maintaining an interorganizational collaboration. Given the dramatic increase in innovations characterized by such collaboration from 1990–94 to 2010, it is surprising that only 5 percent of the Class of 2010—the same percentage as of the 1990–94 semifinalists—cited difficulty maintaining a collaboration as a significant shortcoming. However, this is consistent with coordination problems constituting only 5 percent of the obstacles cited by the Class of 2010 in table 5-1. An obvious progression can be inferred: as the incidence of and therefore the experience with interorganizational collaboration increases, knowledge of smart practice emerges and spreads, making future instances more successful, leading to a greater incidence of interorganizational collaboration. Finally, regressing the most significant remaining shortcomings for the 2010 semifinalists on those of the 1990–94 semifinalists resulted in a slope close to and not significantly different from 1, an insignificant intercept, and a statistically significant R^2.

It is clear from the accounts provided by applicants of the obstacles and criticism their initiatives encountered and the tactics adopted to address them that these innovations of necessity evolved in the course of their implementation and operation. Question 4 on the semifinalist questionnaire asked applicants about this evolution explicitly: "How has the implementation strategy of your program or policy initiative evolved over time?" and also requested an outline of "the chronology of your innovation and . . . the key milestones in program or policy development and when they occurred." Although this shifts the focus away from obstacles and criticism to more neutral ground, there is obviously some overlap. An innovation encountering either obstacles or criticism or both was typically reconfigured to some degree to respond effectively, as our previous findings have shown. Table 5-9 shows the categories of program evolution that were coded on the basis of the 2010 semifinalists' answers to this question. The table also shows that 97 percent of the semifinalists provided some kind of time line, which facilitated coding this question. Regrettably, despite the presence of a similar question in previous semifinalist questionnaires (Borins 1998, 296), I did not code answers to it in previous research. I had not yet made the link between narrative and innovation that I have subsequently explored. The "stories" of the innovations interested me less than their characteristics and outcomes. This was not the first time I've revisited earlier work and thought, "If only I'd known." In *Innovating with Integrity* I coded initiation by frontline staff and middle managers together, but in subsequent research I have coded them separately. Research always involves a

Table 5-9. *Changes in Implementation of Innovation over Time as Percentage of 2010 Semifinalists*

Implementation change	Percentage of semifinalists
Existing services have grown steadily	89
Program has taken advantage of new opportunities	33
Program has launched new services	49
Adjustments have been made in program	31
Program has encountered opposition and has made major modifications	1
Total responses (percent)	203
Narrative time line	
Detailed time line provided	54
Some time line provided	43
No time line provided	3
Total responses	100

Source: 2010 applications coded by author and Kaylee Chretien.

process of learning. Sometimes a question turns out to warrant more attention than you had previously given it.

An average of two responses regarding program evolution was coded per semifinalist for the Class of 2010. Almost all of them (89 percent) said that existing services had grown steadily; half said that the program had launched new services; and a third said that it had taken advantage of new opportunities. A third reported that adjustments had been made in the program, and only 1 percent—one program—said that it had encountered opposition and made major modifications. This was one of the first three charter schools in Ohio, which faced a lawsuit filed in opposition to the very creation of charter schools and as a result had its initial contract with the school district terminated. On balance, though, the answers to the question regarding evolution are positive, with far more citing growth of existing or new services than admitting that adjustments had to be made. Given that these are innovations that have chosen to apply to an awards competition and that have emerged from the first round of the judging process, it should not be surprising that their stories are ones of progress and expansion.

An Archetypal Innovation Story?

In previous research (Borins 2012, 178), based on a small sample of thirty-one finalists to the 2008 and 2009 HKS Awards, I outlined a dominant innovation initiation story. As the title of that article, "Making Narrative Count," suggests, I drew extensively on narratological theory in my analysis. I consequently used the term "fable" there to connote a core structure—a common "plot," as it were—instantiated in a variety of different, specific accounts. That fable focused on interorganizational cooperation, positing difficult policy challenges that cross organizational boundaries as a motivating factor and senior elected or appointed officials who take the initiative or provide support for collaborative programs or policies as protagonists. We can now attempt something similar for the implementation of innovations in government, suggesting an archetypal story derived from the detailed data about the Class of 2010 presented here and about the 1990–94 semifinalists presented in *Innovating with Integrity* (Borins 1998). It is further supported by available data for the 1995–98 finalists and the two sets of Commonwealth awards applicants. Indeed, it is impressive that in almost every instance the regression analysis shows that the patterns of variables are similar, in a statistical sense, for all four groups of innovations.

The story begins with the fact that even successful innovations such as these awards applicants face obstacles. The most common obstacles come from within the bureaucracy because innovations are by their nature disruptive. They challenge occupational patterns, standard operating procedures, and power structures. Inadequate resourcing is another significant obstacle, whether of bureaucratic or political origin. Less frequently, innovations face obstacles emanating from the political arena, such as existing laws that present hurdles to new initiatives, outright political opposition, or the prospect of new political leadership that may withdraw support. Finally, innovations face obstacles from the public sphere, such as resistance from or difficulty reaching target groups or skepticism on their part.

Innovators necessarily prove resourceful in responding to these obstacles. Their two main tactics are persuasion, explaining the need for and benefits of their initiatives, and accommodation, finding ways to take into account the concerns and interests of potential opponents, particularly those within the bureaucracy. Innovators also are imaginative in finding possible sources of funding when their resources are inadequate; indeed, their ingenuity is supported by an increasing variety of alternative funding sources and an increasing comfort among those sources with assuming a shared role in an innovative enterprise. These successful innovators are organizationally astute. They tend not to confuse or conflate the bureaucratic and political arenas. They devise bureaucratic solutions for obstacles in the bureaucracy and political solutions for obstacles in the political arena. Finally, these innovators persevere. They accommodate, demonstrate, educate, reformulate, articulate, and persist. Consequently, they resolve most of the obstacles they encounter and their innovations survive and prosper.

The story makes plain, however, that innovators face criticism as well as obstacles. The criticism is most often philosophical, based on opposition to the theory or model of practice in a particular policy area that underlies an innovation.

Sometimes the criticism is self-interested, arising from the (perceived) negative impact of the innovation on the critic. Criticism constitutes an ongoing dialogue, and, ultimately, the innovator's best response to criticism is to produce impressive results. While deflecting external criticism, innovators nonetheless perceive short-comings in their own programs. Some may only require fine-tuning but others are more serious such as inadequate resources or inadequate growth.

Throughout this chapter, I have made reference to elements of storytelling and narrative, casting the innovations and their initiators as the protagonists in a plot that includes obstacles, antagonists, and challenges successfully met. The next chapter brings the innovation narrative forward to the question of outcomes. Do these innovation stories have happy endings? If so, for whom? To put the question another way, are these public sector actors actually creating public value?

6

Creating Public Value,
Receiving Public Recognition

At the height of the New Public Management debate, in 1995, Mark Moore in his book *Creating Public Value* coined the term "public value" to encapsulate an essential difference between the public and private sectors. Moore argued that private value can be measured by the market test, but public value cannot because it involves pure public goods, or at least goods that politicians have decided will be provided by the public sector without charge to users (technically, "merit goods"). Moore was supportive of New Public Management because he saw it as a means of increasing public value, and he advanced the view that public servants should be imaginative in using the capacity of their organizations to enhance service and in negotiating with their authorizing environment to get approval for their initiatives, both familiar NPM tropes. Moore's book generated a great deal of academic debate about whether the concept of public value could be operationalized and whether concepts developed for the U.S. context could be applied to parliamentary systems. Moore responded in a new book, *Recognizing Public Value* (2013), in which he proposed the idea of a public value account, putting the resource costs of a public sector program on one side of a notional ledger and its beneficial outcomes (including social outcomes, mission achievement, unintended positive consequences, and client satisfaction) on the other.[1]

Borrowing Moore's formulation enables us to ask an essential question about the innovations and innovators we have been examining so closely: Are they pro-

---

1. Moore stressed that his public value account schema differs from private sector accounting because public sector programs have multiple categories of costs and of benefits. He did not make reference to an older tradition of evaluation of public sector programs developed by economists—benefit-cost analysis—which attempts to translate all costs and benefits into the common denominator of money, so that the evaluation can ultimately produce a single measure of public value.

viding public value? It is easy to see how an innovation could become a "vanity project," an initiative driven by the professional egos most directly involved. More charitably, it might be conceived and implemented in a spirit of pure experimentation—innovation for novelty's sake. In this chapter I provide a number of answers to the central question of value provided, looking at a variety of possible gauges of value: the applicants' own impact measures; their self-reported most significant achievements; the results of formal external evaluation; and external recognition in the form of awards, media attention, and transfer of the innovation itself.[2] Even though self-reported "most significant achievements" inevitably are subjective, they are also revealing for what they tell us about innovators' motivations and their own perceptions of what constitutes achievement—which is not always synonymous with success. Formal evaluations and external recognition offer more objective measures to balance the data categories.

In this chapter I also offer econometric analysis exploring which attributes of the 2010 semifinalists were likely to have been responsible for their winning public recognition. To do this I created indexes measuring the extent of media attention, awards, and transfer achieved by the innovations and then used their characteristics to explain their scores on the indexes. I also looked to the HKS Awards program itself, seeking to account for the outcomes of the two rounds of assessments—the selection of semifinalists from the initial applicant pool and the subsequent selection of the top-tier twenty-five and the six finalists—on the basis of various characteristics of the applications at each round. This last aspect of econometric analysis provides a point of comparison between recognition by the HKS Awards program and other forms of external recognition. Returning here to the question of the sustainability and credibility of the program raised in chapter 3 also allows us to probe whether the program is fair, in the sense of following its own stated criteria in the judging process, or whether other factors are at work in the choice of semifinalists and finalists.

The Applicants Speak

Question 7 of the HKS Awards semifinalist questionnaire asked applicants "What are the three most important measures you use to evaluate your program's success? In qualitative or quantitative terms for each measure, please provide the outcomes of the last full year of program operation and, if possible, at least one prior year" (see appendix, "Semifinalist Application Questions," for all references to questions on the HKS Awards semifinalists questionnaire). Table 6-1 charts the 2010

2. The cost side of the ledger would be found in the discussion of the 2010 semifinalists' average capital and operating budgets in chapter 3 (see pp. 55–56). For any particular innovation the public value account would involve comparing its budgetary and other costs with its benefits.

Table 6-1. *Outcomes of Innovations as Percentage of Total Innovations*
for Each Group
Percent except as indicated

Outcome	2010 semifinalists	1990–94 semifinalists
Clients better off	85	NA
People using program	67	52
Program setting and meeting goals	31	70
Costs being reduced	26	19
Service improving	25	32
Satisfaction (in formal surveys)	18	22
Informal expressions of support	15	19
Program receiving awards	9	NA
Improved productivity	7	5
Experimental design	1	6
Increased revenue	0	6
Too early to tell	0	2
Other	0	5
Total responses as percentage of number of innovations	284	238
Number of innovations	127	217
Estimated slope (s.d.'s from 1)		.74*** (1.4)
Estimated intercept		insig[a]
R^2 (goodness of fit)		.65***

Sources: 2010 applications coded by author and Kaylee Chretien; 1990–94 semifinalists: Borins (1998, table 6-1).

NA = Not available

*** $p < .01$ for slope and intercept estimates and R^2.

a. insig = insignificantly different from 0.

and 1990–94 semifinalists' answers to this question. The table shows that most applicants reported three outcomes: an average of 2.8 per applicant in 2010 and 2.4 per applicant in 1990–94. A wide variety of answers was given about how public value was created, including the improved well-being of the user (clients better off), the demand for the service (people using program), reduction in the cost of running the program (costs being reduced), service improving, improved productivity of the resources used in delivering the program, and expressions of satisfaction in surveys. For the 1990–94 semifinalists the category most frequently coded was programs setting and meeting goals (Borins 1998, 104–05); it occurred in 70 percent of the applications. In coding the 2010 semifinalists my research assistant and I observed fewer applications that could fit into that category (31 percent), and we added a more general category of clients better off. This applied to the vast majority of the programs (85 percent). Nonetheless, regressing the outcome measures for the 2010 semifinalists on those for the 1990–94 semifinalists produced a slope close to and not significantly different from 1, an intercept not significantly different from zero, and a statistically significant R^2.[3]

Only 2 percent of the 1990–94 semifinalists indicated it was too early to tell what the outcomes of their program were. None gave that answer in 2010. Informal expressions of support by stakeholders, if coded alone, would have been a very weak claim for public value creation. Among the 1990–94 semifinalists, all but one of the applications for which that category was coded also had at least one more objective measure (Borins 1998, 107), and that was the case for all of the 15 percent of semifinalist applications for which it was coded in 2010.

Since nine different outcome variables were applicable to more than 1 percent of the 2010 semifinalists, I used factor analysis to explore whether they could be reduced to a smaller set of internally related measures. Unfortunately the factor analysis was inconclusive. Improved service, cost reductions, and improved productivity—three conceptually related measures—loaded most heavily onto the first factor, but its eigenvalue was too low (.69) and uniqueness measure (.85) too high for it to be useful for further analysis. All the other factors provided low eigenvalues, small loadings, and no clear interpretation.

The EC Innobarometer survey (Gallup Organization 2010, 24–31) makes a useful comparator here, since it asked respondents about the positive and negative impacts of their innovations. Regarding service innovations, major positive impacts were improved user satisfaction (71 percent of innovating organizations) and faster delivery of services (54 percent). For process innovations, major positive impacts included improved employee satisfaction (62 percent), faster service delivery (62 percent), and reduced cost (51 percent). The Innobarometer survey differed from the HKS Awards questionnaire because it used different categories of innovation and surveyed a much larger sample; nevertheless, increased user satisfaction, improved service, and cost reduction are all frequently mentioned outcomes in responses to the HKS Awards questionnaire too. The Innobarometer survey also asked whether there were negative impacts of innovations. Sixty-six percent of innovating organizations said there were none. The two most frequently mentioned negative effects were additional administration cost (18 percent of innovating organizations) and user resistance or dissatisfaction (12 percent). This picture is confirmed by some of the recent literature on innovation (Damanpour, Walker, and Avellaneda 2009; Walker, Damanpour, and Devece 2010; Salge and Vera 2012), which has used statistical analysis to show that the

3. In the regression, the 2010 measure "clients better off" could not be used because it was not used for the 1990–94 semifinalists.

Table 6-2. *Most Important Achievement of Innovators as Percentage*
of Total Innovations for Each Group

Percent except at indicated

Achievement	2010 semifinalists	1990–94 semifinalists
Implemented the innovation well	76	8
Facilitated collaboration	31	17
Operationalized theoretical model	29	16
Same as a measure of success	16	44
Educated the public about a problem	10	11
Initiated a public discussion	6	3
Used in unforeseen ways	2	2
Getting technology to work	1	1
Other	0	6
Total responses as percentage of number of innovations	171	125
Number of innovations	127	217
Estimated slope (s.d.'s from 1)		insig[a]
Estimated intercept		insig
R^2 (goodness of fit)		.02[a]

Sources: 2010 applications coded by author and Kaylee Chretien; 1990–94 semifinalists: Borins (1998, table 6-2).

a. insig = insignificantly different from 0.

overall level of organizational innovation has a positive impact on aggregate measures of organizational performance.

In question 6 the HKS Awards semifinalist questionnaire requested applicants to identify their "single most important achievement . . . to date" (see table 6-2). "Achievement" is a term worth pausing over. It is broader in its scope than outcome, encompassing the intentions of the organization implementing the program or of the individuals initiating it. It also makes room for a possible distance from "success," since the fact of implementing a complex, perhaps collaborative, initiative may in itself constitute an important internal achievement for the organization without necessarily producing the outcomes that would mark it as a success. There is clearly a place here for internal benchmarks when one is assessing the net effects of an innovation, and for a more nuanced understanding of what both success and failure might mean. Many applicants responded to the question about achievement with one or more of their outcome measures. For the 1990–94 semifinalists this was coded as "same as a measure of success." "For the 2010 semifinalists we coded "same as a measure of success" when the response was identical to one or more outcome measures and "implemented the innovation well" when the response indicated that outcome measures were being achieved because the program was working well. Removing these answers still left many semifinalists presenting achievements that differed from the measured outcomes of the innovations themselves.[4] These achievements related to the innovation process and included facilitating collaboration, operationalizing a theoretical model, educating the public about a problem, and initiating a public discussion. Given the greater incidence of collaboration in the 2010 semifinalists, it is not surprising that facilitating collaboration appeared almost twice as frequently in this data set as it did for the 1990–94 semifinalists. Successful collaboration in particular can reasonably be viewed as an important organizational achievement, since it is likely to have an effect on the success of future initiatives by creating alliances, structures, networks, and a shared history.

As a consequence of both the differing interpretations of "implemented the innovation well" and of "same as a measure of success" as well as differences in the frequency of the other responses, the regression of the most important achievement for the 2010 semifinalists on that of the 1990–94 semifinalists yielded insignificant slope and intercept terms as well as a statistically insignificant R^2 of .02—in effect, no statistically significant relationship at all between the two groups of semifinalists.

External Measures of Value Creation

Throughout our analysis we have found that marked changes in response patterns between our comparators have tended to ramify beyond the specific categories in which they manifest themselves. The most obvious example of this is the increase in interorganizational collaboration, whose implications have been traced in virtually every chapter. Comparing responses to question 11, on formal evaluation or audit "by an independent organization or group," reveals an equally significant difference. Applicants are requested to self-report the results of the formal evaluation—the temptation to filter or interpret too freely being reduced by the questionnaire's also asking for contact information to enable verification. Table 6-3 presents the various types of formal evaluation that applicants mention in answer to this question. It shows a dramatic change in the extent of formal

---

4. For the 2010 semifinalists, total responses (171 percent) minus implemented innovation well (76 percent) and same as measure of success (16 percent), equals 79 percent, or an average of .8 responses per semifinalist. For the 1990–94 semifinalists, total responses (125 percent) minus implemented innovation well (8 percent) and same as measure of success (44 percent), equals 73 percent, or an average of .7 responses per semifinalist.

Table 6-3. *Formal Evaluation of Innovations as Percentage of Total Innovations for Each Group*

Percents except at indicated

Formal evaluation	2010 semifinalists	1990–94 semifinalists
Policy analysis by consultants, nonprofits, or foundations	42	25
Evaluation in government (central agency, inspector general)	24	14
Academic research	23	12
Financial audit	12	20
Accreditation review	6	NA
None	28	38
Responses per semifinalist	1.49	1.18
Number of innovations	127	217
Completely supportive evaluations	42	NA
Partially supportive evaluations	16	NA
Results of evaluations NA	15	NA
Estimated slope (s.d.'s from 1)		insig[a]
Estimated intercept		insig
R^2 (goodness of fit)		.12[a]

Sources: 2010 applications coded by author and Kaylee Chretien. For 1990–94 semifinalists, see Borins 1998, Table 6-3, p. 112.

NA = Not available

a. insig = insignificantly different from 0.

external evaluation between 1990–94 and 2010. Policy analysis increased by 17 percent, evaluation within government by 10 percent, and academic research by 11 percent. Accreditation review (6 percent) was added as a new category. The only type of evaluation to decrease was financial audit, by 8 percent. Financial audit, however, is the least valuable form of external evaluation. It deals only with whether money was used for the purpose for which it was appropriated, not whether the program achieved its objectives, still less whether the program might constitute an achievement for the organization regardless of its outcome. For the semifinalist initiatives that were evaluated, the average number of types of formal external evaluation also increased, from 1.18 to 1.49. The percentage of programs receiving no formal external evaluation decreased from 38 percent to 28 percent. These changes were so substantial that regressing formal evaluations of the 2010 semifinalists on those of the 1990–94 semifinalists yielded insignificant slope and intercept terms and an R^2 of .12—no significant relationship between the two groups of semifinalists.

A change of this magnitude invites speculation about causes. Arguably one legacy of New Public Management was the institutionalization of the practice of performance measurement, a practice that has grown increasingly easy to execute through digital feedback mechanisms. Robert Behn (2014) has referred to this phenomenon as "PerformanceStat," the ongoing measurement and analysis of government performance by both departmental managers and central leadership (the mayor or governor) to achieve continuing performance improvement. And the same technologies that enable the gathering of data provide forums for their display to the general public on web portals and social media sites. Additionally, as public sector innovators turn to foundations for support, they are increasingly obliged to provide performance data for scrutiny. (The Gates Foundation, which has made education one of its priorities and has funded a number of the education innovations that are discussed in chapter 7, is known to be exigent in its requirements.)

What were the overall results of the external evaluations for the 2010 semifinalists? Forty-two percent summarized their external evaluations as being completely supportive of their innovations and 16 percent as partially supportive, meaning they indicated grounds for improvement in some areas. For 15 percent of those that were evaluated, we could not find an overall summary of the assessment, though it may be reasonable to assume that those associated with an initiative that had already received positive external reviews would be more likely to apply to an awards program than those whose external reviews were either strongly mixed or mostly negative. For the 28 percent of applications that did not have an external evaluation, this was coded as NA.

The semifinalist questionnaire probed for three other sources of external recognition: transfer of the innovation, awards, and media attention. We coded the 2010 semifinalists in much more detail about these areas, but can also provide some overall comparisons with the 1990–94 semifinalists and Commonwealth awards applicants. Referring to potential for replication, question 12 of the semifinalist questionnaire asked: "To what extent do you believe your program or policy initiative is potentially replicable within other jurisdictions and why? To your knowledge, have any other jurisdictions or organizations established programs or implemented policies modeled specifically on your own?" Though the questionnaire uses the term "replicability," I prefer "transfer" or "transferability," which connotes adaptation of a program to a different context rather than undifferentiated reproduction.[5]

5. The importance of adaptation to the transferee's context was stressed by Hartley (2008, 176–86) in her discussion of inter-organizational learning in the Beacons Scheme, and by Behn (2008) in a paper arguing that "tacit knowledge" is a key component to any effective program and that the successful transfer of tacit knowledge requires considerable contact between the transferring and adapting organizations.

Table 6-4. *Transfer of Innovations as Percentage of Total Innovations for Each Group*

Percent except at indicated

	2010 semifinalists	1990–94 semifinalists	1998 and 2000 Commonwealth awards
Local interest in transfer	10	27	NA
National interest in transfer	44	54	NA
International interest	15	14	NA
Any interest	54	65	NA
Evidence of local transfer	27	27	11
Evidence of national transfer	42	24	13
Evidence of international transfer	11	1	18
Evidence of any transfer	58	42	38
Transferable, but no actual transfer	31	NA	NA
Other	2	0	NA
NA	1	0	NA
Number of innovations	127	217	56
Estimated slope (s.d.'s from 1)		.79*** (1.1)	insig[a]
Estimated intercept		insig	insig
R^2 (goodness of fit)		.71***	.42[a]

Sources: 2010 applications coded by author and Kaylee Chretien; 1990–94 semifinalists: Borins (1998, table 6-5); Commonwealth awards: Borins (2001a, table 6).

NA = Not available

*** p <.01 for slope and intercept estimates and R^2.

a. insig = insignificantly different from 0.

Table 6-4 shows transfer of innovations for the 2010 semifinalists, 1990–94 semifinalists, and 1998 and 2000 Commonwealth awards applicants. In coding the U.S. applications I distinguished between expressions of interest in transfer and actual transfer and also among local, national, and international transfer. The 2010 semifinalists show 18 percent more actual transfer at the national level and 10 percent more actual transfer at the international level and, as a consequence, 16 percent more transfer overall than the 1990–94 semifinalists. The 2010 semifinalists, however, show 11 percent fewer applicants receiving any expressions of interest in transfer than the 1990–94 semifinalists. Interest in transfer was not coded for the Commonwealth awards applications, but an actual transfer rate of 38 percent was observed—20 percent lower than the overall transfer rate for the 2010 HKS Awards semifinalists. Despite the differences in specific rates, regressing the components of transfer for the 2010 semifinalists on those for the

Table 6-5. *Awards Received by Innovations as Percentage of Total Innovations for Each Group*

Percent except at indicated

Awards	2010 semifinalists	1990–94 semifinalists	1998 and 2000 Commonwealth awards
Own level of government	25	NA	NA
Local awards (nearby)	32	NA	NA
National awards	53	NA	NA
Any award	70	63	53
No awards	30	37	47
Number of innovations	127	217	56

Sources: 2010 applications coded by author and Kaylee Chretien; 1990–94 semifinalists: Borins (1998, table 6-4); Commonwealth awards: Borins (2001a, table 6).

NA = Not available.

1990–94 semifinalists produced a slope close to and not significantly different from 1, an intercept that was not significantly different from zero, and a statistically significant R^2. In this instance I think the differences in components of the pattern are more meaningful than the overall similarity of the patterns. The significantly higher levels of transfer—nationally, internationally, and overall—represent broader interest in public sector innovation and greater connectedness on practitioner communities on both the national and international levels. In contrast, regressing the components of transfer for the 2010 semifinalists on those of the Commonwealth awards applicants produced a statistically insignificant slope, intercept, and R^2.

Transfer may be the sincerest form of flattery, but there is no doubt that awards are welcome, too (see table 6-5). Question 14 explicitly asked HKS Awards semifinalist applicants whether their "program or policy initiative received any awards or other honors" and here, too, details and contact information were required. In coding the 2010 semifinalists, I distinguished among awards by the government (national or otherwise) of the location in which the program is based, nongovernmental local awards, and nongovernmental national awards. These distinctions were not made for the 1990–94 semifinalists. Comparing the three groups, 70 percent of the 2010 semifinalists received awards of any of three types, which was higher than the 63 percent of the 1990–94 semifinalists receiving awards and the 53 percent of the Commonwealth awards applications receiving awards. These differences in one measure are statistically significant, but there were too few observations for regression analysis of the patterns. One reason that the 2010 semifinalists received

Table 6-6. *Media Attention for Innovations as Percentages of Total Innovations for Each Group*

Percent except as indicated

Media attention	2010 semifinalists	1990–94 semifinalists	1998 and 2000 Commonwealth awards
Local or state media	74	NA	NA
Professional, trade	62	NA	NA
National media	43	NA	NA
National media, liberal	33	NA	NA
National media, center	17	NA	NA
National media, conservative	14	NA	NA
Any media attention	89	46	73
No media attention	11	54	18
Media attention NA	0	0	9
Number of innovations	127	217	56

Sources: 2010 applications coded by author and Kaylee Chretien; 1990–94 semifinalists: Borins (1998, table 6-4); Commonwealth awards: Borins (2001a, table 6).

NA = Not available.

more awards than their predecessors is that more awards programs are in existence now, a reflection of the increased interest in public sector innovation that we will discuss in more detail in relation to media attention.[6]

Media attention is a more diverse measure of recognition than winning, or not winning, an award (see table 6-6). But in this instance, the adage that there is no such thing as bad publicity does not hold. HKS Awards semifinalists were asked whether their program "received any press or other media coverage to date." Question 15 then requested them to "briefly describe relevant coverage" and, again, list the sources for possible verification. Overall, 89 percent of the 2010 semifinalists received some media attention, vastly more than the 46 percent of 1990–94 semifinalists and considerably more than the 73 percent of the Commonwealth awards applicants that reported some media attention. Both of these differences were statistically significant. Because media attention was coded only on an aggregate and not on a detailed level for the 1990–94 HKS Awards semifinalists and Commonwealth awards applicants, calculating regressions was not possible. Media attention for the 2010 semifinalists was classified as either local or state media (74 percent), professional or trade media (62 percent), and national media (43 percent). It is possible that the increase in media attention reflects a more general heightening of

6. Borins (2000c) documents a substantial increase in the number of public sector awards programs in Canada during the 1990s, and it is likely this was also the case in the United States.

awareness of public sector innovation, its greater presence on the cultural radar as something other than the proverbial oxymoron. It may also be part of a shift in perceptions of public sector organizations following the terrorist attacks of September 11, 2001, and the global financial crisis of 2008–09 leading to a new sense of their value and potential positive influence on individual citizens' lives.

National media attention was subdivided still further, between media considered to have a liberal orientation (*New York Times, Huffington Post,* MSNBC, NPR), media having a centrist orientation (CBS, CNN, *Time, Newsweek,* AP), and media having a conservative orientation (*Business Week, Forbes, Wall Street Journal,* Fox News). These categorizations were based on those used on the website www.left-right.us/about.html, coupled with some subjective correction of the site's occasionally idiosyncratic judgments. Liberal media are more receptive to the idea of government implementing innovative and effective programs than conservative media; conversely, conservative media are more likely to believe that government intervention is likely to be ineffective. Consequently, I hypothesize that stories of public sector innovation would be more consistent with liberal than conservative preconceptions and thus more likely to be covered by liberal than conservative media.[7] The data are consistent with my hypothesis: one-third of the 2010 semifinalists were covered by liberal media, 17 percent by centrist media, and only 14 percent by conservative media. I tried to drill down further to see if there were patterns regarding specific innovations—for example, whether innovations more consistent with liberal policies, such as health insurance reform innovations funded by a tax on employers and applicable to all individuals not otherwise covered, were more likely to be covered by liberal media and those more consistent with conservative policies, such as health reform innovations emphasizing health savings accounts and requiring co-payments, were more likely to be covered by conservative media. No such pattern appeared consistently. Liberal media may have a higher overall level of interest in public sector innovations than conservative, but neither media orientation is exclusively interested in innovations that are consistent with its own ideological orientation or preferred policies. Some conservative media do seek out dramatic examples of failing or eccentric "boutique" programs for polemic purposes, employing them as part of a more general attack on the wastefulness, inefficiency, impracticality, and even, in extreme cases, sheer pointlessness of the public sector. They are looking for "straw man" programs to ridicule, not for innovations operationalizing their own ideological assumptions.

7. In their study of the innovativeness of American municipal governments, Damanpour and Schneider (2008) found that having a city manager with a liberal orientation increased the innovativeness of the municipality. I interpret this as further evidence that innovation in government aligns more closely with liberal than conservative values.

Table 6-7. *Value of Components of Transfer, Awards, and Media Indexes*

Transfer component	Value	Award component	Value	Media component	Value
None	0	None	0	None	0
Potential transfer	.5	Own government	1	Trade, professional	1
Local interest	1	Local	2	Local	1
National interest	1.5	National	4	National	3
International interest	2				
Local transfer	5				
National transfer	7				
International transfer	9				
Average Score	6.5		3		2.6

Source: Components of index determined by author.

Who Notices? The Determinants of Public Recognition

Tracking data concerning reception of awards and media recognition leads naturally to questions as to which innovations receive awards, and why. After tabulating the results for transfer, awards, and media attention for the 2010 semifinalists, I turned my attention to their determinants, beginning by creating indexes that would assign a value to the extent of transfer, the nature of the awards, and the source of the media attention received by each semifinalist. In creating the indexes I chose weights that reflected my judgment about the importance of each aspect of these three variables (see table 6-7). Actual transfer, therefore, is viewed as more important than interest in transfer, and the further the transferee institution is located from the transferring innovation, the more important the transfer. Similarly, national awards are held to be more important than local ones, and national media recognition more important than local or trade media. The average score for all semifinalists is shown in the last line of table 6-7.

After establishing the three indexes, I correlated the distribution of semifinalist scores for each pair of two of the three indexes and found that they were all significantly correlated: the correlation coefficient between awards and media was .36, between transfer and media, .27, and between transfer and awards, .33. I then performed a factor analysis on the three indexes to see if they could be reduced to one or two. The loadings for each of the three indexes on the first factor were approximately .55. Because the factor's eigenvalue was low (.80) and its uniqueness score high (.77), I retained the three indexes rather than attempting to combine them.

I used the three indexes I had initially created as dependent variables in an ordinary least squares (OLS) regression analysis. I did not change them after the first few runs to improve the goodness of fit of the equation. The index scores are an accurate reflection of my original thinking, and this should not be changed after the fact to improve the statistical results.

I chose as independent variables the outcomes of the innovations, the most important achievements of the innovations, formal evaluation, and the duration of the program in years since inception. The use of outcome variables is based on the assumption that programs that achieve outcomes are most likely to receive recognition and to be transferred. It was necessary to use all nine outcome variables because factor analysis did not create a smaller number of factors to represent them (see earlier discussion, p. 111). I used the most important achievements as identified by the applicants to test whether there were any process achievements that would lead to external recognition and transfer. Because there were high levels of intercorrelation among the different types of evaluation and strong negative relationships among the different types of evaluation and the absence of evaluation, I used "absence of evaluation" as an independent variable representing formal evaluation, hypothesizing that it would have a significant negative influence on the three dependent variables. Finally, I used the duration of the program as an independent variable because programs that have been in existence longer have had more time to be transferred, to receive awards, or to attract media attention.

Table 6-8 presents the results of the OLS regression analysis. The absence of formal evaluation is, as expected, negative and strongly significant for all three dependent variables. To obtain a measure of the extent of its influence, I compared the impact of a change in absence of formal evaluation from 0 to 1 (that is, a change from having a formal evaluation to not having it) to the average value of each index (6.5 for transferability, 3 for awards, and 2.7 for media), which involves simply dividing the regression coefficient by the mean.[8] The impact was .4 for transferability, .57 for awards, and .45 for media, which indicates that a change in formal evaluation has a substantial influence on the three dependent variables. Formal external evaluation provides a measure of validation for innovations, and this validation may be recognized by other governments considering which innovations to adopt, by judges of innovation awards programs deciding which applicants to recognize, and by journalists writing about public sector innovations. These results can also be interpreted in terms of the innovation diffusion model, with measures of evaluation reducing the cost of diffusion (Berry and Berry 2007). When an innovation comes with the imprimatur of positive external evaluation from accredited sources as well as awards and positive media

---

8. Because the independent variables are dummies, taking the value of either 0 or 1, it would not have been meaningful to have calculated their elasticity at the mean.

Table 6-8. *Determinants of Transfer, Awards, and Media Attention for 2010 HKS Awards Semifinalists*[a]

Independent variable	Transfer	Awards	Media
Making clients better off	1.47 (1.05)	−.45 (.71)	−.26 (.53)
Program setting and meeting goals	.48 (.45)	−.23 (.48)	−.21 (.55)
People using program	1.1 (1.1)	−.56 (1.25)	.0 (0)
Service is improving	3.23 (2.9) ***	−.24 (.50)	−.07 (.19)
Costs being reduced	.70 (.62)	.60 (1.19)	−.31 (.78)
Satisfaction with program (survey)	−1.33 (1.06)	.64 (1.15)	.10 (.23)
Informal expressions of support	1.5 (1.1)	1.6 (2.7)***	.89 (1.9)*
Improved productivity	−.87 (.47)	.25 (.30)	−.20 (.31)
Program receiving awards	3.05 (1.8)*	1.1 (1.39)	.26 (.44)
Enabled collaboration	−1.6 (1.55)	.26 (.54)	−.05 (.15)
Operationalized theoretical model	2.32 (2,1)**	1.0 (2.0)**	.79 (2.1)**
Educated public about a problem	−.16 (.1)	.23 (.30)	.37 (.64)
Implemented innovation well	−2.0 (1.69)*	.24 (.47)	.01 (.01)
Initiated a public discussion	1.4 (.66)	.80 (.84)	−.26 (.35)
Duration of program	.15 (2.1)**	.07 (2.1)**	.02 (.65)
No formal evaluation	−2.6 (2.25)**	−1.7 (3.3)***	−1.3 (3.1)***
Constant	4.1 (1.9)*	2.7 (2.7)***	2.9 (3.8)***
Mean VIF	1.2	1.2	1.2
Observations	127	127	127
R^2	.274	.264	.178

Source: Regression analysis performed by author and Elizabeth Lyons.
*$p < .1$; ** $p < .05$; ***$p < .01$.
a. *t*-statistics are in parentheses.

coverage, would-be adapters in other jurisdictions are likely to believe that the probability it can be implemented successfully is high, hence reducing the expected cost of failure.

Duration of the program is positive and significant for transferability and awards, but not for media attention. Using the average duration of the semifinalist programs of 6.6 years, the average values of the transferability index (6.5) and the awards index (3), and their respective coefficients, I calculated elasticities at the means, which were .15 for both. This indicates that the extent of the impact of duration is not large. Innovations that have been in existence longer are slightly more likely to have been transferred and to have received awards. The effect of duration of the program on media attention might be insignificant because media attention for public management innovation has increased in recent years (see earlier discussion, pp. 118–19). There was simply less media attention available for older programs to attract.

Of the five most important achievement variables—operationalized theoretical model, enabled collaboration, educated the public about a problem, initiated a public discussion, and implemented the innovation well—the only one that is positive and significant for all three dependent variables is "operationalized a theoretical model." To get a measure of the extent of its influence, I compared the impact of a change in "operationalized a theoretical model" from 0 to 1 (that is, a change from not having it to having it) to the average value of each index (6.5 for transferability, 3 for awards, and 2.7 for media), which involves simply dividing the regression coefficient by the mean. The impact was .36 for transferability, .33 for awards, and .30 for media, which indicates that operationalizing a theoretical model has a substantial influence on the three dependent variables. This variable may be significant because innovations based on a theoretical model possess a clear "philosophy" or informing idea that may often be controversial. If nothing else, the theoretical model endows the innovation with a clear identity or profile. This in turn may facilitate transfer, offering adopters a template to adapt and apply to their own situation. For the media, controversy of any sort is an attraction, so a controversial theory or method would make an innovation story that much more appealing. Judging panels are perhaps more likely to be drawn by the spectacle of a theoretical model being put into practice and certainly more likely to have the contextual knowledge to be engaged by any resulting theoretical debates. The variable "implemented the innovation well" is negative and significant once, for the transfer index. The three other achievement variables are never significant.

In contrast to the most important achievement variables, the nine outcome variables provide less clear patterns of influence. "Service is improving" and "program is receiving awards" are both positive and significant for the transfer index, but not for the other two indexes. Informal expressions of stakeholder support is positive and significant for the awards and media indexes, but not for the transfer index. The other outcome variables are never significant. Inspection of the data shows that the frequency of the different outcome variables differs considerably by policy areas, which would explain why they were rarely significant when all six policy areas, into which the semifinalists were categorized, are pooled. The natural response to this problem—estimating separate models for each of the policy areas—is not possible because the areas provide at most twenty-six observations, which would provide insufficient degrees of freedom given the large number of independent variables in our models.

Finally, the three regression equations all show very low variance inflation factors, so intercorrelation among the independent variables is not a problem. The R^2 measures are respectable for cross-sectional analysis such as this.

Innovators may initiate innovations for intrinsic reasons, but they may also want external recognition. This statistical analysis of the determinants of recognition for HKS semifinalists provides some guidelines for any public sector innovator who is seeking external recognition. First and foremost, ensure that your program is externally evaluated. A supportive evaluation will strengthen the case for recognition, and an evaluation that points out shortcomings will help you improve the program.[9] Second, use a relevant theoretical model in developing the innovation. The search for a theoretical model will drive you to learn more about leading-edge programs, which will help in program design. As discussed earlier, having a theoretical model makes it easier to explain the essence of the innovation, engage the judges of innovation awards, and attract external attention. Third, realize that getting recognition, especially transfer and awards, will take time, although media attention may well come faster.

Few Are Chosen: Determinants of Award Selection

To this point, our analysis has been treating selection for the HKS Awards semifinalist and finalist ranks as an unquestioned marker of merit. That assumption makes it all the more necessary to understand the process by which the selection and ranking occurs. In their discussion of criteria to assess the effectiveness of innovation awards, Hartley and Downe (2007, 348) argue that "the short listing and final selection [should be] based on evidential rather than political criteria." In the context of the HKS Awards, this means that selection should be on the basis of the awards' four stated evaluation criteria rather than any other factors. After explaining the process itself, in particular the evaluation criteria that are used, statistical analysis of the determinants of selection provides a test of whether the selections made are consistent with the criteria or are the result of other factors that might be considered biases. This information will be of interest to both the organizers of the HKS Awards and future applicants. Finally, the determinants of selection for the HKS Awards can be compared to the determinants of other forms of recognition for HKS Awards semifinalists discussed in the previous section.

The analysis that follows will consider all three levels of the HKS process: the selection of semifinalists from initial applications; the selection of the top 25 semifinalists and 6 finalists from all 127 semifinalists; and the selection of the winning program. There are sufficient observations at the first two levels to model them statistically. Because they are based on different application forms and hence different information, they must be modeled separately. The selection of the win-

9. Cels, De Jong, and Nauta (2012, 29) observed that the innovators they studied requested objective third-party evaluations for these reasons.

ner involves too few observations for quantitative analysis, so I discuss the process qualitatively.

Selection of Semifinalists

The discussion of the selection of semifinalists draws heavily on an article coauthored with Richard Walker of the City University of Hong Kong entitled "Many Are Called but Few Are Chosen: Modeling the Selection Process for the Innovations in American Government Awards" (Borins and Walker 2011). I am deeply indebted to Professor Walker for his contributions as coauthor of that article and for his consent to my incorporation of material from the article here. The title of this entire section, "Few are Chosen," is a further acknowledgment of the article's influence on this section.

The initial application form used for the 2010 awards asked for three things: a short statement of the essence of the innovation; the story of the innovation, encompassing its development and ongoing operations; and evidence of how the program meets the selection criteria of novelty, effectiveness, significance, and transferability (see appendix, "Initial Application Questions"). In two interviews, Christina Marchand, associate director for outreach for the HKS Awards, summarized the semifinalist selection process: Applicants self-identify in one of seven policy areas defined by the HKS Awards program staff. The staff then selects panels of two or three judges in each of the seven policy areas. The judges are either academics or practitioners with expertise in that area. In any given year, some judges will have been involved in the program before and others will be new to it. The panels are charged with assessing all the applicants in their area in terms of the four criteria. They are not required to produce numerical scores, nor are the criteria assigned numerical weights. Rather, the judges use their own discretion in evaluating the applications. The program staff tries to ensure that a comparable percentage of the initial applications is selected for semifinalist rank for all seven policy areas.[10]

In modeling the selection process, the HKS Awards criteria were included as independent variables with expected positive signs. The application question requesting the innovation's "story" suggested the use of characteristics related specifically to narrative elements (a timeline, the use of "human interest" anecdotes, cases, or examples) to test for their influence. The staff's concern to ensure that a comparable percentage of applications from each policy area were selected implies that representation in any policy area should have no influence on selection, so the regression coefficients for all policy areas should not be significantly different from zero. There were applications from all three levels of government.

10. Christina Marchand, interviewed by the author on July 26, 2011, and May 7, 2013.

We hypothesized that level of government should have no influence on selection, hence that the regression coefficients for level of government should not be significantly different from zero (Borins and Walker 2011).

Another set of possible influences would be the characteristics of the innovations that were presented in table 3-1. If the presence or absence of a characteristic has no impact on selection, its regression coefficient should be zero, but it might be the case that judges favor certain characteristics. If judges believe networked government is the wave of the future, they might well prefer applications demonstrating collaboration. In other words, expert knowledge might result in selection bias. Table 3-1 demonstrated a very similar distribution of characteristics among applicants selected as semifinalists and those not. This led us to expect that innovation characteristics would not have an impact on selection. Before we can confirm this expectation it is necessary to examine the influence of the characteristics in a multivariate context.

Prior experience as a semifinalist or finalist might influence selection positively. Although the application form shows only whether an applicant has applied previously, without requiring disclosure of result, some judges who have served in previous years may remember which applicants were past semifinalists or finalists and may favor them accordingly. (Of course, judges with good memories might also remember programs that failed to make the cut.) If a program had been selected previously, those involved in preparing the new application may be able to benefit from institutional experience with the application process, and possibly feedback from it, something that could enable them to prepare a stronger application. It therefore seems reasonable to expect that applications that were selected as semifinalists or finalists previously would be more likely to be selected again.

Duration of an innovative program is also likely to influence its chances of being selected as a semifinalist. This relationship is anticipated to be nonlinear, because the programs that apply when they have just begun operation are at a disadvantage: they will not have demonstrated results and will show weakness in terms of the criterion of effectiveness. Conversely, programs initiated a considerable time before they apply will likely show weakness on the criterion of novelty.

One final factor we might anticipate would influence the choice of semifinalists is the size of the organization applying. The research evidence on the impact of organizational size on innovation is becoming more robust, particularly in relation to process innovation (Walker 2014). Larger organizations are associated with access to more complex and diverse facilities, more professional and skilled workers, more slack resources, and higher technical potential and knowledge (Damanpour, Walker, and Avellaneda 2009; Rogers 2003). Given the growing body of evidence on size, it can be hypothesized that judges would expect larger governments—whether the federal government, the larger states, or the larger cities—to be more innovative than smaller governments.

To test all these hypotheses, we requested that HKS program staff randomly select two-thirds of those chosen as semifinalists (108) and one-third of those not chosen (126). These were put into a single list, ordered alphabetically. This ensured that we could not distinguish between semifinalists and non-semifinalists while coding, to minimize attribution bias. After the coding was completed, the staff notified us as to which applicants had been chosen as semifinalists.

The dependent variable here is dichotomous: zero for a non-semifinalist and 1 for a semifinalist. We operationalized three of the four HKS Awards criteria by creating a measure for each.[11] Novelty was coded on a four-point scale: zero for no answer, 1 for a restatement of the nature of the innovation, 2 for either an explanation of how the innovation is novel or making the case that the innovation isn't being done elsewhere, and 3 for both explaining how the innovation is novel and making the case that it isn't being done elsewhere (mean 1.7). Significance was coded on a three-point scale: zero for no answer, 1 for arguing that this is a problem in other places or that this is a major problem, and 2 for arguing that this is a problem in other places and that it is a major problem (mean 1.1). Transferability was coded on a five-point scale: zero for no transfer, 1 for an argument about potential transferability, 2 for expressions of interest in transfer, 3 for evidence of actual nearby transfer, and 4 for either widespread nearby transfer or some transfer to distant locations (mean 2.0). The fourth criterion, effectiveness of the innovation, was the most difficult to operationalize and it was not possible to establish a unidimensional scale.

The effective use of stories was operationalized by specifying six characteristics, each of which was observed in some cases. The characteristics were derived from my previous analysis of a small sample of finalist applications (Borins 2012) and the narratological theory that informed it. Simplifying radically, I considered two defining dimensions here: a meaningfully related sequence of events and the presence of a human agent central to the events being related (effectively, a protagonist). These generated six story-related variables:

1. Discussion of the initiation of the innovation
2. Discussion of its establishment or implementation
3. Discussion of opposition or challenges to the innovation
4. The provision of a timeline

---

11. The judging process is confidential, and we did not have any access to records or to the judges themselves. We therefore chose readily measurable evidence in the written applications that we felt would be indicative of the judges' assessments.

5. The presence of a named protagonist

6. The use of cases or examples of how the innovation affects individuals

The first four variables are all aspects of meaningfully sequencing events. The use of cases or examples can be seen as personal stories with identifiable protagonists (even if not named) embedded within the larger innovation story. It is comparable to policy advocates' practice of using individuals' experiences to dramatize their arguments.

The HKS Awards staff divided the applications into the seven policy areas. Because the seven policy areas are mutually exclusive and collectively exhaustive, six dummy variables were created for them. Level of government is also mutually exclusive and collectively exhaustive, so only two levels were used, federal and local. Organizational size was operationalized by using the logarithm of the population of the jurisdiction. The population of a jurisdiction is a proxy for the size of its government. Population was used because it is readily accessible.[12] Using a logarithm reduces the disparity in size between the federal government, which serves a population of more than 300 million, and any state or city.

Prior experience is a categorical variable. Therefore, dummy variables were created for programs that applied previously and were not selected (previously unsuccessful) and for programs that applied previously and were selected as a semifinalist or finalist (previous semifinalist or finalist). Time between the program's initiation and its application to the HKS Awards was operationalized in two ways. First, a dummy for programs initiated two to four years ago was specified. Second, the number of years since inception was recorded and a quadratic term was also derived from this. The nonlinear specification requires two steps: testing whether the length of time since a program was initiated was significant and, if it was, rerunning the equation with the squared term added.

Fourteen innovation characteristics were coded. Four types of interorganizational collaboration were distinguished: collaborations within one level of government; collaborations across levels of government; collaboration with nonprofits; and collaborations with the private sector. Six innovation characteristics deal with internal program design, of which five are organizational process innovations (use of volunteers in program delivery; improvement in the marketing of a public service; improvement of a management or production process; organizational change; and empowerment of the public sector workforce) and one is a technological process innovation (use of information technology). Four characteristics pertain to the interaction between the program and its context or environment: the use of market incentives in place of regulation; empowerment of, or

---

12. Walker's (2014) meta-analysis of the determinants of innovation in local government shows that operationalizing organization size by population or actual number of employees offers very comparable results.

consultation with, citizens; solving a problem or preventing a problem from worsening; and changing public attitudes. Each of the fourteen characteristics was coded as a dummy variable, equal to one for an observation where the characteristic is present in an application and zero when it is not.

The multiple regression equation was estimated as a logit. Simple correlations among most independent variables were small (less than 0.2). The one exception was that the correlation between the log of population and federal government was 0.58 and between log of population and local government was –0.56.[13]

Table 6-9 shows four regression models. Because there were a total of forty-five independent variables, I have not included coefficients for those that were statistically insignificant (they are available). Model 1 includes both the log of population and level of government, as well as a dummy for applications made two to four years after inception. Model 2 drops the latter variable and includes time since inception. Because time since inception was not significant, time since inception squared was not added to any of the models as an independent variable. Models 3 and 4 deal with the correlation between log of population and level of government by dropping the level of government variables because they were insignificant in models 1 and 2, while retaining the log of population, which was strongly significant.[14] Model 3 includes the two-to-four-year time since inception variable, and Model 4 substitutes time since inception. Presenting four similar specifications of the model shows the impact on the coefficients of slight differences in specification. If a variable is robust, its coefficient and significance level will not change much from one equation to another: the overall pattern of results for the four equations supports this notion.

The first variables to consider are the four awards criteria. If other variables did not influence the awards, it would be expected that all these coefficients would be positive and statistically significant, and all other variables should be insignificant. There is strong support for the novelty and transferability criteria, but the significance criterion is statistically insignificant. The result for the significance criterion may be due to measurement error on our part or a lack of clarity on the part of the judges as to how to operationalize the concept, a possibility suggested by the HKS Awards staff based on their observation of the judging process. The innovation effectiveness measures do not add much to the models: five are insignificant; one, recognition from other awards, is at the margin of significance

---

13. Variance inflation factors (VIFs) were also tested, and initially those for log of population and novelty were greater than 10. These two variables were centered and the equations were re-estimated. All the coefficients and their significance levels were virtually identical, but all VIFs were below 10, and the average VIF for all models in Table 6-9 was reduced from 3.5 to 2.5. The models with the two centered variables are presented in table 6-9.

14. The levels of government variables were not significant when the log of population was excluded.

Table 6-9. *Determinants of Selection of Semifinalists, 2010 Innovations Awards*[a]

Independent variable	Model 1	Model 2	Model 3	Model 4
Transfer or transferability	.53 (3.9)***	.46 (3.4)***	.53 (3.8)***	.46 (3.4)***
Novelty	.86 (2.6)**	.82 (2.5)**	.87 (2.6)**	.82 (2.5)**
Significance	insig[b]	insig	insig	insig
Satisfaction in surveys	−1.13 (1.9)*	−1.35 (2.2)**	−1.09 (1.9)*	−1.32(2.1)**
Recognition	.75 (1.7)*	.71 (1.6)	.75 (1.7)*	.70 (1.6)
Other effectiveness measures (five)	insig	insig	insig	insig
Timeline provided	2.29 (2.8)***	2.15 (2.7)**	2.28 (2.8)***	2.14 (2.7)***
Discusses opposition to innovation	−.87 (2.0)**	−1.00 (2.2)**	−.87 (2.0)**	−1.00 (2.2)**
Uses cases or examples	−1.00 (1.9)*	−.97 (1.8)*	−1.03 (2)**	−.99 (1.9)*
Other story features (three)	insig	insig	insig	insig
Policy areas (six)	insig	insig	insig	insig
Log of population	.18 (2)**	.21 (2.2)**	.22 (3)***	.22 (3.1)***
Federal government innovation	insig	insig	—	—
Local government innovation	insig	insig	—	—
Two to four years since inception	insig	—	insig	—
Time since inception	—	.04 (1.5)	—	.04 (1.5)
Previously unsuccessful application	insig	insig	insig	insig
Previous semifinalist or finalist	1.19 (1.9)*	1.11 (1.8)*	1.19 (1.9)*	1.13 (1.8)*
Collaboration within a level of government	.55 (1.5)	.60 (1.64)	.54 (1.5)	.60 (1.65)*
Uses information technology	−.71 (1.8)*	−.72 (1.8)*	−.69 (1.7)*	−.71 (1.8)*
Organizational change	−2.86 (1.8)*	−2.90 (1.9)*	−2.74 (1.8)*	−2.79 (1.8)*
Other characteristics (eleven)	insig	insig	insig	insig
Constant	insig	insig	insig	insig
Number of observations	234	234	234	234
R^2	.258	.263	.257	.263

Source: Regression analysis performed by author and Elizabeth Lyons.
* $p < .1$; ** $p < .05$; *** $p < .001$ (two-tail).
a. *t*-statistics are in parentheses.
b. Coefficient statistically insignificant.

with the expected (positive) sign, while another, satisfaction with the program as indicated in surveys, is significant but negative. It is likely that the innovation effectiveness measures performed poorly because, like the outcome measures in the regressions explaining transfer, awards, and media attention, they differ across policy areas. The natural response to this problem, estimating separate models for each of the seven policy areas, is not possible because the areas have approximately thirty-five observations, and the models also have thirty-five independent variables (excluding the policy areas), which provides too few degrees of freedom.

The coefficients for the six variables that operationalize the contribution of the presence of a strongly told story to selection as a semifinalist are lackluster: providing a timeline is positive and strongly significant, discussing opposition to an innovation and using cases or examples are negative and significant, and the three remaining ones are insignificant. Perhaps the judges consider an admission in the initial application that there was opposition to an innovation to be a sign of weakness and the use of cases or examples an attempt to mask the absence of rigorous objective evidence regarding the selection criteria.[15]

None of the dummies for the policy areas are significant. This finding indicates that when judges make decisions about which initial applications will progress to the semifinal stage they are not influenced by the policy area of the innovation.

We anticipated that size of the applicant organization, proxied by the population of the jurisdiction, would be a predictor of semifinalists. Although this is not a stated criterion, the literature has found that larger organizations are faster adopters of innovations. The HKS Awards draw applications from governments of diverse sizes, from small municipalities up to the federal government. It was expected that judges would view applications submitted by larger governments more favorably. The statistical results show that this variable was significant. Neither federal nor local government was statistically significant so the level of government (as distinct from size of jurisdiction) does not influence selection of semifinalists.

Neither approach to the operationalization of time (a dummy for years two to four, or actual time and a quadratic term for time) led to statistically significant results. Prior experience of the awards program is an important explanatory variable. The coefficient for previously unsuccessful applications is never significant. The coefficient for applications that were previously semifinalists or finalists, however, is always positive and significant in a two-tail test at close to five percent.[16]

Eleven of the fourteen innovation characteristics (see pp. 128–29) are never significant and thereby offer strong support for the hypothesis that characteristics did not influence the judges' thinking. The insignificant ones include three types of collaboration: across levels of government, with the nonprofit sector, and with the private sector. Only one collaboration variable, collaboration within a given level of government, is barely significant at 10 percent in a two-tail test once

15. A number of efforts were made to modify the story and innovation effectiveness variables. For story, an index equal to the sum of all the scores on the six story variables for a given application was created; for effectiveness, an index equal to the total number of different innovation effectiveness variables coded for a given application was created. Neither was significant. Factor analyses were undertaken for both the sets of effectiveness and story variables. In both, the first three factors had no evident interpretation and were not significant.

16. It could be argued that since our expectation is that having previously been a semifinalist or finalist couldn't hurt an application, the appropriate test would be one-tailed, which would allow this variable to clear the hurdle of significance at five percent.

(model 4). It is interesting that although the data confirm the growth of networked government over the last two decades (see table 3-1), the judges of the 2010 competition did not favor applications characterized by this type of innovation.

Two other innovation types were negatively associated with likelihood of proceeding to the semifinals. Organizational change and use of information technology were negative and significant at better than 10 percent, suggesting that entrants to the HKS Awards program would be less likely to be selected as a semifinalist if they focused on these characteristics. This suggests something of the ubiquity and familiarity of information technology in the public sector. Fifteen years ago, its presence alone conferred a degree of novelty and innovativeness. That is clearly no longer the case.

The regression analysis should serve as the basis for discussion on the part of the organizers of the HKS Awards. They should be pleased that two of the four stated criteria, novelty and transferability, as we operationalized them, are significant in explaining selection. The statistical insignificance of the significance criterion and most of the effectiveness variables suggests it would be worthwhile for the program to discuss with its judging panels how they define and measure significance and how each policy area defines and measures effectiveness. The organizers should also be pleased that so many potential sources of bias (policy area, most characteristics, level of government, time since inception) have no impact on selection. It is not surprising that previous semifinalists or finalists are more likely to be selected again. The organizers might be concerned because applications from larger jurisdictions appear to be advantaged and that those that are characterized by information technology or organizational change appear to be disadvantaged. These issues, too, should be discussed with the judges. It is important for the organizers of any innovation award to review their selection criteria and how they are put into practice by judges. Statistical analysis such as this can test whether selections are being made on the basis of stated criteria or on the basis of other factors, and thus inform self-examination.

These regression results might be read by would-be applicants to the HKS Awards as a "how-to" guide to getting selected as a semifinalist. We would caution against reading too much into these results. To begin with, applicants to the HKS Awards and other innovation awards might not necessarily be primarily looking for recognition but instead may be applying because of the intrinsic value of telling their own story, both externally and internally, and of learning from other applicants. Even if they are "in it to win it," it is not clear that the results of an analysis based on 2010 applications will continue to be relevant to future years. In addition, regression results assume that everything else is held constant. In this case, it would mean that these results apply to one applicant when all other applicants do not change their behavior. But if all applicants changed their behavior because of these regression results (including a time line, not discussing opposition, and not providing cases or examples), then the changed behavior would no longer provide any advantage.

The primary piece of advice we have for applicants to the HKS Awards or to any innovation award is to carefully and accurately document their program's achievements in terms of the award's criteria. For the HKS Awards, it appears to be particularly important to show how an innovation is novel and where it has been transferred. It is not clear from the regression analysis how the judges interpret significance. Similarly, the analysis does not show what kind of evidence of effectiveness would be relevant to all policy areas, and compelling evidence of effectiveness probably varies from policy area to policy area. In terms of telling their stories, the results suggest that it helps initial applicants to present a timeline, but not to discuss opposition to an innovation or to use cases or examples.

Selection of Top Twenty-five Semifinalists and Six Finalists

The selection process for the top twenty-five innovations and six finalists is similar to that for the semifinalists.[17] The semifinalists, previously assigned to one of seven policy areas, are evaluated by new judging panels of three experts. New members are used to ensure that the semifinalists are seen by fresh eyes. The members of the new panels have expertise comparable to the previous ones. Using the four criteria for the award, the judging panels are asked to recommend one finalist and four to six runners-up for their policy area. The judging panels may make a recommendation that is contingent on the program staff's doing some additional due diligence research to resolve concerns about claims made or possible gaps in the written application. The judging panels may provide candid critical assessments of the quality of the finalist and runners-up they are nominating. The HKS Awards director, Stephen Goldsmith (a Kennedy School faculty member who is a former mayor of Indianapolis), and staff review the judging panels' nominations. Taking into account the candid comments, additional research undertaken by the staff, and a desire to provide some geographic and thematic balance, Goldsmith and the staff produce the list of six finalists and the other nineteen in the top twenty-five. In the 2010 competition, all six finalists recommended by the policy area judging panels were accepted.

The methodology to model the selection of the top twenty-five semifinalists and six finalists builds on the initial study of the selection of semifinalists (Borins and Walker 2011). To avoid attribution bias while coding the semifinalist applications, my research assistant and I again deliberately avoided learning the outcome of the selection process. Two alternative specifications were used: a logit

---

17. Christina Marchand, interviewed by the author on July 26, 2011, and May 7, 2013.

model, in which the two categories were the top 25 and the 102 not selected, and an ordered logit comprising three groups, the 6 finalists, the other 19 in the top 25, and the 102 not selected. In both specifications, higher values of the dependent variable denoted higher outcomes.

Some of the independent variables used were the same as those employed in the semifinalist selection study. Taking advantage of the more comprehensive information about outcomes, achievements, and external recognition in the semifinalist questionnaire than in the initial questionnaire, I added a number of additional independent variables in this study. I used six policy areas rather than the seven used for the initial applicants ("children and family services" was merged into "health and social services"), but at the finalist selection level the staff make no effort to maintain equal representation for the different policy areas. The population of the jurisdiction was found to have a positive influence on semifinalist selection, so it was used in this study. There were two independent variables for repeat applicants: those that were not selected as semifinalists and those that were selected as semifinalists or higher. Again, I used the characteristics of the innovation as independent variables.

Given the weak results for the story-related aspects of the initial applications, only two narrative features were used: providing a detailed timeline (assessed on a scale of 0 for none, 1 for some detail, and 2 for substantial detail, with a mean of 1.5) and using a human interest story (relating to either an individual delivering or receiving the program), a narrative strategy that was employed by 25 out of 127 semifinalists.

Three of the four selection criteria (novelty, transferability, and effectiveness) were also operationalized. Significance was not, being neither statistically significant in the semifinalist study nor addressed directly in the semifinalist application. An index for novelty was created, based on the results of table 4-1. In this index, adding features to an original innovation or extending the reach of an original innovation each received .5 points (and could be added together) and not having heard of anyone else doing this received 1.5 points. The average score for the novelty index was .97. Transferability was assessed by using the transfer index (see p. 120). Effectiveness was assessed by using the nine outcomes presented in table 6-1 as well as external evaluations, the awards index, and the media index. Finally, the achievement of operationalizing a theoretical model was included because, as discussed earlier, it was significant as a determinant of all three of the indexes: awards, transfer, and media. The results of this analysis are shown in table 6-10. The second column shows the regression results for the ordered logit and the third for the dichotomous logit. They are very similar, both in terms of the estimated coefficients and their significance levels. As in the previous table, because of the large number of independent variables, those that

Table 6-10. *Determinants of Selection of Top Twenty-Five Semifinalists and Six Finalists, 2010 HKS Awards*[a]

Independent variable	Ordered logit (semifinalists and finalists)	Logit (semifinalists)
Policy areas (five)	All insignificant	All insignificant
Log of population	Insignificant	Insignificant
Applied previously, didn't advance to semifinals	–2.1 (1.67)*	–2.4 (1.8)*
Applied previously: semifinalist, top fifty finalists	Insignificant	Insignificant
Uses information technology	–1.8 (2.1)**	–1.5 (1.7)*
Citizen empowerment	1.5 (1.7)*	1.6 (1.7)*
Other characteristics (four)	All insignificant	All insignificant
Novelty index	Insignificant	Insignificant
Detailed narrative	Insignificant	Insignificant
Use of example	2.5 (2.5)**	2.6 (2.5)**
Program met goals	2.0 (2.5)**	2.0 (2.3)**
Costs being reduced	–2.0 (1.8)*	–2.4 (1.8)*
Informal support	–2.2 (1.7)*	–2.0 (1.4)
Other outcomes (six)	All insignificant	All insignificant
External evaluation measures (five)	All insignificant	All insignificant
Transfer index	Insignificant	Insignificant
Awards index	Insignificant	Insignificant
Media index	.7 (2.8)***	.68 (2.4)**
Operationalizes theoretical model	2.1 (2.4)**	1.8 (1.9)*
Cut 1	Insignificant	NA
Cut 2	Insignificant	NA
Constant	NA	Insignificant
Mean VIF	1.6	1.6
Number of observations	127	127
Pseudo-R^2	.358	.358

Source: Regression analysis performed by author and Elizabeth Lyons.
NA = Not available
* $p < .1$; ** $p < .05$; *** $p < .001$ (two-tail).
a. *t*-statistics are in parentheses.

were statistically insignificant were not reported, but full results are available on request.

The coefficients on the policy areas are not significant, which is consistent with a judging process that attempts to produce one finalist and three or four applicants within the top twenty-five for each policy area. Unlike the regression for semifinalist choice, large jurisdictions (as proxied by the log of their population) have no advantage here. Applicants who applied previously and did not make it to the semifinals then appear to be at a disadvantage. On the other hand, those that applied previously and made it to the semifinals or beyond have no advantage when they applied again.

Of the six innovation characteristics, four (collaboration within government, collaboration outside government, use of volunteers, improvement of a management or production process) do not have a statistically significant influence on selection to the top twenty-five or finalists. The use of information technology has a negative and statistically significant influence, as it did on selection as a semifinalist. Citizen empowerment has a positive and significant influence on selection at this level, in contrast to having been insignificant at the semifinalist selection level.

The novelty index is insignificant. This might be because at the finalist selection level the judges rely on their own views about what is novel rather than on the claims made by the applicants, which were the basis of the index I developed. One of the story-related variables, the use of an example, is positive and statistically significant. This contrasts with semifinalist selection, where the use of a case or example was negative and statistically significant. The use of a detailed timeline is insignificant at the top twenty-five or finalist level, which also contrasts with the semifinalist selection level, where it had a positive and statistically significant impact.

Of the nine outcome measures, six (clients were made better off, people use the program, service is improved, satisfaction is expressed in formal surveys, program receives awards, productivity is improved) are insignificant. A program's setting and meeting goals has a positive and significant influence, though cost reduction and informal expressions of support are negative and significant. These results differ from those for semifinalist selection, where receiving awards is positive and significant and satisfaction expressed in formal surveys is negative and significant. Had it been possible to reduce the nine outcome measures to a smaller number of factors, the regression results for outcome measures might have been more meaningful.

All five external evaluation measures (policy analysis, financial audit, evaluation within government, accreditation review, and academic research) were insignificant, as was the absence of external evaluation when it was used alone in place of the five external evaluation measures. The transfer index was insignificant, which contrasts with the transfer index at the semifinalist selection level, which was positive and significant. The awards index was also insignificant, but the media index was positive and strongly significant. The media index might be picking up on the novelty criterion as it is applied by the judges. Put simply, an innovation is likely receiving media attention because it is novel.

Finally, I used the achievement of operationalizing a theoretical model, and it is positive and significant. This is identical to the finding that operationalizing a theoretical model had a positive and significant impact on transferability, awards, and media attention (see table 6-8). It appears that the judges in the HKS Awards, like judges for other awards, are drawn to the spectacle of a theoretical model being put into practice and have the contextual knowledge to be engaged by any debate it stimulates.

In considering the implications of these results, the organizers of the HKS Awards can take satisfaction from the knowledge that several possible sources of bias—policy area, population of the jurisdiction, most innovation characteristics, and previous status as a semifinalist or higher—do not advantage or disadvantage semifinalists. This would particularly be the case for population, which did have an impact on the selection of semifinalists. However, the use of information technology does disadvantage applicants at both the semifinalist and finalist selection levels. The fact that most of the outcome variables are not statistically significant for the entire set of semifinalists is an argument for entering into discussions with the judges at the finalist selection level about which types of outcomes they consider most important for each policy area. The statistically insignificant results for the novelty, transfer, and awards indexes are all problematic, because these indexes are germane to the HKS Awards' four criteria. Perhaps this is due to measurement error on my part. Nevertheless, the statistical results could serve as a starting point for a discussion among the organizers and judges at the finalist selection level about how to define and measure concepts such as novelty and transfer.

These regression results, like the previous ones, might be read by applicants selected as semifinalists as advice about how to write their detailed applications. Here, too, results based on the 2010 semifinalists may not be relevant in future years. Recognition is an important motivator for some public servants; the following are inferences they might draw from these results. Operationalizing a theoretical model is positive and significant, as it was for the regression analyses of external recognition for semifinalists. HKS Awards applicants should be aware of and consult theoretical models in planning their innovations, and should not be reluctant to refer to the theoretical models they used. Because the media index is positive and significant, they should make sure to include detail about coverage, particularly by national media. Finally, the variable "use of an example" is positive and significant, so applicants should provide an example of how the innovation has affected a particular member of its target population. I direct this advice specifically toward applicants to the HKS Awards, but it applies to any public sector innovator. Theoretical models are valuable for planning; media interest in public sector innovation has increased, so be prepared to tell your story; and using a personal example is always an effective storytelling technique.

Selection of a Winner

Before a winner is selected, the six finalists are required to host a one- or two-day site visit from a nationally recognized expert in their policy area, who meets with managers of the innovative program, its political sponsors, and its critics. The site visitor then writes a confidential report discussing the history of the innovation, evaluating how innovative it is, what its accomplishments are, how well it runs, whether it has been or can be transferred, and what its overall strengths and weaknesses are. The winning program is selected by a high-profile national selection committee that includes academics, practitioners, and politicians. They review the semifinalist and site visit reports. On the selection day they also have ten-minute confidential meetings with the site visitors and hear five-minute public presentations by the finalists, followed by a five-minute question-and-answer session.[18] The selection committee then deliberates privately to choose the winner, and the result is subsequently announced by the Harvard Kennedy School.

I studied the selection process for winners in 2008, 2009, and 2010. In 2008 there were fifteen finalists and six winners; in 2009, sixteen finalists and six winners. In 2010, owing to budget cuts to HKS programs, this was reduced to six finalists and one winner. In my article analyzing the 2008 and 2009 competitions, I discussed the nature of the information provided by the site visitors to the national selection committee and the nature of the content and rhetoric employed by finalists in their oral presentations (Borins 2012, 171–77, 179–84). The semifinalist applications are usually written to be read by policy area experts, and the site visitors sometimes provide a clearer explanation of the nature of the innovation for the generalists who populate the national selection committee. They also often offer a more candid account than the applicants themselves either can or will provide of the politics of an innovation's initiation, ongoing operations, and future survival. Finally, the visitors provide an assessment of the innovation's achievements in terms of the selection criteria.

Although the assessments based on site visits are positive—as would be expected given the thoroughness of the review process to that point—site visitors often do point out weaknesses regarding unresolved operational problems. These include political factors, such as whether an innovation is likely to survive the transition from the political leadership that founded it to new political leadership; weaknesses in the evaluative data in the application, perhaps because the program has not been in operation long enough to provide more robust data; and doubts about transfer because the program either responds to unique local needs or takes advantage of local resources unlikely to be found in other jurisdictions. If we return to the "story" of an innovation, site visitors are offering an

18. PowerPoint presentations are not permitted.

alternative narrative, perhaps making explicit a dimension that had either been omitted or glossed over.

The rules for the public presentation delivered on the day of selection permit two people associated with the innovation to speak. The most frequent presenters are the program managers, but other possible spokespeople include someone at a higher organizational level such as a governor, mayor, or cabinet secretary or, at the opposite end of the institutional spectrum, a client of the program or a front-line worker involved with its delivery. The thirty-one finalists in 2008 and 2009 all devoted some of their time to explaining the nature of the innovation itself. Twenty-one presenters included some account of their innovation's impact and some quantitative measures. Two other features of the presentations, each used in about a third of the applications, were a short historical narrative about how the program was initiated and developed and a brief testimonial by a client of the program or a frontline worker explaining how he or she personally benefited from the program. The most compelling historical narrative I heard was Director of National Intelligence Mike McConnell's one-minute history of American intelligence from George Washington to the present, emphasizing the importance of cooperation within the intelligence community in response to the threat of networked terrorism (Borins 2012, 183). Several of the personal narratives were equally memorable in quite different ways, effectively giving voice to the human dimension of the innovation. Including client or frontline worker voices in the oral presentation is a shrewd dramatic strategy, but one that carries certain risks. Do you rehearse and control the first-person accounts to ensure that speakers remain on message, compromising the spontaneity and authenticity that are their most effective contributions to the story you seek to tell? Or do you surrender control over this part of your story and hope that your "characters" do what is needed, or at least remain within approximate narrative bounds? Ultimately, the oral presentation component of the selection process gives applicants an opportunity to craft a further story about their innovation, an advocacy narrative designed to persuade a more generalist audience of its merits.

Finalists might read this section, like the previous two, from an "in it to win it" perspective, so I shall offer them some advice based on my observation of the two-part selection process. Applicants should recognize that site visitors are knowledgeable and savvy enough to find any weaknesses in their written materials. Prepare for the site visit as you would for a debate or a job interview. Anticipate the difficult questions and develop answers for them. Site visitors often want to interview a wide range of people associated with the innovation, including the leadership of the organization(s) sponsoring the innovation and critics of the innovation. Although you have no control over an innovation's critics, you can at least communicate a common perspective about and generate enthusiasm for the innovation.

The oral presentation to the national selection committee is particularly demanding because the committee consists of generalists and because of the constraints on time (five minutes) and the number of presenters (two). Ideally, the content should include a short explanation of the innovation in nonspecialist language, a short history of the innovation or its context, and a nontechnical explanation of its impact that uses a modicum of quantitative measures. Careful drafting is necessary to say all this in five minutes. One of the two presenters will be the person most deeply involved with the innovation, for example, the originator or program manager. If the other presenter is an organizational leader, such as a cabinet secretary, mayor, or governor, she should be sufficiently conversant with the details of the innovation that she can participate in the presentation and the five-minute question-and-answer session that follows. Clients or frontline staff, too, should be able to participate in the presentation and question-and-answer session.

Advice for Innovation Skeptics, Innovators, and Award Organizers

The best way to summarize this chapter's extensive and detailed statistical analysis is to consider its implications for three potential readers: the innovation skeptic, the would-be innovator, and the innovation award organizer. The innovation skeptic might be a long-standing critic of New Public Management or an academic who, having recently discovered public sector innovation, approaches it with standard professional skepticism. In previous chapters I have taken issue with the image of public sector innovators as loose cannons, rule breakers, and power politicians that has been promulgated by the critics of New Public Management. The data from the HKS Awards presented in chapters 3, 4, and 5 demonstrate that innovators are creative and proactive problem solvers who prefer to plan and who respond to obstacles and criticism with persuasion and accommodation. In this chapter I reply to the criticism that innovations are "vanity projects" that do not produce outcomes of value to society.

When asked about outcomes, virtually none of the HKS Awards semifinalists in either 1990–94 or 2010 responded that it was too early to tell or provided only informal expressions of support; almost all semifinalists provided quantitative outcome measures. The 2010 semifinalists provided an average of approximately three such measures. The 2010 semifinalists also reported more formal evaluations than those of 1990–94, with substantial increases in the percentages being evaluated by consultants, nonprofits, or foundations, by evaluators within government, and by academic researchers. The percentage reporting no evaluation declined from 38 percent for 1990–94 semifinalists to 28 percent for those in 2010. The percentage of semifinalists reporting any transfer of their programs increased from 42 percent in 1990–94 to 58 percent in 2010. Media attention for innovations also increased, with the percentage reporting no media attention dramatically declining from 54 percent in 1990–94 to 11 percent in 2010. In other words, the 1990–94 semifinalists set a high standard in all these areas of evidence of public value, and the 2010 finalists handily exceeded it. A multiple regression analysis of the determinants of transfer, awards, and media attention for 2010 HKS Awards semifinalists showed that the absence of formal evaluation was a significant negative determinant. The skeptical reader might argue that these results pertain only to HKS Awards semifinalists, which are the "crème de la crème" but not to other, and it is assumed, less successful innovations. The EC Innobarometer study—a survey of 4,000 public sector organizations in twenty-seven countries dealing with their experience as innovators—found that the innovations it surveyed produced similar outcomes to those cited by HKS Awards semifinalists and that their positive impacts strongly outweighed negative ones. The conclusion to draw from the weight of this evidence? Surely it is a powerful refutation of the skeptical view regarding the outcomes, and external validation of the outcomes, of public sector innovation.

These results imply three clear lines of advice for managers of innovative programs who would like to apply to innovation awards in general, or the HKS Awards in particular:

1. Establish quantitative outcome measures that are appropriate to your policy area, and then measure them for several years.

2. Look for external validation for your program and then learn from the reviewers' feedback, which may well include suggestions for improvement in addition to praise.

3. Use relevant theoretical models, which will help in designing your program, choosing appropriate outcome measures, and attracting attention to your program.

This advice, directed at managers who are applying to innovation awards, is just as useful to those who have no intention of applying for awards. These are simply the right things for innovators to do.

Applicants to the HKS Awards should focus on presenting strong quantitative evidence for the program's four criteria of novelty, effectiveness, significance, and transferability. What is evidence of effectiveness varies from one policy area to another, making it important for you to be familiar with outcomes and measures considered appropriate by its community (or perhaps communities) of practice. There is an inherent conflict between novelty and the other criteria, because applying very early in the life of a program restricts the evidence it can provide of effectiveness, significance, and transfer. For those who are "in it to win it," the regression results provided some evidence of what constitutes effective persuasive technique at different stages in the competition. Initial applicants should focus on using the limited space in the application to present a clear definition of their program and show how it meets the four criteria, rather than on telling its story. For semifinalists completing the more detailed application form for recognition as finalists, using examples or stories becomes a positive factor. Also at that level, the statistical results encourage recounting in detail media coverage of the innovation. At the ultimate selection level, the five-minute oral presentation to the national selection committee should offer, geared to a general audience, a clear description of the program, a brief history of the program or its context, and a case or example, expressed in the words of a client or frontline staff person participating in the presentation.

Innovation awards organizers and judges make up the third, and most specialized, audience for this chapter, both generally and at HKS. It is important that they be clear on what their criteria are and how they measure them. If the award encompasses all policy areas, then the conclusions, particularly in areas such as novelty and effectiveness, will depend on practice within the policy area. If the awards have developed some clarity about definitions of the criteria, then the question of how to measure them should also be clarified. This would result from discussions between organizers and judges, especially on a policy area basis. Award organizers should also undertake some retrospective analysis—if they have enough data, perhaps regression analysis—to find biases, in the sense of factors other than the criteria that have an independent effect on determining which applicants are selected. For the HKS Awards, the two main sources of concern appear to be that innovations from larger jurisdictions are advantaged at the initial selection level and that innovations for which the use of technology is a characteristic are disadvantaged at both the semifinalist and finalist levels.

In the discussion in this chapter, I have noted in several places that appropriate outcome measures for innovations appear to vary among policy areas. In addition, throughout the book I have included references to individual programs as exemplars. Chapter 7 carries this approach further by disaggregating the data of the previous chapters tracking the changing patterns of innovation within each area and focusing on specific examples of innovations within each. If a policy area can be seen as constituting a community of practice, looking at its patterns of innovation can also be a means of grasping changes in practice within the area as a whole. That, too, constitutes a focus for our discussion about how public management innovation in the United States has changed or remained constant in the last twenty years.

7

From Data to Stories: Innovation Patterns in the Six Policy Areas

The research methodologies we use shape our thought processes as much as they are shaped by them. Throughout this analysis I have grouped all the HKS Awards semifinalist applications together to create a data set with enough degrees of freedom to support statistical analysis, which would not have been possible had I analyzed the six policy areas separately. And I have consistently conceived of and discussed public sector innovation as a single, though never simple, phenomenon with identifiable characteristics that cross policy areas. It is now time to disaggregate. Public sector innovators in different policy areas confront different types of problems, engage different groups within the population, use different specialist vocabularies, and draw on different bodies of theory and practice. In this chapter I change focus to consider each of the six policy areas defined by the HKS Awards program, identifying and describing the initiatives within each one.

This creates an inevitable forest-and-trees dilemma, since 127 semifinalist programs across six policy areas add up to a lot of trees. My solution is to employ both cumulative and comparative approaches. I begin with comparison, delineating how each policy area's semifinalists differ from the entire set we've been considering to this point, using the innovation characteristics presented in chapters 3 to 6 as descriptors. Shifting to a cumulative analysis, I also present the major "themes" evident within each area's set of innovations—the issues they focus on. An underlying question throughout this analysis is the degree of homogeneity each area displays. Are there a few common foci, or even a single one? Are there discernible trends, or are the areas more internally disparate? Finally, I return to longitudinal comparison and the landscape of public sector innovation as a whole by comparing each policy area's profile in 2010 to its counterpart in

1990–94, noting both changes and continuities. My descriptions of individual programs are of necessity cursory, generally amounting to little more than a thumbnail portrait that scarcely begins to suggest either their achievements or their back stories. Yet I hope that even these brief sketches make it plain that this study has never been dealing with abstractions—that there are flesh-and-blood realities behind each table entry and data point. I hope, too, that I provide sufficient identifying information to enable readers to pursue the initiatives that interest them— my contribution toward diffusion. Many of the programs have their own websites.[1]

The HKS Awards staff assigned the semifinalist applications to the six policy areas, and I accept both their definition of the policy areas and their assignments of the applicants to them. There are good reasons for doing so beyond convenience. The staff has long-standing familiarity with the policy communities that exist in the public sector in the United States, which gives them a good sense of where a given application fits best. The policy areas they have defined involve some degree of aggregation within an area, and this is necessary if we are to generate any useful generalizations for six areas and only 127 semifinalists. Were I to establish a larger set of policy areas, the number of observations in each policy area would be too small to support general conclusions.

We can begin to distinguish among policy areas by the particular populations they engage. Table 7-1 presents the target populations for the six policy areas and compares them to those for all semifinalists. Semifinalists in Management and Governance (MG) predominantly target government bodies and the general population; those in Transportation, Infrastructure, and Environment (TIE) focus on the general population and on business; those in Community and Economic Development (CED) target business and low-income populations; those in Education and Training (ET) focus on young people and students; those in Health and Social Services (HSS) target high-risk and low-income populations as well as young people; and those in Criminal Justice and Public Safety (CJ) focus on people with dysfunctions. Table 7-1 shows the estimated slopes and intercepts for regressions of the distribution of target groups for each policy area on the distribution of target groups for the entire sample. The results deviate sharply from the pattern in evidence for most of the tables in chapters 3 to 6, with slopes either insignificant or very significantly different from 1, statistically significant intercepts, and some statistically significant R^2. These measures all indicate that the pattern of target groups for each policy area is considerably different from the pattern of target groups for all policy areas taken together. The numbers of semifi-

---

1. I can also supply readers with more information on specific programs if desired. Readers can contact me by email at borins@utsc.utoronto.ca

Table 7-1. *Target Populations as Percentage of Each Policy Area's Innovations*[a]
Percent except as indicated

Target population	All 2010 semifinalists	MG	TIE	CED	ET	HSS	CJ
General population	36	52	80	38	7	4	35
Businesses	28	22	40	52	29	15	17
Government bodies	19	61	20	5	0	8	13
Nonprofit organizations	7	13	10	10	0	8	0
High-risk populations	24	13	0	10	29	62	22
Low-income populations	26	17	5	38	29	50	13
Young people	18	17	5	5	29	31	22
Students	18	9	15	5	79	23	0
Elderly people	5	0	5	0	0	19	0
People with disabilities	6	4	5	5	7	8	4
People with dysfunctions	11	0	0	0	0	4	52
Other	2	9	0	0	0	4	0
Number of semifinalists	127	23	20	21	14	26	23
Estimated slope (s.d.'s from 1)		.34** (4.7)	.32** (7)	.46*** (4.5)	insig[b]	insig	insig
Estimated intercept		10.5**	11.7***	10.2***	13.7***	12.8**	12.2**
R^2		.38**	.49**	.60***	.14[b]	.13b	.21[b]

Source: Applications coded by author and Kaylee Chretien.
** $p < .05$, *** $p < .01$ for slope and intercept estimates and R^2.
a. MG = Management and Governance; TIE = Transportation, Infrastructure, and Environment; CED = Community and Economic Development; ET = Education and Training; HSS = Health and Social Services; CJ = Criminal Justice and Public Safety.
b. insig = insignificantly different from 0.

nalists by policy area are too small for statistical analysis, from a low of fourteen in Education and Training to a high of twenty-six in Health and Social Services. The heterogeneity of the policy areas' target populations would lead us to expect marked differences in other aspects of each area's profile. And this will prove to be the case. Let's look more closely at these differences.

Management and Governance

Innovations in the area of Management and Governance are characterized by a strong focus on the internal operations of the public sector. As shown in Table 7-1, 61 percent target government bodies, compared with 19 percent for all semifinalists. A number of other distinctions flow from this. Management and Governance innovations involve more use of information technology than all semifinalists (56 percent versus 41 percent) and are initiated more frequently by middle managers (55 percent versus 40).[2] Their success measures involve cost reduction more often (47 percent versus 25 percent) and improved productivity more often (26 percent versus 6 percent). These are internal measures as compared to external measures such as user satisfaction. MG innovations receive much less media coverage than other semifinalists: 48 percent local or state media stories versus 73 percent for all semifinalists, and 26 percent national media stories versus 44 percent for all semifinalists. Thirty percent of MG innovations had no media coverage, versus only 12 percent for all semifinalists. The local, state, and national media consider these innovations to be the public sector equivalent of "inside baseball," a somewhat arcane pursuit interesting only to those die-hard enthusiasts for whom it is a passion. Professional and trade media, however, are in the business of reaching just such niche audiences, so it is not surprising that these innovations do receive the same level of attention in trade media as all semifinalists (60 percent).

MG initiatives are clearly dominated by two main themes: applications of information technology (IT) and improvements to internal management. IT applications demonstrate considerable uniformity, with seven out of nine programs seeking to improve citizens' access to and interactions with various levels of government. Boston's Citizens Connect is an iPhone app enabling residents to communicate with the city government about services and to track their delivery: say, photographing a pothole, submitting the image, and tracking when the pothole has been filled. In Orange County, California, the SECURE system is similarly service-oriented, allowing users to record real estate transactions electronically. It has been expanded to Los Angeles, Riverside, and San Diego counties.

Focusing more on outreach, the federal government established "regulations. gov" through its eRulemaking program, using the website to support citizen feedback to proposed regulations. Similarly, in Charlotte County, Florida, Smart Charlotte 2050 software facilitates public participation in its planning process. In Orange County, California, the Online Voter Information Program provides Web 2.0 applications on the website of the county's Registrar of Voters. All of these initiatives clearly involve both transparency and access, but two programs explicitly make increased transparency their goal: Open Book Texas, an aptly named website making detailed information about state revenues and expenditures avail-

---

2. In addition to calculating statistics for the entire group of 127 semifinalists for the variables discussed in chapters 3 to 6, we also calculated these statistics of each of the six policy areas. These calculations are the basis for the discussions in this chapter showing how four of the policy areas—management and governance, community and economic development, education and training, and health and social services—stand out from the entire group. Statistics for the policy areas have not been included in the book, but are available on request.

able to the public, and Kentucky's Open Door portal, which makes an even wider range of financial, managerial, and demographic information available. Two IT innovations are designed for internal use rather than citizen access or service. The federal government's Budget Formulation and Execution Manager is open-source software available for departments to use in preparing budget submissions. Denver's Human Services Work Management System is, as its name suggests, a backroom service integration system that uses data provided by the state.

One possible epigraph for this chapter could be "There are always outliers." In the Management and Governance policy areas the anomaly is In-Q-Tel, a CIA-funded venture capital fund that invests in small technology companies developing software of value to the intelligence community. For security reasons, the application provided no information about its budget and few examples of its investments. This is a familiar paradox with federal security innovations: the more successful they are, the less people should know about them. This is not the case with policing innovations and leads one to wonder, if security programs were to win innovation awards, would they tell anyone?

In contrast to the IT initiatives, programs whose goal was improvement of internal management were much more diverse. Although they had few common themes, it is worth noting—given our frequent references to the rise of the "PerformanceStat" culture within the public sector—that four of eleven such programs involved some aspect of quantitative research, data collection, or performance measurement. New York City's Center for Economic Opportunity, the winner of the competition, was mandated by Mayor Bloomberg in 2006 to improve the effectiveness of antipoverty initiatives. The center is funded by both the city's budget and private foundations and supports a wide variety of initiatives, including the creation of a new measure of poverty. It requires evaluation of the programs it supports, often using randomized trials, to determine whether they are effective. Programs that pass the test are scaled up and those that do not are terminated. In Somerville, Massachusetts, SomerStat is a performance management system based on Baltimore's CitiStat, but with a more integrated approach to the relationship between statistical analysts in the mayor's office and the departments than the original, and with greater emphasis on involving the community in providing feedback. The Florida Benchmarking Consortium enables forty-eight small Florida municipalities to compare cost and performance for their services, and Washington State's Municipal Research and Services Center provides exactly what its name suggests for municipal governments. In a similar spirit, Maine's Bend the Curve program applies continuous improvement principles to the operations of the Department of Labor and the Department of Health and Human Services.

Four MG initiatives applied some principle of collaboration, cooperation, or coordination. Seattle's Funders Group coordinates twenty-two organizations involved in funding housing or service programs for the homeless. Georgia's Department of Human Services' Limited English Proficiency/Sensory Impaired Program is a partnership of the firms providing it with translation services. Winston-Salem, North Carolina, pooled all its investment funds to lower management costs and improve returns. In New Hampshire, the Multi-jurisdiction Assessing program enables three small towns to share one full-time real estate assessor. This list highlights an often intriguing aspect of the judges' selection of semifinalists: their quite striking differences in scale.

Two other MG initiatives focus on employees rather than on measurement or process. The U.S. Department of Labor's Customized Employment Program (also known as flexible work arrangements) is designed to make it easier for people previously considered unemployable to participate in the workforce. In King County Washington, where Seattle is located, Workplace Health Initiative offers confidential health risk assessments to workers in the municipal government as part of a package aimed at improving employee health. It also supports local initiatives such as lunchtime yoga classes.

And now the MG outliers: Two semifinalist applications involving volunteering. Chicago's Civic Consulting Alliance, a partnership between the city and the major management consulting firms, enables the latter to make their professional staff available for pro bono consulting assignments dealing with the city's major priorities. New York City's NYC Service, a finalist in the competition, provides the organizational infrastructure for thousands of New Yorkers to volunteer their efforts in areas of highest priority, for example, assisting with vaccinations for the H1N1 virus.

Although a considerable proportion of these initiatives were launched by middle managers and frontline staff, there were a number of instances of high-profile political involvement. Mayor Bloomberg launched both the Center for Economic Opportunity and NYC Service. Governor Steve Beshear of Kentucky made a campaign promise to establish the OpenDoor Transparency Portal and Texas Comptroller Susan Combs made a similar commitment that led to Open Book Texas. In Orange County, California, Recorder Tom Daly spearheaded the SECURE Electronic Recording Delivery System, and the mayor of Somerville, Massachusetts, Joseph Curtatone, launched SomerStat. Just as there is no single "innovator type" among public sector workers, there is none among politicians. The category includes policy aficionados, driven hands-on problem solvers, and those fulfilling specific campaign commitments—who may subsequently prove either "one-trick ponies" or committed innovators.

How does this profile of initiatives and initiators within the Management and Governance policy area in 2010 compare to the 1990–94 cohort? Two chapters in *Innovating with Integrity* are relevant here, one dealing with information technology (Borins 1998, 131–51) and the other with organizational change (152–87). In the early 1990s, public sector IT was at a critical transition point from the use of mainframes for back-office functions to the application of a wide range of new technologies in a host of different functions. Itemizing the initiatives offers a useful reminder of the speed with which cutting-edge technologies become either standard or simply obsolete. A list of IT-based semifinalists between 1990 and 1994 includes seven geographic information systems, six databases, five interactive television projects, five smart cards, four electronic data interchanges, four mobile communications projects, four computer control systems, three video-based projects, three hotlines, two projects involving barcodes, two electronic kiosks, two expert systems, two voice-mail systems, two projects to network PCs, and one each involving imaging, photo radar, electronic highway pricing, e-mail, and management information systems. Some of these technologies, such as kiosks, have now been superseded, others (barcodes, voice mail, e-mail) are so commonplace that no one would think of submitting them to an innovation award, and others, such as road pricing, have latest-generation versions that are significantly more sophisticated. Certainly, new technologies continue to proliferate, but the 2010 semifinalist programs focusing on IT show a much narrower focus, perhaps indicative of a maturing understanding within the public sector of the pitfalls of the "solutions in search of a problem" mentality—the desire to use new technologies, regardless of necessity.

Thinking longitudinally, we can posit that the 2010 semifinalists in the Management and Governance area represent the norm that has emerged out of the transitions reflected in the earlier cohort. This plays out slightly differently in the area of internal improvement, where the focus in the earlier applications is primarily on workplace restructuring. The 1990–94 semifinalists included a handful of organizational turnarounds, where the application highlighted both the turnaround process and the technological or managerial innovations that were part of it (Borins 1998, 153–64). In addition to turnarounds, there were also initiatives to increase autonomy for frontline managers, such as the New York City subway system's Station Manager Program; initiatives to cross-train frontline regulatory staff in the Massachusetts Department of Environmental Protection; performance measurement such as Oregon Benchmarks; gainsharing for public servants; the introduction of competition through outsourcing, such as Indianapolis's Competition and Costing Program; public consultation initiatives such as North Dakota's Consensus Council; and large collaborative partnerships, such as the San Francisco Bay Area's Joint Urban Mobility Program, involving thirty-six agencies involved in the transportation system. Some of these innovations—Oregon Benchmarks, Competition and Costing, and the Station Manager Program—subsequently received widespread attention and recognition.

As we've seen, the organizational change initiatives among the 2010 semifinalists are a more limited set. First, there were no turnarounds among the 2010 semifinalists (and only one, the Arizona prison system, in the 2008 or 2009 finalists.) None of the innovations, except possibly the application of continuous improvement principles in Maine, affected the workplace as deeply as the 1990–94 initiatives in gainsharing, frontline management autonomy, cross-training, and outsourcing. Oregon Benchmarks can be seen as a precursor to Baltimore's CitiStat or Somerville's SomerStat, which the later initiatives improved upon by making much more fine-grained data available much more frequently and analyzing them continuously. The emphasis on evidence-based program evaluation embodied in New York City's Center for Economic Opportunity is certainly a new development since 1994, as are large-scale volunteer programs such as NYC Service and Chicago's Civic Consulting Alliance. Clearly, there has been as marked a shift in the emphasis of organizational change innovations as there has been in those employing IT. Where change in IT use is arguably an inevitable reflection of the trajectory of new technologies (from cutting-edge to standard to obsolete), the shift in the emphasis of organizational change innovations seems likely to be the result of broader social and political changes: the emergence of the performance measurement culture and an increased role for volunteer service inspired by both presidential appeals and a renewed spirit of post-9/11 patriotism and sense of urgency. And of course today's public sector workplace is the direct beneficiary of the innovations introduced in the earlier period. No need to reinvent that aspect of government again.

Transportation, Infrastructure, and Environment

Unlike the MG semifinalists, the Transportation, Infrastructure and Environment (TIE) semifinalists look very much like the entire set, varying little from the patterns typical of the group as a whole. When one considers this subset of applications, it quickly becomes apparent that the triple-barreled title is inaccurate. There is a consistent focus here on two primary, conceptually related objectives: environmental sustainability, in particular initiatives to reduce the production of greenhouse gases, and energy efficiency. Very few concern transportation or infrastructure. Of course, individual initiatives showed considerable diversity in both novelty and scale, with some considerably more modest and local in orientation than others. Two applications within this area were more tangentially related to the dominant "green" theme, both involving statewide land-use planning. But though this differs in focus, it clearly has implications for, and overlaps with, both sustainability and energy-related concerns. Then there were the inevitable outliers. The federal government's Aircraft Icing Prediction Initiative uses geostationary satellite data to more accurately predict aircraft icing hazards. The North Coast Geotourism Program is a partnership among the Department of the Interior's Bureau of Land Management, the National Geographic Society, and California's North Coast Tourism Council to build a tourism website for the region that is respectful of its geographic character.

The three most significant energy-related programs were the U.S. Environmental Protection Agency's Smart Way Program, the state of Maryland's Generating Green Horizons Program, and Denver's Greenprint Environmental Management System. The Smart Way Program is intended to encourage truck operators to reduce their emissions of greenhouse gases. It uses as policy instruments recognition for trucking and shipping companies who participate and increased access to capital for small trucking companies to retrofit their fleets. Maryland's initiative contracts out for the establishment of four facilities intended to produce 133 megawatts of wind or solar power. The goal of Denver's Greenprint Environmental Management System is to achieve ISO 14001, the most demanding standard for environmental management, for as many of Denver's municipal government departments as possible. By 2009 fifteen departments had been certified, and the final thirteen were to be certified in 2010. Clearly, despite the ongoing political controversy over global warming, public sector jurisdictions at all levels have not hesitated to launch "green" initiatives and to call attention to their efforts.

Not all energy-related initiatives were on this scale. In a more modest effort, Florida provided information to encourage its agricultural sector to participate in producing renewable fuels such as ethanol, and Sonoma County, California, subsidized projects to improve energy or water efficiency on private properties. The state of Missouri, together with the city of Columbia, Missouri, used a private sector partner's generation of landfill gas to provide power for the city and for two prisons. Marin County, California, adapted a British program to encourage students to bicycle or walk to school and their parents to carpool. These innovations may have a less wide-ranging impact than the more ambitious projects described above, but they are clearly motivated by the same environmental concerns that dominated the TIE policy area in 2010.

Three of the cluster of semifinalist programs addressing issues of environmental sustainability stand out for the sheer scale of their undertaking: the Northeast Regional Greenhouse Gas Initiative; the Orange County, California, Groundwater Replenishment System; and the Santa Ana Watershed Authority's One Water One Watershed Program based in Riverside County, California. Each involved large budgets, extensive coordination of high-level collaborators, and significant logistical challenges. The Northeast Regional Greenhouse Gas Initiative is a carbon emission reduction program for two hundred power plants in ten northeastern states that is the first mandatory cap-and-trade system in the United States. The program has raised more than $700 million in auction fees, much of which has been reinvested in increasing energy efficiency. Governor Pataki of New York took the initiative in inviting his counterparts to establish the program in 2003. Mitt Romney was governor of Massachusetts at the time. His administration participated in planning the project, but he refused to sign the agreement itself, apparently because participation would have conflicted with the "severely conservative" image he sought to establish to win the Republican presidential nomination.[3] (Presumably, the very name of the project would have been enough to damn it in some circles.) The Orange County, California, Groundwater Replenishment System involved an agreement between the county sanitation and water districts to build a $500 million treatment plant to produce 70 million gallons per day of drinkable water by recycling wastewater using microfiltration technology. The One Water One Watershed Program involves integrated regional planning for the Santa Ana Watershed encompassing more than one hundred agencies and nongovernmental organizations.

Within the TIE policy area, the awards judges also clearly recognized the value of small-scale local initiatives, some of which were only in the planning stages. The California Air Resources Board submitted an application for its initiative to reduce the production of ozone-depleting gases, most notably by allowing a credit for the destruction of ozone-depleting substances under a future cap-and-trade program. Oregon's Solar Highway, mentioned earlier (see pp. 67–68), is an initiative to locate solar panels on interstate rights-of-way and use the energy they generate to power highway lights. Other local initiatives included Salt Lake City's program to encourage businesses to be environmentally sustainable; a Mesa County, Colorado, initiative to produce a map of its energy reserves to show which can be accessed with the least detrimental environmental impact; a regional program in upper New York State to restore the wetlands of the headwaters of the Susquehanna River; and a San Antonio, Texas, regional watershed management program that was still in the planning process at the time of application.

I include an extremely ambitious integrated land-use planning initiative here because its animating spirit and a number of its components clearly overlap with these environmental sustainability innovations. Oregon's Statewide Land Use Program was put in place through legislation in 1974. Though the HKS Awards make novelty one of their criteria, it was selected as one of the six 2010 finalists. The initiative instituted wide-ranging planning controls that encompassed protection of the coast and the Willamette Valley, integrated land-use and transportation planning, and limits on urban sprawl, particularly in the Portland area.

---

3. Sheryl Stolberg, "Romney Shifted Right on Energy as Presidential Politics Beckoned," *New York Times,* September 29, 2012.

The program has been controversial and is unusually ambitious in comparison with other U.S. land-use planning programs. Its presence as a 2010 finalist speaks to the robustness of the program and its continued—indeed increased—relevance. A second planning initiative, Envision Utah, includes similar long-term planning goals, but functions as a forum for public discussion and involvement in the planning process.

Taken as a policy set, how do these initiatives compare to those of the early 1990s? We can answer the question broadly before examining comparators in more detail. First, TIE innovations in 2010 focus on one large, and controversial, problem: environmental protection and sustainability, however multifaceted its manifestations. This tends to give them a shared focus as a set that contrasts with the diversity of their earlier counterparts. Despite the concern with greenhouse gases, however, transportation largely drops out of view in 2010 as a target of innovation. Finally, it is notable that the 2010 initiatives make more extensive use of regulation as a policy instrument. *Innovating with Integrity* (Borins 1998) included a chapter on environmental and energy management (188–209) and a section of a later chapter (230–32) on economic development and transportation, which can form the basis for a more detailed comparison. The 1990–94 semifinalists the book analyzed included several transportation projects: electronic tolling technology on the Oklahoma Turnpike; partnerships to fast-track road and bridge projects in Cleveland and public transit projects in the San Francisco Bay Area; and a program to encourage greater use of public transit in Boulder, Colorado. The only transportation initiative among the 2010 semifinalists was the U.S. Environmental Protection Agency's Smart Way Program. It does not actually deal with transportation issues but rather with gas emissions produced by one component of the transportation system.

Reviewing the environmental and energy innovations among the 1990–94 HKS Awards semifinalists evokes something of the same time warp we experienced revisiting their "cutting-edge" IT innovations: recycling and clean-up initiatives play a large role. Seattle, Washington, developed a pioneering curbside recycling program, and Burlington, Vermont, provided advice to help businesses comply with mandatory recycling as well as subsidizing recycling containers. A suburb of Minneapolis instituted curbside recycling using barcode records, and a multistate initiative supported procurement of recycled xerographic paper. Focusing on environmental cleanup, Minnesota launched a program to provide technical assistance to help businesses or individuals clean up contaminated urban land, and Wichita, Kansas, used tax incentives to support a local environmental cleanup. A number of other initiatives were largely educational in aim: Iowa developed a center for research in sustainable agriculture initiatives, Georgia provided information to residents of rural areas about drilling dry hydrants and using no-till planting technology, and the California Air Resources Board distributed comic-book-style handbooks to industry to encourage self-inspection of equipment. Finally, in a somewhat more forward-looking spirit, Harwich, Massachusetts, developed a small greenhouse-based sewage treatment plant.

The initiatives are diverse, but it is possible to find common themes. The projects on this list were generally small in scale and often located in rural areas. They dealt more often with groundwater or soil pollution than with atmospheric pollution. Greenhouse gas emissions barely register as an issue. Recycling and education were major themes. And these projects used voluntary compliance, encouragement, and occasionally tax incentives much more than regulation or the establishment of public sector institutions to achieve their objectives.

Clearly, the 2010 semifinalist innovations differ in a number of ways. They accord much more attention to atmospheric pollution—in particular, the production of greenhouse gases—than to soil or water pollution. None of them involves recycling, which has now been established as standard practice. They are tightly focused on either environmental sustainability or energy efficiency, in contrast to the diversity of the 1990–94 semifinalists. Although many of the 2010 energy and environment semifinalists were small projects, a number were operating on a very large scale, such as the northeastern states' Regional Greenhouse Gas Initiative, the new Orange Country water treatment plant, Oregon's land-use planning initiative, and the EPA's Smart Way Program. There is simply nothing comparable in terms of budget or logistics in the earlier set. Many of the 2010 programs, like the earlier programs, employ encouragement and exhortation to achieve their goals, but now some include more stringent regulation, such as the imposition of cap-and-trade environmental management systems. The California Air Resources Board has abandoned comic book manuals for a more regulatory approach to reducing the production of ozone-depleting gases. Innovation is a responsive phenomenon. Changes in expert knowledge and common practice within a policy area will result in the emergence of new priorities and the recognition of new challenges. The nature of the innovations that emerge to address them inevitably changes as well.

Community and Economic Development

The semifinalist programs within the Community and Economic Development (CED) area frequently target business in general or businesses serving low-income populations. Comparing their characteristics with those of the entire set of semifinalists makes it very clear that the target groups are not passive recipients of public sector largesse but instead are deeply involved in the design, implementation, and financing of the innovations. Business is, in fact, a uniquely "advantaged" target population, with resources of knowledge and capacity to harness. Seventy-one percent of the CED initiatives involve collaboration with the private sector, 17 percent higher than all semifinalists. Forty-two percent of originators are participants in the collaboration, which is 15 percent higher than for all semifinalists, and 21 percent are members of interest groups, which is 10 percent higher. Forty-two percent of these innovations employed a planning process involving public consultation. That is 15 percent higher than for all semifinalists. Almost half (48 percent) of the CED applications report that their most important achievement was enabling individuals or groups to collaborate, which is 17 percent higher than for all semifinalists. Twenty-nine percent cite the business lobby as one of their strongest supporters, which is 17 percent higher than for all semifinalists. Forty-three percent report that the private sector provided some financing, which is 18 percent higher than for all semifinalists. Finally, 24 percent of CED semifinalists report that national media associated with the political right have reported on their innovations, which is 10 percent higher than for all semifinalists. Apparently, though the more conservative media may be relatively uninterested in public sector innovation (except in the case of programs deemed egregiously eccentric or conspicuous failures, which then become useful sticks to beat opponents with), they do pay attention when the business community is involved.

CED semifinalist applications cluster around four dominant themes: support for the new economy; urban development, which encompasses business, housing, and parks; rural development; and responses to the mortgage foreclosure crisis that began in 2007. The two outliers here are cases of a slightly awkward fit more than complete anomalies. The Lancaster, Pennsylvania, Property Code Enforcement initiative provides property inspectors with hand-held computers and access to the city's database so that they can quickly produce notices, similar to parking tickets, of violations of quality-of-life regulations, such as overgrown lawns, excessive trash, abandoned vehicles, or graffiti. The Pennsylvania Council of the Arts' Cultural Data Project has developed templates for cultural organizations to generate financial or organizational reporting to government or stakeholders; it is now being used by 9,300 organizations in eight states.

Littleton, Colorado, a suburb of Denver, experienced an economic crisis in 1987 with the departure of its two major employers, Marathon Oil and Martin Marietta. Rather than following standard practice and offering incentives to encourage business to relocate, the city adopted an approach it called "Economic Gardening." This involved support for existing businesses by providing critical business information and accompanying analytics such as cyberspace tools, as well as enhancing public sector infrastructure and facilitating networking among businesses and between businesses and educational and social institutions. Economic Gardening was originally an HKS Awards semifinalist in 1992, when the competition was open to state and local governments only (Borins 1998, 231). The program has endured, becoming more sophisticated in its strategies and demonstrating continued success through more recent economic challenges. Its continued relevance was recognized in 2010 when it was chosen as an HKS Awards finalist.

Sharing Littleton's emphasis on technological infrastructure aimed at business generally, Santa Monica, California, built a local broadband fiber-optic network, which it made available to local businesses at lease rates that were much lower than the rates of private sector carriers. The price and availability of the network attracted several businesses to Santa Monica, in particular, large users of broadband such as film production companies. The originator of this innovation, Santa Monica's chief information officer, Jory Wolf, was also the originator of an information technology innovation in 1993 (Wolf is discussed in chapter 8 as an example of a "serial innovator").

Adopting a more narrowly focused approach, Pennsylvania used funds from the Tobacco Settlement Act of 2001 to establish three biotechnology centers. One of these, the Life Sciences Greenhouse, located in central Pennsylvania, was a semifinalist for the 2010 award. Ohio, also using Tobacco Settlement funds, worked closely with the university sector to establish its Third Frontier Program to support technology-based economic development.

Initiatives relating to urban development show more diversity, though understandably engage more directly with low-income populations than the more general business-oriented innovations discussed above. All of them share a concern with generating both economic and social benefits. Demonstrating durability similar to Littleton, Colorado's Economic Gardening, a program established by the Clinton administration in 2000 was a semifinalist in 2010. The New Markets Tax Credit Program allows investors to claim a credit against federal income tax for investing in business or real estate projects in distressed communities. The program uses a competitive process to determine which proposals are funded—the $5 billion it made available in 2010 was oversubscribed by a factor of 5. Originally the program funded investments primarily in urban areas, but in order to retain congressional support in 2006 it started directing 20 percent of its funds to be invested in rural areas.

Philadelphia's Transit-Oriented Development Gap Financing Program was established in response to the 2008 economic crisis. To help small businesses cope with the difficulty of finding private sector financing, the city partnered with a private nonprofit lender to create a loan fund of $11 million to provide loans to small businesses located near transit hubs. Also addressing the issue of financing, Arlington, Virginia, provided loan guarantees to a housing development at Potomac Yards, a former regional railroad center. The development included sixty-four affordable housing units located above a new state-of-the-art fire station.

Three semifinalist initiatives involved with park development differ significantly in scale and in the demographic profile of their most likely beneficiaries. The most ambitious project was New York City's Bryant Park Corporation, a private nonprofit corporation that restored, gentrified, and now operates Bryant Park, adjacent to the New York Public Library (Donahue and Zeckhauser 2011, 176–89).[4] The city of Louisville's City of Parks initiative also involved private and public funding to renovate the city's park system, which had originally been planned in the 1880s by Fredrick Law Olmsted. The initiative included acquisition of 8,000 acres of parkland, building a 100-mile trail looping around the city, improving facilities in existing parks, and establishing an environmental education program, measures aimed at improving access and facilities for all. In Davenport, Iowa, River Vision on the Mississippi is an initiative to improve its riverfront parkland. The project is still in the stage of planning and initial projects; it is unclear whether it will take either the Bryant Park Corporation or Louisville's City of Parks as a model in pursuing public-private partnerships.

When we look at rural development initiatives, it is clear that all three semifinalist programs are responding to changing demographic and economic patterns in rural areas. The Kentucky Agricultural Development Fund was an initiative launched by Governor Paul Patton in 1998 to take a comprehensive approach to rural development, especially tackling the difficult problem of reliance on tobacco as a major crop. When funding from the Tobacco Settlement Act became available, this program began providing grants that supported transition to other crops, research, and a renewable energy initiative. Oregon's Urban and Rural Reserve initiative flowed from the Statewide Land Use Program, discussed earlier as an environmental initiative. In this case the planning process dealing with the extent of urbanization in the Portland area ultimately designated 29,000 acres of urban reserves and 267,000 acres of rural reserves, which will be protected from urban development for the next fifty years. Finally, Virginia's Return to Roots Program was initiated by rural counties in southern Virginia with shortages of skilled labor. The state has developed a website with social media capability to encourage people who have left those regions to return to them to fill vacant positions.

---

4. Donahue and Zeckhauser (2011, 156–76) also discuss two other New York City partnerships: the Central Park Conservancy and Harlem's Swindler Cove Park and Peter Jay Sharp Boathouse. They conclude that these partnerships have increased the resources for the park system far beyond what the public sector could provide. These investments have immensely improved the capital, maintenance, and public safety of the parks, but have given private sector donors considerable control over how the parks are used. The authors question the value of establishing a world-class boathouse in a park in Harlem and argue that the community would have preferred a very different pattern of investment. Lisa Foderaro ("New York Parks in Less Affluent Areas Lack Big Gifts," *New York Times*, February 17, 2013) has written that parks in the less affluent areas of New York City are ignored by the major donors.

The mortgage foreclosure crisis that began in 2007 produced a tragically wide range of economic and social aftershocks. It is not surprising to find that programs responding to it run the gamut from those attempting to prevent foreclosures to those intended to quickly return foreclosed properties to the housing market to those that attempt to deal with properties that have long been abandoned.

In Detroit, Wayne County's Mortgage Foreclosure Prevention Program works with fourteen nonprofit agencies to provide advice to help people facing foreclosure understand their options and choose the best one for them. The Massachusetts Housing Partnership developed the SoftSecond Loan Program in 1990. It supports lower-income first-time home buyers with an interest subsidy provided by the state, and homeownership classes. The mortgage foreclosure crisis generally had its origin in the overexpansion of mortgage credit, but this program appears to have avoided that problem.

The harsh reality of the effects of the crisis is made clear by three programs dealing in somewhat different ways with vacant properties. The Minneapolis Community Stabilization First Look Pilot Program works with the federal Department of Housing and Urban Development's Neighborhood Stabilization Program to give nonprofit or for-profit organizations partnering with the city a two-week window to acquire foreclosed properties at a discount before the properties become available to speculative investors. The purchaser participating in the program would then be expected to renovate the property and attempt to resell it. In Wilmington, Delaware, the Vacant Property Registration Fee Program put in place a schedule of registration fees that increase the longer a property has been vacant, with a one-year waiver if the owner of the property rehabilitates it, rents it, or demolishes it. The Philadelphia LandCare Program takes abandoned and blighted properties and turns them into parklets, managing them as urban green space.

Initiatives in the CED area show considerable diversity in both target populations and objectives, but one thing many of them have in common is collaboration of the public sector with the private or nonprofit sectors. Private sector investment was essential for Bryant Park, the New Market Tax Credit Program, the Massachusetts SoftSecond Loan Program, Philadelphia's Transit Oriented Development Gap Financing Program, and the Minneapolis Community Stabilization First Look Pilot Program. Although the role of the public sector could involve subsidy or regulation, in addition there were instances of direct public funding. Two important sources were Tobacco Settlement Act funding—essential to the Kentucky Agricultural Development Fund, Ohio Third Frontier, and Pennsylvania Life Sciences Greenhouse—and the Recovery Act, which contributed to the Kentucky Agricultural Development Fund, Philadelphia Transit Oriented Development Gap Financing program, Wayne County Mortgage Foreclosure Prevention Program, and Minneapolis Community Stabilization First Look Program.

Innovating with Integrity discussed CED initiatives together with community policing—a revealing juxtaposition (Borins 1998, 210–35).[5] In the 1990–94 set of applications, both economic development and policing showed an almost exclusive focus on community mobilization, whether to fight crime in the urban ghetto or to improve housing and build social capital, with modest financial support from state or local government. Typical development initiatives included community organizing and empowerment in Massachusetts public housing; neighborhood revitalization with the assistance of small municipal government grants in Savannah; a Cleveland program to speed foreclosure of vacant properties so they could be redeveloped; and a Baltimore initiative to subsidize restoration of vacant inner-city houses. There are relatively few such examples to cite.

Economic development innovations among the 1990–94 semifinalists did not address the new economy (with the exception of the early version of Economic Gardening in Littleton, Colorado), nor did they include urban park initiatives such as the restoration of Bryant Park, major urban development initiatives like the New Markets Tax Credit, nor major rural development initiatives like the Kentucky Agricultural Development Fund. The opportunities created by the information economy and new funding opportunities such as the Tobacco Settlement Fund were not yet available, with the result that public sector innovation was of much less significance in economic development and was generally small in scale.

What is more, these programs were animated by a very different social narrative than comparable initiatives in 2010. The innovative programs of the early 1990s were attempting to build social capital in impoverished neighborhoods and were founded on the optimistic assumption that such a reconstructive venture was possible. The innovative programs in the years following the mortgage foreclosure crisis had the much harder task of trying to stabilize communities that were collapsing because so many residents were being forced to leave. These innovations were born of fatalism or desperation and a pressing need to mobilize scarce resources in the face of an overwhelming crisis. Looking at Community and Economic Development overall, it is clear that although economic development has seen the emergence of new opportunities, new resources, and new types of partnerships, the field of urban development, in particular in low-income communities, has experienced no such renewal. Dealing with the economic and social

---

5. Community policing is defined as the establishment of close relationships between police departments and the communities they serve.

fallout of the mortgage crisis has necessarily absorbed much of the public sector's attention and crowded out other possibilities.[6] It is a stark illustration of the double-edged effect of a crisis of such magnitude: as a catalyst, it forces innovative thinking and a flurry of problem solving, but it also monopolizes the public sector's creative and fiscal capital, elbowing out many other important issues.

Education and Training

Education is everybody's business, a point I made first in *Innovating with Integrity,* where I used the phrase as the title of a chapter on educational innovation. It is even truer today. It is not only that we have all had formative experiences in the educational system ourselves, or even that many of us have reencountered that system through the experiences of our children—although both experiences are likely to engender strong opinions about questions of failure and reform. It is also that the past two decades have seen educational innovation become a topic of widespread public debate and controversy. *Governing Fables,* my book on narratives of the public sector (Borins 2011, 27–61), devotes a chapter to "teacher fables," both heroic and antiheroic, noting the complex relationship between cinematic treatments of the theme, whether fiction or documentary, and current policy debates.

The fourteen semifinalists in the 2010 Education and Training (ET) area represent the smallest set overall. And they manifest other differences that reflect the policy area's public visibility, the high importance attributed to it, and its increasingly controversial character. Ninety-three percent of the 2010 educational innovations involve collaboration with nonprofits, 26 percent higher than for all semifinalists. Thirty-eight percent are initiated by frontline staff, 17 percent higher than for all semifinalists, and 23 percent are initiated by interest group members, 12 percent higher. Educational innovation tends to be theory driven, with 50 percent of the semifinalist innovations reporting that their most important achievement was operationalizing a theoretical model, as compared to 30 percent for all semifinalists. Public interest groups are among the strongest supporters of educational innovations, registering support for 57 percent of the innovations, 28 percent higher than for all semifinalists. On the other hand, professionals are often in evidence as critics of educational innovations, playing that role in 29 percent of the educational innovations, compared to 14 percent for all semifinalists. The main criticism, expressed for 61 percent of the educational

6. Austen (2013) provides a compelling account of the ongoing magnitude of the crisis in the southern and western suburbs of Chicago, seen through the viewpoint of the Anti-Eviction Campaign, a group that helps renovate abandoned properties and enables homeless people to occupy them on a squatters' rights basis.

innovations, is opposition to the informing philosophy. This is 12 percent higher than for all semifinalists.

The presence of a theoretical model, then, operates as a mixed blessing: it focuses the work of the innovator and the approval of its supporters, but equally galvanizes the opposition of its critics. Given the close relationship of the elementary and secondary educational systems to institutions of higher education, which train a large proportion of the teachers in their faculties of education, it is no surprise that 43 percent of the educational innovations report that they have been the subject of academic research, 20 percent higher than for all semifinalists. Finally, educational innovations are of intense interest to the media: 79 percent were covered in professional or trade media, 16 percent higher than was the case for all semifinalists; 79 percent were covered in national media, 35 percent higher than for all semifinalists; 43 percent were covered by national media on the political left, 10 percent higher than for all semifinalists, and 43 percent were also covered by media of the political center, 26 percent higher than for all semifinalists. Interest group and nonprofit organization engagement, theory, principled opposition to theory, and intense media coverage—to a significantly greater degree than any other category of innovation, educational initiatives are characterized by specialist interest, external scrutiny, and theoretical controversy.

Among the six policy areas, Education and Training involves perhaps the broadest range of target populations (from pre-kindergarteners to later-life learners, all of whom may also display a range of exceptionalities and face a variety of linguistic, cultural, and financial barriers to access), institutions, and personnel, so it is not surprising that the fourteen ET semifinalist programs demonstrated considerable diversity. Even so, we can identify five major themes: teacher quality initiatives, charter schools, drop-out recovery, distance education, and English as a second language. And the outliers? There were three that did not fit easily into any of these thematic clusters. The New England Common Assessment Program is a collaboration among Maine, New Hampshire, Rhode Island, and Vermont to develop and use common instruments for testing under No Child Left Behind. The Texas Master Naturalist Program trains volunteer naturalists to work in Texas state parks, and Raven Island is computer software developed in Alaska to teach children about fire safety.

In 2003 Boston's superintendent of schools, Tom Payzant, was approached by a private foundation willing to support his top organizational priority. Identifying his most important problem as improving the overall quality of teaching—in particular, reducing the turnover rate for new teachers in the Boston public school system—Payzant spearheaded the establishment of an in-house teachers' college (what the corporate world would call backward vertical integration). The Teacher Residency Program trains teachers by combining courses taken at the

University of Massachusetts, Boston with mentored instruction in the classroom, using a medical residency model. The program pays for the teachers' tuition and offers a stipend and health insurance in exchange for a commitment to teach in the Boston public schools for three years. The Teacher Residency Program receives approximately ten applicants for every individual it admits, now trains approximately one-third of the new teachers the Boston public schools hire every year, and has also been able to increase the supply of visible minority, special education, and ESL teachers. The program was one of the 2010 HKS Awards finalists.

A contrasting approach to improving teacher quality is based on the establishment of pay-for-performance compensation. Two of the semifinalist applicants operationalized this model. Minnesota's Quality Compensation System for Teachers, instituted by the legislature in 2005, allows local school districts and teachers' unions to design a compensation system that uses objective teacher evaluations to allocate performance pay. A considerable percentage of school districts have now opted into the system. Denver's public school district and the Denver Classroom Teachers Association established a professional compensation system for teachers that links teacher compensation more directly to student achievement outcomes and provides rewards for serving in high-poverty schools and teaching hard-to-staff subjects. Like virtually every other aspect of educational reform, the issue of improving teaching quality is highly contested and frequently highly politicized. We might compare the very different routes chosen by Boston and Minnesota and Denver to the contrasting solutions adopted by various jurisdictions to the problem of citizens lacking health insurance (discussed on pp. 165–66) where direct intervention is ranged against more "market-oriented" solutions.

Three of the fourteen ET semifinalists were charter school initiatives. High Tech High is a charter school in San Diego that uses the Coalition for Essential Schools' philosophy of personalized education and connection to the adult world through an emphasis on individual student projects. The school's curriculum puts considerable weight on math, sciences, and engineering, and it also attempts to increase the enrollment of women and minority groups. The founder of High Tech High was Larry Rosenstock, who had previously founded CityWorks, a similar program based at Rindge School of Technical Arts in Cambridge, Massachusetts, which was an HKS Awards winner in 1992 (Borins 1998, 264, 268, 271, 278). (Rosenstock is discussed in chapter 8 of this volume as an example of a "serial innovator.") Improved Solutions for Urban Systems is a charter school based in Dayton, Ohio, that focuses on dropout recovery, combining classroom work with training for the construction industry. The Boston Day and Evening Academy, which also focuses on dropout recovery, started life as an evening school to better reach its students and later added daytime classes. Like High Tech High, it follows the Coalition of Essential Schools' approach with its emphasis on research projects and links to the community. What all three schools share is a commitment to making education both more accessible and more meaningful and deemphasizing standardized results in favor of creating strong connections between the schools and the larger community, especially the working community.

Charter schools such as Improved Solutions for Urban Systems and the Boston Day and Evening Academy included drop-out recovery among their objectives, but the 2010 semifinalists also had single-focus programs dealing solely with the challenges of recovery and reentry. Philadelphia's Project U-Turn takes a multi-component approach that includes a summer workforce development program, making spaces available in the school system for over-age and under-credited students, providing a hot line for dropouts seeking to return to school, and establishing a drop-in reengagement center for counseling. Washington State's Integrating Basic Education and Skills Training (I-Best) Program is aimed at remedial adult learners and works through the community and technical college system, providing grants to support fifteen students at each college who are taking both adult basic education and vocational training courses.

The two distance education programs among the semifinalists pursue a different form of outreach. Florida's Virtual School initiative began in 1997 as an early user of broadband Internet. The program provides a wide variety of courses to 100,000 students, 40 percent of whom live in rural areas and belong to minority communities. It is now the largest program of its kind in the United States. Access Alabama, which began operation in 2005, took the Florida program as a model but pursued a narrower focus, putting a special emphasis on making available advanced placement (AP) and other advanced courses, including language courses. It now has 32,000 students participating. Access Alabama is particularly concerned with improving educational offerings for rural schools, to put them on a par with suburban schools and offset the disadvantages of geography.

So far, only one HKS Awards semifinalist, Nashville's International Newcomer Academy, makes English language training its primary focus, but changing demographic patterns will likely make this an increasingly important area of innovation. The Boston Teacher Residency Program made increasing teacher capacity in ESL one of its priorities, and Washington State's I-Best program also served many ESL students. Nashville's program provides full-time English language training for two semesters for students prior to their entry into the school system. The program is small, serving only thirty-nine students in 2009–10, but was accommodating 50 percent of the demand for comprehensive ESL education in the Metropolitan Nashville Public Schools district.

Has educational innovation changed significantly since the early 1990s? Much of the analysis in *Innovating with Integrity* (Borins 1998, 261–82) suggests a profile similar in many ways to the one just outlined. Then as now, educational innovations had strong support from outside government from nonprofits such as the Rockefeller, Taubman, and Kellogg Foundations. Education innovations were often theory driven and often were criticized by professionals who opposed the theories being implemented. One innovation, New York City's Peer Intervention Program, attempted to improve teacher quality by engaging experienced teachers to provide counseling and skills development to teachers rated unsatisfactory—fewer than 1 percent of the 45,000 teachers in the New York City system. Several schools developed innovative curricula: CityWorks at Rindge School of Technical Arts, and two others using the Coalition for Essential Schools' model, Central Park East Secondary School in New York and Thayer Junior/Senior High School in New Hampshire. There were technology-based innovations, such as the use of interactive television in Kentucky, Hawaii, and Oklahoma, as well as a program providing a computer lab in a public housing project in Lansing, Michigan. A program in Los Angeles aimed at combating truancy by bringing to the table a variety of professionals to deal with the problems of a truant's family.[7] Massachusetts' Student Conflict Resolution Experts program trained students in mediation so that they could play a role in reducing gang violence in the schools. Finally, the Michigan Partnership for New Education was a comprehensive educational reform program that partnered selected schools with university faculties of education to restructure curriculum and develop teacher skills.

Comparing the 1990–94 and 2010 ET semifinalists more closely we can see shifts that reflect changes in the educational policy landscape and its major players. The innovative magnet schools of the early nineties are now more likely to be charter schools. Interactive television as an educational tool has gone the way of the Walkman: innovations in program delivery now use the Internet. Foundations are still involved in supporting innovations, with the difference that the Gates Foundation has become preeminent in supporting educational innovations that are consistent with its own results-based reform agenda. Two charter schools among the 2010 semifinalists, High Tech High and Improved Solutions for Urban Systems, acknowledge Gates support, as does Washington State's college-based Integrated Basic Education and Skills Training Program.

There is, additionally, a significant element of the current educational policy agenda that was not much in evidence two decades ago. Improving teacher quality has been increasingly identified as a prerequisite to educational reform, and initiatives have proliferated in that area. A remedial counseling program for failing teachers such as New York City's Peer Intervention Program would now be seen as woefully inadequate in comparison with the much more comprehensive

7. The 2010 semifinalists include a comparable program in Arlington, Virginia, to combat truancy by using multi-agency collaboration to respond to the entire set of problems underlying truancy. This program was classified in the Health and Social Services policy area; nevertheless, it demonstrates the ongoing existence of programs focusing on truancy.

solution of pay-for-performance for all teachers, an innovation that is now being diffused nationally. Like Boston, other school systems, too, have begun to play a larger role in specialized training for their own teachers. The 2010 education semifinalists also included initiatives in dropout recovery and ESL, two areas that were not represented in the earlier set. Both are likely to be the focus of future innovations as educational priorities continue to shift to reflect demographic, economic, theoretical, and cultural changes. The point bears repeating: innovation is a responsive phenomenon, reacting to the changing realities around it.

Health and Social Services

Health and Social Service innovations (HSS) that were semifinalists in 2010 targeted a unique subset of Americans. Only 4 percent focused on the general population, 33 percent lower than all semifinalists. In contrast, 62 percent targeted high-risk populations, 38 percent higher than all semifinalists; 50 percent targeted low-income populations, 25 percent higher than all semifinalists; 19 percent were aimed at the elderly, 15 percent higher than all semifinalists; and 30 percent were aimed at young people, 12 percent higher than all semifinalists. Beyond the unique demographic profile of the groups they deal with, HSS innovations, like educational innovations, are strongly theory driven, with 46 percent of them citing as their most important achievement operationalizing a theoretical model, 17 percent higher than for all semifinalists. Their measures of success are primarily external, with 46 percent citing increased user satisfaction with the program, 28 percent higher than for all semifinalists; 42 percent mentioning improved service, 17 percent higher; and 96 percent responding that their programs have made their clients better off, 10 percent higher.

HSS innovations formed the largest group within the semifinalist bloc, encompassing twenty-six semifinalists, seven within the top twenty-five, and one finalist. The twenty-six semifinalist programs can be grouped around five dominant objectives: improving access to the health-care system, especially for those without health insurance; youth health and fitness; support for youth in troubled families; enhancing the ability of citizens to receive benefits to which they are entitled; and improving the effectiveness of organizations in the health-care sector. Only one outlier resisted categorization: New York City's court-administered Prevention Services Law Project enables families who have received eviction notices to meet with social workers and counsel to obtain comprehensive legal, financial, and social services to prevent them from becoming homeless.

The issue of access can be addressed in a variety of ways, either through broad-based measures aimed at uninsured populations within a given jurisdiction or through more narrowly targeted initiatives to meet the health-care needs of specific groups. Healthy San Francisco, one of the six finalists in the 2010 competition, provides universal comprehensive health care for 54,000 uninsured adults in San Francisco, more than 70 percent of that city's uninsured population of 77,000. Run by the San Francisco Department of Public Health, the plan works through a network of thirty primary-care medical "homes." Participants may choose to enroll in any one of them. The eligibility limit is 500 percent of the federal poverty line, and fees are modest and geared to income. The program is funded primarily out of the city's budget, with contributions from the federal government and a health-care spending requirement for local employers.

Healthy San Francisco can be seen as a type of single-payer system favored by the political left because participants pay their fees to the program and the program reimburses the medical "homes." Healthy Indiana represents the political right's approach to expanded health care for the noninsured because it emphasizes a consumerist approach, making participants conscious of cost by requiring them to pay their share. The program is funded by an increase in the state's cigarette tax. Its budget can cover 51,000 individuals, only 15 percent of Indiana's 350,000 uninsured. The program has a $1,100 deductible, mandates co-payments for use of emergency departments, and requires participants to make monthly payments to their health savings accounts, which are also subsidized. The two approaches reflect the very different political cultures of two very different regions as they tackle the same urgent problem.

Access to health services is no guarantee of access to medications. West Virginia Rx is a charitable pharmacy that provides free prescriptions for 20,000 low-income state residents. Operating out of the state's largest free clinic, West Virginia Health Right in Charleston, the program has built a database of drug manufacturers' patient assistance programs (which provide free medications for those with low incomes) and can quickly access the appropriate drug and manufacturer for each participant.

Children represent a special health-care target population, with prevention and proactive support particular priorities. Three semifinalist initiatives are designed specifically for children. New Jersey's Evidence-Based Home Visiting Initiative sends nurses to visit pregnant women and parents of infants and children to the age of three who are at higher risk for child abuse, neglect, or youth violence, on the basis of an assessment of the parental situation made by community agencies or HIV programs. The Massachusetts Child Psychiatry Access Program provides primary-care physicians with telephone consultations about psychiatric issues in or treatment for children they are seeing. The program identifies treatment options, in particular alternatives to the use of prescription drugs, for example counseling, and attempts to ensure that the preferred treatment option is covered by insurance. The Rhode Island Pediatric Practice Enhancement Project enlists experienced parents of children with special needs to act as consultants to other families, helping the latter to navigate the complexities of the health-care system.

Three other programs within the semifinalist group narrow their focus still more. The Washington, D.C., Automatic HIV Counseling Program works with the corrections system to provide automatic testing as part of normal medical screening for inmates at intake (with an opt-out rather than opt-in option). The results of the screening can be used in planning counseling and treatment options both within the prison system and upon discharge. Money Follows the Person is a Texas program that has enabled 21,000 individuals who were in Medicaid nursing facilities to use the funding they were already receiving to relocate into the community. Finally, 911 Telehealth addresses the issue of use of emergency medical resources. The Houston program diverts nonemergency 911 calls from hospital emergency rooms to clinics and provides a subsidized no-cost taxi, rather than an ambulance, to take callers there.

As childhood obesity, with all of its social, educational, and health implications, has become an increasingly pressing public health concern, it is not surprising to discover two innovative programs seeking to promote youth fitness among the semifinalist group. Both initiatives were also selected for the top twenty-five. Arkansas's Act 1220 was a 2003 act of the legislature requiring schools to measure the body mass index of students and report it confidentially to parents. Shape Up Somerville represents something very different: a single initiative with a strictly limited focus that grew into a holistic approach to the problems its own results identified. The program began with a study of the health and weight of grade one to three students in Somerville, Massachusetts, schools. It then became an obesity prevention campaign in the schools, ultimately evolving into a comprehensive campaign to encourage physical activity and healthy eating for residents of all ages, along with a program of infrastructure improvement— for example, parks and bicycle paths—to encourage physical activity.

Maintaining a focus on youth and adopting a similar proactive stance, six semifinalist programs seek to identify and support young people at risk due to family circumstances, mental health issues, or socioeconomic pressures. The variety of targets and delivery mechanisms speak not only to the resourcefulness of the initiators but also to the complexity of the problems they seek to address. Michigan's Family Resource Centers are located in fifty-two schools identified as priority schools by their failure to meet progress milestones under No Child Left Behind. The centers provide integrated case management (counseling, health care, day care, Medicaid, food stamps) for children who are in difficulty academically or socially and for their families. Safe Passages is a formal partnership (known under California law as a Joint Power Authority) of the City of Oakland, Oakland Unified School District, and Alameda County, in which Oakland is located. Here, too, the focus is on integration, providing services in areas such as mental health, violence prevention, and juvenile justice for children and youths from low-income families.

Neighborhood for Kids is a San Diego program for abused children that places them in familiar surroundings with people they know and trust, such as relatives, rather than removing them to foster care. It also provides integrated services that focus on concerns such as safety and academic performance. Georgia's One System of Care for Grandparents Raising Grandchildren supports these families (of which there are 103,000 in Georgia), using caseworkers to deal with the complexity of the welfare system as administered by Georgia's Department of Human Services.

Two initiatives offer children and youths positive recreational and work opportunities. Safe Summer is a Prince George's County, Maryland, program based in schools and community centers that provides free accessible late-night recreation during the summer for children and young adults ages twelve to twenty-four. It began as a program to make basketball courts available but evolved to include health and physical education, arts and culture, and social events. The trajectory is similar to Shape Up Somerville: a narrowly focused initial program broadening to a more holistic approach. Summer Work Experience is a rural Nevada program that used Recovery Act funding to hire forty at-risk youths identified by the juvenile justice system, teach them job readiness skills, and employ them to clean up illegal dumpsites in the desert.

Three semifinalist programs addressed the complexities of the benefits system, adopting different means to simplify and improve access. Michigan's Online Electronic Benefit Transfer Program for WIC (women, infants, and children) welfare benefits was the first of its kind. Participants in the program—women with low incomes who are either pregnant or have children up to age five—receive a card with a magnetic stripe that they can swipe at the grocery store. The innovation succeeded in incorporating the complexity of the WIC program's rules into the online system and has reduced the administrative cost. Equally important, it has eliminated the stigma of paper food stamps. The Ohio Benefits Bank was established by the Ohio Association of Second Harvest Foodbanks with the intention of helping those with low incomes, particularly in the Appalachian southeast of the state, to access all the government benefits to which they are entitled. The program uses a web-based software system to identify and claim benefits, and VISTA (Volunteers in Service to America) volunteers provide the outreach. Finally, Wyoming's Healthy Families Succeed program pools data from a number of state government departments (Health, Corrections, Family Services, Employment) to identify high-risk families that are heavy users of public services. It then develops integrated case management solutions for them, ensuring that they can access the services most suited to their needs.

All four of the 2010 semifinalist initiatives aimed at improving the performance of health sector organizations emphasized training, often in combination with new or improved performance measures. Integrated Ethics is an initiative of the Veterans Administration hospitals that applies continuous improvement principles to the work of hospital ethics committees by defining national standards, providing training, and developing and reporting performance metrics. The Massachusetts Department of Mental Health's Restraint/Seclusion Prevention Initiative is a quality improvement effort designed to reduce the use of restraint or seclusion for patients behaving violently in mental health institutions. The program has developed alternative treatment options and trained staff and has been able to dramatically reduce the use of restraint and seclusion. The Rhode Island Department of Health's initiative to promote resident-centered care in nursing homes developed a regulatory inspection process to monitor the quality of life for residents of nursing homes, for example, by enhancing resident choice of daily activities. It uses the results of the inspection to provide feedback, targeted technical assistance, and training. North Carolina's New Organizational Vision Award (NOVA) seeks to improve recruitment and retention of direct-care workers in home-care agencies, adult-care homes, and nursing homes. It is a voluntary comprehensive state licensure pilot program. Nine of 1,900 agencies have met its criteria, and they have been able to make significant reductions in their turnover rates.

This detailed account of the Health and Social Services semifinalists in 2010 should make clear both the number and variety of innovations undertaken in this policy area. Looking back to 1990–94, the profile is the same. Then, too, HSS innovations formed the largest policy area, with sixty-five semifinalists (Borins 1998, 236–60), and the applicant programs addressed an equally wide range of target populations and issues. These included programs focusing on reducing infant mortality and ensuring healthy births, supporting the victims of child and sexual abuse, reducing youth violence and delinquency, preventing AIDS and dealing with its consequences, addressing the issues of seniors' health, substance abuse, disabilities, comprehensive care for and preservation of troubled families, and job training for workers in the health sector. Comparing these concerns to those of the 2010 semifinalists, we find some that are common to both periods and others that are unique. The 2010 cohort includes an AIDS program, although recent progress in both prevention and treatment means the disease is less of a policy focus. There is also one program aimed at infant health, New Jersey's Evidence-Based Home Visiting Initiative. Other initiatives seek to assist troubled families: Michigan's Family Resource Centers, Oakland's Safe Passages,

San Diego's Neighborhood for Kids, Georgia's One System of Care for Grand-parents Raising Grandchildren, and Wyoming's Healthy Families Succeed. The technology-based semifinalists such as Michigan's Online Electronic Benefit Transfer Program for WIC and Ohio Benefits Bank can be seen as a later genera-tion of initiatives first reported in 1990–94 under the category of Information Technology, namely programs seeking to move the payment of benefits online (Borins 1998, 133–34).

The 2010 HSS semifinalists include programs reflecting distinctly new prior-ities. There was a greater emphasis on expanding health care for the uninsured, whether by a single-payer approach (Healthy San Francisco) or a consumerist one (Healthy Indiana), or by increased access to free prescription drugs (WVRx). These innovations reflect the momentum for health insurance reform that has been building since the failure of the Clinton administration's proposals in 1993. Unlike the earlier applicants, the 2010 set also includes youth fitness initiatives (Arkansas's Act 1220 and Shape Up Somerville). This, too, is a policy area that has been receiving increased attention in the last fifteen years, as part of a more generalized awareness of the social and economic consequences of rising obesity rates. First Lady Michelle Obama's promotion of healthy nutrition and an active lifestyle has drawn further attention to the issue. The 2010 HSS semifinalists also include some internal quality improvement initiatives, a focus not evident in 1990–94. Given our understanding of public sector innovation as a respon-sive phenomenon, we would expect to see the emergence of new objectives and approaches. This is particularly true within a field as closely linked to scientific and therapeutic research as health care and social services must be. Within this policy area, however, the profile is one of overlap with the past rather than a complete break. Certain health- and family-welfare-related issues remain ongo-ing priorities.

In terms of process and structure, there were several important continuities between the 1990–94 HSS semifinalists and those of 2010. Interorganizational collaboration remains important, particularly for programs involving integrated care (Borins 1998, 233–34). Case managers continue to play an important role in bringing together the efforts of different bureaucracies and sets of entitlements. Theories such as those dealing with family functioning and appropriate treatment options continue to drive innovation in this area (Borins 1998, 249–52). The the-oretical models operationalized here seem to provoke less controversy than edu-cational theories, which can attract as much criticism as support for the innova-tions they underpin. Charitable foundations still continue to play a key role in supporting and driving change. The Robert Wood Johnson Foundation was a major supporter of the 1990–94 innovations (Borins, 1998, 248–49, 251), and it was involved in supporting and shaping several 2010 semifinalists: Healthy San

Francisco, Shape Up Somerville, Oakland's Safe Passages, New Jersey's Home Visiting initiative, and North Carolina's New Organizational Vision Award. Its ongoing role in the health and social services area is comparable to that of the Gates Foundation in the educational sector. Representing as they do the largest single group within the 2010 semifinalist programs, the applicants in the Health and Social Services policy area allow us to anticipate a summary finding we'll consider in more detail in the next chapter: within public sector innovation, persistent processes and structures may coexist with radically shifting goals and priorities.

Criminal Justice and Public Safety

Criminal justice and public safety innovations (CJ) differ from all other types of innovations in that 52 percent of them target people with dysfunctions, especially those already within the corrections system or those in trouble with the law and therefore on its margins. Otherwise, however, the profile of the applicants within the CJ policy area does not differ markedly or systematically from that of the entire group of semifinalists. The twenty-three innovations are internally diverse, though clustering around five major focuses: the corrections system, including prisons and parole; the juvenile justice system; innovations in policing; innovations in public security; and innovations in the judicial system. Only two of these initiatives were included among the top twenty-five, and this was the only policy area that was not represented among the six finalists.

All of the programs addressing issues relating to the prison system share a focus on rehabilitation, a reflection perhaps of a growing awareness of "incarceration inflation" to the point that the incarceration rate in the United States is among the highest in the world, with huge costs in both human and financial terms.[8] Florida's Pinellas County (Tampa and St. Petersburg) is home to one of the two CJ semifinalist innovations selected for the top twenty-five. The Mobile Inmate Video Visitation bus is a reconditioned bus now used for online video visits by family and friends of inmates who would have difficulty visiting them in prison. The bus stops at four locations in the county and is available every weekday. In Arizona, the correctional system, focusing on prisoners rather than their families, has established partnerships with a number of private sector companies for which prisoners may work in manufacturing, agriculture, and at a call center. Prisoners receive the minimum wage, with 30 percent of their earnings deducted to pay for the cost of incarceration and another 30 percent for restitution. The Angola, Louisiana, State Penitentiary, in partnership with the New Orleans Baptist Theological Seminary, provides training for a small group of inmates to become certified as ministers, as

8. See http://en.wikipedia.org/wiki/List_of_countries_by_incarceration_rate.

a means to their own rehabilitation and development of their qualifications to provide counseling to other inmates.[9] The Montgomery County, Maryland, Pre-Release and Reentry Services program prepares seven hundred inmates per year who are within twelve months of leaving prison, developing individualized reentry plans that address transition needs in terms of housing, employment, family contact, and medical services. The program uses electronic monitoring and substance abuse testing to hold participants to a zero-tolerance policy with respect to drugs, alcohol, and criminal activity. Oklahoma's Regimented Treatment Program established a dedicated treatment facility for adult male drug offenders using a highly structured paramilitary approach ("boot camp") together with therapeutic treatment and reentry and after-care services. The facility is located in the small town of Alva, in northwestern Oklahoma, which remains supportive of the program. Communities are understandably often highly suspicious of parole programs. The support this initiative was able to gain and retain is a testament to the careful implementation strategy of its initiators.

Three programs targeting parolees share an emphasis on holistic and integrated approaches. New York City's Reentry Court, based in Harlem, assists recently released prisoners with the transition to full parole. It provides services such as assessment and treatment using cognitive behavioral therapy and close monitoring, an approach that has been demonstrated to reduce the chances of reoffending. New Jersey's Female Offender Reentry Group Effort (FORGE) provides one-stop reentry centers that offer a full range of gender-sensitive rehabilitation programs, focusing on issues such as drug and sexual abuse, mental health, and responsibilities such as caregiving for children. Missouri's Community Supervision Centers encompass seven thirty- to sixty-bed parole centers located in smaller communities throughout the state, rather than just in Kansas City and St. Louis. The centers provide wraparound services for parolees in the areas of health, substance abuse, anger management, mental health, and financial management. They have been able to reduce the rate of revocation of parole and, like the Oklahoma program, maintain community support.

Two programs addressing institutions within the juvenile justice system offer an interesting contrast: one is a broad-based initiative with an emphasis on standardized metrics and the other is a highly targeted "boutique" innovation, a somewhat unusual choice for semifinalist selection. The broad-based initiative is Arizona's Standardized Program Evaluation Protocol, developed by the state supreme court to measure the state's 100 juvenile justice court programs against evidence-based guidelines based on a meta-analysis of a large number of programs through-

9. Angola State Penitentiary, infamous as the setting for the memoir and subsequent movie *Dead Man Walking*, has a history of brutality and violence and was under federal court supervision for twenty years.

out the country. The court established a rating protocol for Arizona programs that can be followed by reviewing data they provide, eliminating the need for costly site visits. The rating protocol also provides performance improvement plans. Programs with the highest scores have been shown to have the lowest recidivism rates. The "boutique" program is in Pendleton, Indiana, where a high-security juvenile correction facility has developed a Future Soldiers Program that prepares approximately fifty participating inmates for enlistment in the military upon release.

There is a similar dichotomy in the two programs targeting youths outside correctional institutions: one is structural/procedural, the other purely client focused. Wayne County's Juvenile Services System in Detroit is based on a memorandum of understanding with the courts and the state, which have agreed to give the county the mandate to operate the juvenile services system. The county receives partial funding from the state and is the single payer for services, contracting with numerous social service organizations to provide services such as case management and probation at home. The system is supported by an Internet-based information system. In contrast, the Miami-Dade County Civil Citation Initiative is a program intended to keep young people who have committed minor offenses out of the traditional juvenile justice system. Instead of being arrested, they are issued a civil citation and sent to the Dade County Juvenile Services Department for case management, which includes assessment, referral for treatment, and customized sanctions. If the treatment is successful, the young person will have no criminal record. Thirty-seven agencies in Miami and surrounding jurisdictions have agreed to participate in the initiative. In three years it has served 7,500 youths and achieved a successful completion rate of 82 percent.

The 2010 CJ semifinalists include only one community policing initiative involving cooperation between police and the community. Michigan's STOPPED program (Sheriffs Telling Our Parents and Promoting Educated Drivers) is intended to enable parents to monitor and influence their children's driving. The program gives an adult car owner the option of registering his or her car in order to be informed if it has been stopped by the police, whether or not a summons was issued to the driver.

Also in the police cluster are two programs in this policy area that, while not directly engaging the general public in policing, engage mental health clinicians in dealing with police cases involving people suspected of having mental illnesses. The Los Angeles Police Department and Los Angeles County Mental Health Department's Mental Illness project established teams of police and mental health clinicians to respond jointly to calls likely involving people suffering some form of mental illness or imbalance such as threatened suicides and hostage takers. The Los Angeles program grew out of a 2001 federal consent decree in which the police department agreed to improve its treatment of encounters with people suspected to be mentally ill. The Framingham, Massachusetts, Jail Diversion Program also established SWAT teams composed of police and mental health clinicians to respond to calls involving individuals believed to be mentally unstable. In Framingham, the initiation of the program was in part serendipitous: the police station was located near Advocates Inc., a mental health clinic, making the conceptualization and implementation of the collaboration literally a "small leap."

The policing cluster also includes two high-tech innovations, one of which was conceptualized as a technology platform for community policing. In East Orange, New Jersey, the Community Safety Information Grid seeks to improve the data available for police use in community policing. It integrates a number of existing technologies such as alarm-based automated dispatching, GPS tracking, surveillance cameras, and crime management dashboards to analyze crime patterns in real time as well as to forecast future incidents. The External Alarm Interface Exchange American National Standard is a partnership of the Central Station Alarm Association and Association of Public Safety Communications Officials to develop a computerized system to provide more efficient and accurate contact between alarm companies and police than is the case for in-person calls from alarm company operators to 911 operators. It was successfully piloted by the Richmond, Virginia, police, Vector Security, an alarm monitoring company, and GE Security, Vector's software provider. Even under the continuing rubric of "community policing," a dominant theme of the previous generation of policing innovations, we note a definite shift in emphasis to the technical and police side of the partnership.

Inevitably, in the post-9/11 era, a number of initiatives within the CJ policy area focus on public security, but they are an extremely disparate group, varying widely in both significance and scope. San Francisco's Citywide Post-Disaster Resilience and Recovery Initiative, the only other semifinalist in this area that placed in the top twenty-five, is a planning exercise convened by the city administration to prepare for a major earthquake. The plan involves cooperation among utilities, the private sector, and nonprofits to build the skill sets and social capital necessary to recover quickly from such a disaster. The state of New Jersey and CSX Transportation have established a partnership utilizing CSX's proprietary online tracking system that follows every rail car and shipment and can make that information available to federal and state agencies. The partnership between CSX and New Jersey is a pilot program that CSX has expanded to several other states. The Center for Applied Identity Management Research is based at the University of Texas at Austin and is supported by a partnership of federal government departments such as Defense and Homeland Security as well as several corporations, universities, and nonprofits. It studies how identity management practices can respond to threats such as cybercrime, fraud, and terrorism. In distinct contrast to these much more ambitious and security-oriented initiatives, Consolidated Fire Services is a Joint Power Authority agreement under California law among three small towns in the San Luis Obispo area to share fire department services, both staff and equipment.

Two semifinalist programs address very different aspects of citizen involvement with the judicial system. In Minnesota's Hennepin County, which includes Minneapolis, the Early Neutral Evaluations program is an alternate dispute resolution initiative, offering spouses engaged in negotiating custody-related issues an opportunity to avoid litigation. It uses a team of male and female mediators who meet in a confidential session with estranged parents and their attorneys to hear their arguments and provide feedback about the probable outcome of a full custody and parenting-time hearing. The hope is that the feedback will lead to an agreement that avoids the stress and expense of litigation in open court. In Travis County, Texas, which includes Austin, iJury is an initiative to enable prospective jurors to communicate electronically with the court system, for example, to complete questionnaires and be screened for exemptions. Ninety-five percent of prospective jurors now use the program, and so their first in-person appearance is at the start of jury selection.

Stepping back to consider the Criminal Justice and Public Safety policy area as a whole, it is clear that there is a very sharp contrast between the 2010 semifinalists and their 1990–94 counterparts in the area of community policing. Only four of the 2010 applicants include what could be called a community policing component: one, the Community Safety Information Grid in East Orange, New Jersey, is primarily a technology project, and the other three (STOPPED and the Los Angeles and Framingham initiatives dealing with cases involving suspected mental illness) are very specialized. In 1990–94, as *Innovating with Integrity* noted in detail (Borins 1998, 211–21), all sixteen semifinalists in the policing area were applications of some aspect of the community policing model. Some programs affected the activities of the police department itself: Reno, Nevada, applied community policing principles to traffic management; St. Petersburg, Florida, divided the city into forty-eight policing districts and established a GIS system to track crime on a district-by-district basis; San Diego recruited noncommissioned officers from immigrant groups to undertake outreach. Others were based on community partnerships, such as in Oakland, California, where the police department worked with community groups to shut down drug houses. Interdepartmental cooperation within government also played a role, but community objectives were always targeted, for example by San Francisco's Code Enforcement Task Force, in which representatives of the housing, building, fire, public health, planning, police, and city attorney's departments inspected suspected drug houses reported by neighborhood residents. The point is not that community policing is no longer engaged in. Just the opposite—it has become accepted practice. New applications of the model no longer self-identify as "novel," which removes them from eligibility for the HKS Awards program.

Both the 1990–94 and 2010 semifinalists include several initiatives enhancing technology in either policing or the courts. Among the 2010 semifinalists were Austin's iJury, the Center for Applied Identity Management Research, and the External Alarm Interface Exchange. Semifinalists in 1990–94 were more varied and, once again, clearly reflect the emerging stage of public sector IT applications. They included the Massachusetts Automated Child Support Enforcement System, which scanned the state's databases to find income or assets to be seized to enforce child support obligations; the Los Angeles County court system's use of interactive video for arraignment hearings; the Chicago police's installing laptops in police cars for wireless connections with law enforcement databases; the Arizona Supreme Court's development of electronic kiosks; and implementation of photo radar in Paradise Valley, a Phoenix suburb. In much the same way that community policing has become so ubiquitous as no longer to feature as innovative, so, too, the wholesale adoption of new technologies within the policy area raises the bar for technology-based innovations in 2010 and may perhaps account for their relatively limited presence.

Two further shifts within this policy area are of note. Holistic or "wraparound" approaches to clients of the criminal justice system are a significant component of a number of programs. These include the Miami-Dade Civil Citation Program, Wayne County Juvenile Services System, Missouri community supervision centers, Female Offender Re-entry Group Effort, Montgomery County's Pre-Release and Reentry Services, Harlem Reentry Court, and the Regimented Treatment Program. A second notable characteristic is the frequent use of collaboration within the public sector. Thirty-seven agencies participate in the Miami-Dade Civil Citation Program, while the Wayne County Juvenile Services System depends on agreement among the county, state, and courts. Collaboration between the public and private or nonprofit sectors also plays a significant role in at least four semifinalist initiatives: Center for Applied Identity Management Research; Angola State Penitentiary partnership with the New Orleans Baptist Theological Seminary; San Francisco's Post-Disaster Resilience and Recovery Initiative; and CSX Transportation's Rail Security Partnership with New Jersey.

Criminal Justice and Public Security may not have accounted for any 2010 HKS Awards finalists, but it offers the clearest example of a policy area in which a previous decade's dominant innovation has become so thoroughly assimilated as to be no longer considered noteworthy. It also illustrates, yet again, the pattern of emergent priorities necessitating innovative responses. The new priorities are not yet as fully theorized as community policing— the bold new paradigm two decades ago—nor are they as likely to be diffused as widely, since they are more tied to local problems and opportunities. What they do give evidence of, however, is enhanced creativity in public management—the persistence of the innovative spirit.

Change Is a Constant

Considering the six policy areas as a whole, there has been considerable change within almost all of them. Some change is the result of new policy priorities that have emerged since the early nineties and led to the creation of new programs now vying for recognition from a major innovation award. Conversely, some change results from previous innovations' having run their course, in the sense of being widely diffused. (Late adopters wisely do not seek recognition from an innovation award that puts a premium on novelty.) The movement is cyclical: within each policy area, new themes appear and established ones fade.

This chapter began with an insistence on the importance of detail, of the trees that make up the forest, but the accumulation of references to so many different initiatives can become overwhelming. Let us end, therefore, with an overview of the forest, recapitulating the significant shifts within the six policy areas and presenting them in order from most changed to least.

New consensus, new objectives. Transportation, Infrastructure, and Environment initiatives are now focusing on increasing energy efficiency and promoting environmental sustainability, in particular by reducing the production of greenhouse gases. This represents an almost complete change in focus. In the early 1990s, environmental initiatives dealt primarily with water and soil pollution. Transportation and infrastructure initiatives are now far less common than in the earlier period.

Diversity and crisis. Community and Economic Development innovations have become much more diverse, including initiatives supporting the technology-driven "new economy"; urban development initiatives, especially nongovernmental support for the revitalization of urban parks; rural development initiatives; and, sadly but necessarily, attempts to deal with the consequences of the mortgage foreclosure crisis, either by preventing foreclosures or, if that is not possible, by maintaining the housing stock or converting it to other productive uses. In addition to private contributions to public parks and new economy initiatives, two major new public sources of funding for community and economic development initiatives have been the Tobacco Settlement Fund and the Recovery Act. Community and Economic Development initiatives in the 1990–94 cohort were undertaken on a much smaller scale and often involved support for community building in urban ghettoes. These are the locations that have been hardest hit by the foreclosure crisis, hence requiring much more extensive public action now.

Diffusion, security and "incarceration inflation." The Criminal Justice and Public Safety policy area is no longer dominated by a single theoretical model as it was in the early 1990s. Community policing innovations are now standard practice, and no other single focus, practice, or theory has taken its place. Instead, a variety of initiatives encompass the corrections system, in both the adult and juvenile justice contexts, dysfunctional target populations at risk of entering the corrections system, and enhancements to public safety in the more challenging post-9/11 environment.

Protection, prevention, and accessibility. The Health and Social Services policy area has witnessed an increase in innovative programs providing better health care for people who are uninsured, programs attempting to enhance youth fitness, and integrated approaches to simplifying and improving access to social benefits. It may be the case that the former will be subsumed under the Affordable Care Act. If so, the act's complexity, as well as the obligations it places on the states, may well spark a new set of state-initiated innovations intended to implement it effectively and equitably.

From magnets to charters. Education and Training initiatives still tend to be focused on innovative schools, now usually structured as charter schools. The major change in this policy area from the early 1990s is the stronger emphasis on programs to improve teacher quality, especially by using pay-for-performance—and, presumably, dismissal for bad performance. Some jurisdictions, such as the Boston public schools, have begun to manage their own teacher training. Dropout recovery, which some charter schools have now begun to focus on, is a new theme. Distance education initiatives that previously used interactive television as a platform are now inevitably and much more comfortably being accommodated by the Internet.

Social media versus restructuring. Management and Governance initiatives continue to be dominated by the application of new technology, which is now focusing on the development of new software or applications, or on applications of social media to the public sector. There are far fewer internal organizational restructuring initiatives as the current generation of innovators benefits from this legacy of their predecessors. The one new theme in this policy area is the establishment of large-scale volunteer programs. Undoubtedly, the new social media technologies, and the crowd-sourcing mentality they foster, play some role in this.

Throughout this chapter, space constraints have imposed a focus on the "what" of public sector innovation, but the innovations in the different policy areas illustrate many of the overarching themes about the "how" of public sector innovation that were explored in previous chapters. There are abundant examples of initiatives launched by chief executives, such as mayors and governors, and numerous initiatives launched by middle managers and frontline public servants. Interorganizational collaboration is often present. This may take the form of collaborations between the public sector and the private and nonprofit sectors, such as in the revitalization of urban parks. In other instances it is enacted through collaboration among governments, for example, by means of formal agreements establishing Joint Power Authorities under California law or working arrangements facilitating the holistic responses to individual problems embodied in wraparound care. Finally, there are instances of ongoing involvement of nongovernmental funding sources (foundations) investing in innovation in particular areas, such as the Gates Foundation in education and the Robert Wood Johnson Foundation in health care. In the next and last chapter I step back still further to consider both the "what" and the "how" in the long view, and also take a look ahead.

8

Summing Up, Looking Forward: Awards, Practitioners, and Academics

I f there is a single point this book has sought to make, from its title onward, it is that public sector innovation is an enduring, ongoing phenomenon. It is fitting, then, that this final chapter stands as a point of departure rather than a conclusion. There is, happily, no final word to say. Innovation in government persists because inspired individuals launch innovations, awards programs recognize them, and scholars study them. It is a three-way partnership, and this book is intended as both a testimony to the potential of that partnership and an argument for its extension.

Innovation begins with ideas and the individual practitioners who instantiate them, as well as the organizational structures that sustain them. Awards programs not only recognize those ideas, they also offer opportunities to publicize and disseminate them, providing data for scholars in the process. Such programs serve a convening function, enabling practitioners to learn directly from one another. The academic research that the programs support introduces these innovative initiatives to a still wider audience, their histories now mediated by scholarly analysis and reflection.

I have always envisioned this book speaking to practitioners and academics alike, even though I recognize how difficult it can sometimes be to bridge the cultural and professional barriers that separate them. Rather than enshrine those divisions in the structure of the book, I have chosen to address both readerships jointly, by interweaving technically detailed accounts of the statistical analysis I've performed with speculation on the implications for practice of the patterns and relationships that analysis has revealed. This concluding chapter bifurcates more sharply. I begin by mapping out the landscape of public sector innovation—how it has changed, how it has not—and summarizing the results of the detailed comparisons previous chapters have explored. I then offer two sets of proposals, one directed to practitioners and the other to academics. These, necessarily, differ significantly in both aim and content. It is my hope that my findings here can be translated into practical advice for would-be innovators, particularly in relation to obstacles to anticipate, strategies of response, and tactics for securing support and recognition. The goal is to assist the important work they are choosing to do. For my academic colleagues, I offer suggestions of research possibilities, specifically new data sources and methodological links, which could in turn yield new support for public sector innovators and their efforts. I wish particularly to encourage other scholars to turn to innovation awards programs as the basis for research on innovations themselves, on public entrepreneurship, and on innovative organizations. I am fully aware of how much more there is to discover and to say.

"The More Things Change . . ."

Using the applications to the HKS Awards program as evidence, I have identified four significant changes in public sector innovation in the United States between the early 1990s and 2010. Do they transform the landscape? Certainly not beyond recognition, but, to push the metaphor a little further, they might be said to constitute important new landmarks. The first and perhaps most far-reaching in terms of its implications is the major increase in interorganizational collaboration the applications document. There have also been marked shifts in the nature of the innovation agenda in each of the six major policy areas the HKS Awards define. If both process and objectives have evolved, so too have the forms and frequency of external evaluation and the extent of both transfer and media attention.

Table 8-1 sums up statistically what has and hasn't changed by including all the results (slopes, intercepts, R^2) for the regressions of the distributions of responses for the 2010 HKS Awards semifinalists on responses for the 1990–94 semifinalists and, when available and comparable, the 1995–98 finalists and 1998 and 2000 Commonwealth International Innovations Awards applicants.

New Partners: Interorganizational Collaboration

The increase in the frequency of interorganizational collaboration as a characteristic of innovations is broad-based and widespread. Since it is evident in both initial applications and semifinalists, it is not a result of a bias in favor of collaboration on the part of HKS Awards judges. It includes all four types of interorganizational collaboration: within one level of government; across levels of government; with the private sector; and with the nonprofit sector. It is evident in all policy areas, in both their characteristics presented statistically (see table 3-2) and the sketches of individual semifinalists presented in chapter 7. Finally, there is considerable evidence

Table 8-1. *Summary of What Has and Hasn't Changed*

Aspect of innovation	1990–94 semifinalists			1995–98 finalists			Commonwealth awards winners, 1998 and 2000		
	Slope	Intercept	R^2	Slope	Intercept	R^2	Slope	Intercept	R^2
Differences									
Characteristics	insig[a]	insig	.29	NA	NA	NA	NA	NA	NA
Formal evaluation	insig	insig	.12	NA	NA	NA	NA	NA	NA
Frequency with which obstacles are overcome	insig	.46**	.11	NA	NA	NA	NA	NA	NA
Most important achievement	insig	insig	.02	NA	NA	NA	NA	NA	NA
Similarities									
Organizational structure	1.1***	insig	.93***	NA	NA	NA	NA	NA	NA
Accountability	1.1***	insig	.93***	NA	NA	NA	NA	NA	NA
Initiator	.9*	insig	.56*	.8**	insig	.60**	.4**	13**	.58**
Conditions leading to …	1.1***	insig	.53***	1.1***	insig	.60***	.8***	insig	.61***
Analysis	.9***	insig	.65***	.9***	12**	.68***	.8**	insig	.31***
Obstacles	1***	insig	.7***	1***	insig	.45***	.9***	insig	.72***
Tactics used	1.1***	insig	.74***	.8***	insig	.44***	.5***	3**	.32**
Critics	.7**	insig	.38**	NA	NA	NA	NA	NA	NA
Criticisms	1.1***	insig	.97***	NA	NA	NA	NA	NA	NA
Outcomes	.7***	insig	.65***	NA	NA	NA	NA	NA	NA
Transfer	.8***	insig	.71***	NA	NA	NA	NA	NA	NA

Source: Statistical analysis by author and Elizabeth Lyons.

NA = Not available

$* p < .1; ** p < .05; *** p < .01$ for slope and intercept estimates.

a. insig = insignificantly different from 0.

of increasing organizational collaboration in other countries, as was noted in reference to Farah and Spink's (2008) study of the Brazilian innovation awards and the European Commission's Innobarometer survey (Gallup Organization 2010).

One important aspect of interorganizational collaboration for the 2010 HKS Awards semifinalists was the diversity of their funding sources, with federal, state, and local governments all funding approximately one-half of the semifinalists, and the private sector and nonprofits together more than a third. In addition, the average semifinalist received funding from two different sources. Fewer of the 1990–94 semifinalists received funding from as many sources or as much funding from nongovernmental sources (Borins 1998, 92–96). This suggests a growing organizational elasticity, likely the product of an accumulating body of experience and precedent, an increasing capacity to accommodate multiple partners within a single initiative. And more possible partners now appear comfortable with a contributing rather than directing role. This is confirmed by the evidence we considered regarding accountability relationships and oversight mechanisms. Collaborations now are often accommodated within existing structures.

New Problems, New Solutions: Changing Forms of Innovation by Policy Area

A policy area as defined by the HKS Awards represents a set of institutions throughout the country with comparable functions, for example, police forces and correctional systems in the Criminal Justice and Public Safety area. At any point in time, innovations are diffusing within those comparable institutions in a process described by Rogers's (2003) logistic curve. Because the HKS Awards include novelty as one of their criteria, it is likely that the semifinalist applications will include many early adopters; conversely, once an innovation has been widely embraced by the entire population of a policy area, it is unlikely to feature prominently. This structural insight can explain the differences in the character of applications to each policy area over the two decades since the early 1990s.

In the 1990–94 period, the HKS Awards program's Criminal Justice and Public Safety policy area was dominated by a wave of community policing applications. By 2010 very few appear, likely because community policing has been widely embraced as an established approach, moving from innovation to fixture. Community policing applications have been displaced by public safety applications that are a reflection of the post-9/11 environment and by corrections applications that are responding to the problems created by the incidence of incarceration in the United States, which is among the world's highest.

Innovations in the Transportation, Infrastructure, and Environment area are now much less diverse than in 1990–94 and are focusing on two key priorities with a clear interconnection: increasing energy efficiency and reducing the emission of greenhouse gases. On the other hand, Community and Economic Development initiatives have become more diverse. Social optimists will point to "new economy" initiatives and large-scale urban programs, such as increased nongovernmental support for the revitalization of urban parks, as signs of the efficacy of public sector innovation. Pessimists will counter by highlighting the role of the mortgage foreclosure crisis in driving innovation, noting that even award-winning innovations are only making small dents in a vast problem.

The Health and Social Service policy area demonstrates a number of programs designed to provide better care for people who are uninsured. With the Affordable Care Act in the process of implementation, it remains to be seen how it will affect the innovation agenda in the health care area. Education and Training, while still including a large number of innovative programs based in magnet or charter schools, is now experiencing a new wave of pay-for-performance compensation programs for teachers. Initiatives involving information technology continue to play a major role in the Management and Governance area: the rapid spread of information technology within the public sector coupled with the speed of its evolution has meant that current awards applications are dominated by new apps, transparency websites, and social media. There are far fewer internal organizational reform initiatives such as gainsharing or job redesign than in the early 1990s. Viewing the applications policy area by policy area enables us to see the evolving priorities that inform innovators' initiatives, reflections of changing social and political realities and cultural values. The objectives change; the impulse to find new and better ways to achieve them does not.

Scrutiny and Validation: Increasing External Review

The 2010 HKS Awards semifinalists underwent significantly more formal external evaluation than their 1990–94 counterparts (see pp. 113–15). More of them were reviewed by consultants, nonprofits, or foundations (42 percent versus 25 percent); by agencies within government, for example, a budget office or an inspector general (24 versus 14 percent); by academic researchers (23 versus 12 percent); or by accreditation bodies (6 percent versus none). The number of programs having no external review at all declined from 38 percent in 1990–94 to 28 percent in 2010, and the average number of reviews for those who underwent them increased from 1.2 to 1.5. Regarding the content of the reviews, 42 percent of the 2010 semifinalists reported their reviews to have been completely supportive, and 16 percent considered them partially supportive. The applications themselves do not provide any information to account for this increase in external review, but I speculate that it is a reflection of a larger culture shift within the public sector, part of a new emphasis on performance measurement. There is a growing expectation that new programs will build performance measurement into their design, facilitating external review, and I have noted, too, the importance of new technologies in both data gathering and the publication of results. Additionally, external donors such as major foundations, whose role as funders of innovation has grown significantly, tend to demand that government programs receiving their grants be reviewed.

Attention Is Being Paid: More Transfer and More Media

The 2010 semifinalists reported considerably more actual transfer (as opposed to interest in transfer) than the 1990–94 semifinalists (see pp. 115–17). Twenty-seven percent of both groups reported local transfer, and 42 percent of the 2010 semifinalists reported national transfer (versus 24 percent for the 1990–94 semi-finalists), 11 percent reported international transfer (versus 1 percent), and 58 percent reported any transfer (versus 42 percent).[1] Again, I can only speculate as to possible explanations. Certainly, the increased availability of information through the Internet makes it easier for public sector managers to look further afield for programs to learn from and ultimately to emulate. The increased number of awards programs offers more exposure for innovations and more opportunities for would-be adopters to discover them. It's possible, too, that there is an increasing "expectation of innovation" within the public sector that is prompting public servants to seek out proven initiatives.

Finally, the 2010 semifinalists reported considerably more media attention than the 1990–94 semifinalists (see pp. 118–19). Only 11 percent of the 2010 semifinalists reported that they received no media attention, far fewer than the 54 percent of the 1990–94 semifinalists who did so. The 1990–94 data were not disaggregated, but the 2010 data were, and showed that 74 percent were covered by local or state media and 62 percent by professional or trade media. A full 43 percent were covered by national media, a preponderance of which have a liberal or centrist orientation. This suggests that public sector innovation is now considered more newsworthy than in the past. We might also link this to changing attitudes toward government in the years following 9/11 and the global financial crisis of 2008–09. At the least, it certainly suggests a greater willingness to investigate new initiatives or innovations in the public sector and to accord them something of the attention and respect typically shown to private sector "visionaries" and their works.

---

1. Transfer is the one instance where the pattern of responses for the 2010 semifinalists is sufficiently close to that of the 1990–94 semifinalists to produce similar regression results, as shown in the last row of table 8-1. However, the results, taken on a number-by-number basis and together with those for awards and media attention (neither of which could be subject to regression analysis because of a lack of degrees of freedom), are more consistent with the conclusion that there is a difference between the two groups of semifinalists.

". . . the More Things Stay the Same"

Clearly, there has been substantial change in the innovation agenda in every policy area. And yet, it is equally clear that the innovation *process* for HKS Awards semifinalists has stayed remarkably constant between the early 1990s and 2010. Statistically, this was illustrated by the results for regressions of the 2010 semifinalists responses on those of the 1990–94 semifinalists (see table 8-1). My previous research had indicated that the process of public sector innovation in the later 1990s in both the United States (Borins 2000a) and in the Commonwealth countries (Borins 2001a) was similar to that in the United States in the early1990s, but I began this research with no expectation that the same characteristics would still be observed a decade later. The fact that they have been adds cogency to the innovation principles I will offer to practitioners. The reason should be clear: if the process of innovation is also persistent, then there is an identifiable trajectory to anticipate and prepare for. Before outlining those principles, I shall review the innovation characteristics that have remained constant.

Although the frequency of interorganizational collaboration has greatly increased between 1990–94 and 2010, the frequency of other characteristics—what I have previously (Borins 2006) referred to as building blocks—has remained approximately constant (pp. 49–50). Specifically, the use of information technology, process improvement, citizen empowerment, the use of volunteers, and the application of market incentives all appear as consistent features of the innovation landscape. In other words, these approaches have proved their efficacy. They continue to be used because they continue to produce results.

The organizational structures used by the HKS Awards semifinalists have also stayed constant, roughly half comprising line operations in one or more organizations and the other half incorporating some sort of formal coordination. I have noted before that this is rather surprising. We might have expected the increase in interorganizational collaboration to have led to an increase in formal coordination. If the finding is surprising, it also seems to me promising. The unchanged level of formal coordination suggests innovative programs have learned how to coordinate informally (pp. 53–54) and organizational structures have developed sufficient elasticity to accommodate such arrangements. An increased institutional comfort level in this area bodes well for future innovative initiatives that continue the collaborative trend.

The scale of the average semifinalist has stayed relatively constant as measured by population reached: 202,000 in the early 1990s and 236,000 in 2010, though the average operating budget has increased almost four-fold, from $6 million to $22 million, slightly more than half of which was due to inflation and the increase in program size (see pp. 55–56). It is tempting to speculate on a possible increase in the willingness of funding sources to "invest" in public sector innovation, and this in turn might be linked to the larger shifts in public perceptions referred to in other contexts, but there is simply no clear answer to account for the rest of the increase.

Although politicians and agency heads have become somewhat more prominent as initiators of the HKS Awards semifinalists, the extent of initiation by middle managers or frontline staff—the local heroes I celebrated in *Innovating with Integrity*—has remained constant, at close to half of the semifinalists.[2] The increased role for politicians and agency heads may be due to the increase in interorganizational collaboration. Those at the top of organizations have more scope to negotiate collaborative arrangements with other organizations than those on the frontlines (pp. 64–65). We've also speculated that politicians may have a greater appreciation now for the benefits to be gained from associating oneself with public sector innovation—finding better ways to make government work—if only as a means of distancing oneself from the political narrative of partisanship and dysfunction emanating from Washington.

This narrative is separate from but often accompanied by an image of government agencies as inflexible and hence prone to crises brought on by an inability to anticipate and solve problems. But the data continue to refute this assumption. Proactive problem solving remains a much more frequent condition leading to the innovation than crisis management (see pp. 70–72). Not surprisingly, comprehensive planning also remains a much more frequent mode of analysis for public sector innovation than Behn's more intuitive "groping along" (see pp. 73–75). One needn't seek far for the explanation: if the catalyst for innovation is *not* a crisis, a state of affairs that by definition is urgent and requires immediate action, there is time for planning, including planning that makes a place for a necessary element of responsive improvisation. The continuing importance of planning as an integral phase of an innovative initiative could also be related to the increased expectation of external evaluation and to the increasing reliance on multiple funding sources, since the unsystematic, improvisational nature of "groping along" might be seen as undermining the initiative's credibility by both reviewers and potential funders.

Like the process of innovation, the pattern of obstacles encountered by innovators has also remained constant, with about 50 percent being internal to the public sector (mainly logistical problems and bureaucratic resistance), 30 percent being external (mainly public doubt and difficulty reaching the innovation's target group), and 20 percent being due to a shortage of resources. Similar tactics

2. The proportion of Commonwealth awards applications initiated by middle managers and frontline staff was considerably higher because a very large proportion of them involved introducing information technology into government operations in the late 1990s, a time when middle managers and frontline staff were much more knowledgeable about IT than senior public servants or politicians.

continue to be used to respond, the most popular being persuasion (showing the benefits of an innovation, social marketing, and demonstration projects) or accommodation (consultation, co-optation, and providing training for public servants affected by the innovation). The overall frequency with which obstacles were overcome has increased from 58 to 77 percent, the most significant component of that increase being greater success at finding necessary resources (see pp. 94–95).[3] This may be attributed to the greater participation by a wider range of funding sources. Without going into detail, the patterns of responses—which tactics tend to be employed to address which obstacles—have also remained constant (see pp. 91–93).

Given the consistency of process, obstacles, and responses, it is not surprising that the pattern of criticism of the HKS Awards semifinalists has remained relatively constant too: the most frequent criticism by far—about half of the total—is of an innovation's philosophy (see pp. 99–101). Arguably, this suggests that public sector innovation has on the whole been fortunate in its critics, who tend to be a community of informed observers and participants with professional expertise, or, at the very least, interested individuals engaging with current theoretical debates and taking the business of both government and innovation seriously.

The character of the self-criticism reported by HKS Awards semifinalists in answer to questions regarding their program's most significant challenges or remaining obstacles has also remained constant. The two most frequently cited are that a program needs fine-tuning and that it lacks resources (see pp. 103–04). This latter is somewhat surprising, given the vast increase in budgets reported.

Finally, the pattern of results reported by the semifinalists has remained relatively constant. These continue to include that the clients of the innovation are being made better off, that a significant segment of the target population is participating in the program, that cost reductions have been achieved, and that service has improved (see pp. 109–11). It is noteworthy that the most commonly cited measures of outcomes are quantitative, a fact that links back to the points I have now made repeatedly regarding both the rise of the "PerformanceStat" culture within the public sector itself and the increase in external review—which might be expected to value numbers over less precise outcome measures.[4]

It is not often in a concluding chapter that one has the luxury of summarizing extended, multifactoral analysis in two phrases, but it is possible here. The *con-*

---

3. That is why the frequency with which obstacles were overcome was one of the areas where the statistical results in table 8-1 show differences rather than similarities.

4. The pattern of most important achievements reported by the 2010 semifinalists changed from that reported by the 1990–94 semifinalists, as indicated by the regressions results shown in the last row under differences in table 8-1.

tent of public sector innovation has necessarily changed over the last two decades as innovators have sought solutions to emerging problems, guided by emerging knowledge and new priorities reflecting shifting public and political values. The *process* of public sector innovation, however, has remained largely constant. And this fact enables me to offer practitioners process-related insights distilled from the common experiences of successful innovators in the United States and also in other countries over two decades.

If You Innovate: Thirteen Precepts for Practitioners

Who is the practitioner to whom this advice is addressed? Few politicians or public servants have the word "innovation" included in their title or even their job description. Unlike staff in the private sector's research labs, their stated function is not to develop new products to boost their employer's profits and market share. Public servants and politicians are drawn to innovate as a way of making progress in solving the myriad policy problems government confronts on a daily basis. The urge to innovate is also born of a committed belief in government as a solution and an impulse to find better ways to make it so. Finally, prospective public sector innovators share a conviction that there is scope for creative problem solving, inspired improvisation, experimentation, and risk-taking within their organizations. And my research has shown that such believers are found at all levels of government. It is to such people that I direct the advice in this section—among them, I hope, future HKS Awards applicants, semifinalists and winners as well as applicants to and winners of innovation awards in other countries.

Considering the landscape of public sector innovation in the past two decades, both its emerging landmarks and its unchanging contours, I have identified thirteen fundamental precepts. The number actually seems auspicious here, evoking as it does the thirteen colonies that collaborated to launch America's founding innovation. I present the precepts in order of their place in the three phases of an innovation: conception, implementation, and operation. Most are derived from the continuities we have observed between the patterns of public sector innovation in the 1990s and 2010; three, however, follow from the significant shifts we have also noted.

At Conception

1. Expect to collaborate. Interorganizational collaboration will likely feature as part of any innovation. The 2010 HKS Awards semifinalists and other innovators elsewhere have shown that creative problem solving in the public sector requires interorganizational collaboration far more often than not, both within the public sector and outside. There are numerous things to consider when undertaking such partnerships.[5] What will be the "glue" that holds the collaboration together? Is an informal agreement sufficient, or is a formal written agreement necessary? Are there senior executives (mayors, governors, agency heads, legislators) who are strongly supportive of the collaboration and committed to its survival? Will the collaboration have some participants at the working level with an especially strong commitment to keeping it together? Will it have neutral mediators for dispute resolution? Is there a process in place for building trust among participants? How will the collaboration be funded? Are there possibilities for financial participation by several levels of government, as well as foundations and the private sector? While there are some high-profile foundations deeply involved in public policy (Gates, Johnson, Bloomberg), the competition for their funds is intense, so would-be innovators might have more success with lower-profile foundations whose scope is regional or local.

2. If it worked, use it. In addition to interorganizational collaboration, consider the other building blocks for public sector innovation: information technology, process improvement, citizen empowerment, the use of volunteers, and the application of market incentives. While none of them appear as frequently in our cumulative data as inter-organizational collaboration, they are used sufficiently frequently that they should be at the front of a problem solver's mind. They are structural features of innovation design that have repeatedly produced significant results. The challenge lies in recognizing how they may be adapted to your specific objective.

3. Speak up and listen hard. Approximately half of the HKS Awards semifinalist programs, both in the early 1990s and in 2010, were initiated by middle managers or frontline public servants. This fact should encourage middle managers and frontline public servants to put their ideas forward. It should equally convince public sector organizations to empower these local heroes and to create an organizational culture that gives them the confidence and the resources to put their ideas into action. And this includes giving innovators permission to fail. Given that so much public sector innovation involves interorganizational collaboration, middle managers and frontline staff not only should be thinking about how to solve problems using the capacity of their own organization but also should be looking beyond their organization's boundaries. In the course of their work they may come in contact with counterparts in other public sector organizations; conversations in the course of these interactions might provide the catalyst of an innovation. Finding opportunities for such conversations increases the likelihood that a spark will be struck.

---

5. I discuss these success factors in terms of a new, collaborative innovation narrative in Borins (2011b, 174–79). Practitioners should also consult Ansell and Gash's (2008) meta-analysis of the case literature on collaboration between government and civil society, which suggests some evidence-based success factors and which does not use quantitative methodology.

4. Proactive beats reactive. Both over time and in a variety of different contexts, public sector innovations are more frequently proactive responses to internal problems or new opportunities than reactions to externally visible crises. This is not an invitation to ignore crises, not usually an easy thing to do in any event. It is rather a reminder of the proven importance of being proactive. Not only is it essential to look for solutions to problems before they become crises but it is even more important to seek opportunities. These might be presented by new technology, new funding sources, an unexpected alignment or overlap with other public sector agencies, a shift in public priorities or values. Any one of these might suggest or support innovations. The point is to keep looking and asking.

5. It's never either/or. I have extensively discussed two contrasting approaches to strategizing an innovation: comprehensive planning and incremental "groping along." My finding is that planning is used far more often than incremental groping. In particular, planning tends to be associated with larger innovations and those involving considerable interorganizational collaboration, while groping along tends to be associated with innovations that are initiated by frontline staff and that involve information technology. Would-be innovators would do well to start with a bias toward planning. This may be particularly important for securing external funding, and may also prove useful when evaluation of the initiative becomes an issue. But recognize, too, that circumstances might dictate groping along, or some combination of the two. In other words, in strategizing, as in so much else in the innovation process, flexibility is key.

6. Models matter. In developing plans for an innovation, you need to ask whether there are relevant theoretical models in your policy area. If so, are they appropriate for your use? My statistical analysis of the 2010 semifinalists indicates that those programs operationalizing a theoretical model were more likely to be transferred to other organizations, to win awards, and to receive media attention. Analysis of the determinants of selection to the ranks of the top twenty-five semifinalists and six finalists in the HKS Awards confirmed the importance of operationalizing a theoretical model: it increased the likelihood of selection. Why do models matter? They undoubtedly increase the clarity and comprehensibility of an innovation's profile, which appeals to agencies interested in transfer, to awards judging panels, and to the media. (If the theoretical model is contested, that may make the innovation controversial, which also makes it more newsworthy.) And they have other strategic benefits. Theoretical models endow an initiative with intellectual credibility, a gravitas that can help it gain both partisans and sponsors. It is essential to be aware of the latest developments in the relevant policy area, to understand the theoretical models that are extant, and to be familiar with ongoing debates about their merits. The best choice for your initiative may not be among them, but the choice must be made (and justified) from a standpoint of knowledge.

At Implementation

7. One size doesn't fit all. Think carefully about the organizational structure and accountability relationship for your initiative. It may be possible to implement an innovation through an existing organization and its accountability structure. But don't be confined by those parameters. If the innovation is more complex, and if it involves many participants or partners, it may require some sort of special arrangement. This could include the establishment of a nonprofit corporation for the initiative, interorganizational coordination directed by a line department or central agency, or an interdepartmental committee. What is more, creating such structures builds organizational precedent, capacity, and knowledge for future innovators to exploit.

8. Anticipate, anticipate, anticipate. This research has demonstrated a consistent set of obstacles to public sector innovation. These include, in order of the frequency with which they occur, internal bureaucratic resistance, external doubt and skepticism, and difficulty finding resources. Forewarned is forearmed. No design can be perfect, and no conception objection- or obstacle-proof. You should assume that you will encounter at least some of these basic difficulties and prepare accordingly. As much as innovators should be planning the nature of their innovation, they should also be conceiving a *defensive* implementation strategy, in terms of gathering support and neutralizing opposition.

9. Persistently flexible, flexibly persistent. This research has demonstrated not only a consistent set of obstacles to innovation but also a consistent set of effective responses to them. This set of responses encompasses persuasion at both the bureaucratic and political levels and accommodation, through consultation, co-optation, training, or some other modification of the features of the innovation so that the skeptics' concerns are addressed sufficiently to gain their participation. An effective response also involves perseverance—in searching for funding and in maintaining a dialogue with skeptics. Often the best response to specific obstacles combines a mixture of all three of these approaches. A vision, even a theory, is not enough. You need buy-in, too.

10. Are we there yet? You know what the goals of your innovation are. Do you know how you will measure progress in achieving them? Being able to do so in an accurate and consistent way offers important benchmarks to those involved in delivering the initiative, to funding sources tracking its progress, to external reviewers who will examine its design and outcomes, and to outside observers looking to adopt, publicize, or judge it. Given the diversity of the innovations in the six main policy areas our research has investigated, there are many results that could be measured: the well-being of clients as reflected in satisfaction surveys;

the extent that the target population is using the innovation; improvements in existing services; cost reductions and productivity increases. The HKS Awards semifinalists in both the early 1990s and 2010 displayed a wide variety of results measures, almost all of which, it should be noted, were formal and quantitative. Over and above the benefits we've just outlined, there is an intrinsic value to measuring outcomes, namely, ensuring that public resources are being used effectively and efficiently. The trend toward transparency for public sector organizations evidenced through the online posting of performance indicators applies to innovations as well, in that the public also expects to know whether innovations, particularly those that are high-profile, are improving public sector performance.

In Operation

11. Find outside eyes. Once your innovation is in operation and has internal performance measures in place, ensure that it has a formal external review. This study has shown that an increasing proportion of HKS Awards semifinalists have been reviewed by consultants, nonprofits, foundations, governmental budget offices or inspectors general, academic researchers, accreditation boards, or financial auditors. Initiatives that are reviewed are the most likely to be transferred to other organizations, to win awards, and to receive media attention. Consider, too, the increased credibility conferred by such a review, and the opportunity it provides to raise your innovation's profile, even to secure for it highly effective external advocates.

12. People are watching. Recognize that the media, whether local, regional, professional, trade, or even national, are paying increasing attention to public sector innovation. At the national level there is evidence that media sources with a liberal orientation tend to be more likely to report on public sector innovation than those with a conservative orientation. Such attention can build support for your innovation, as well as increasing the likelihood of transfer. Look for the human stories embedded within your program's history, whether among clients or implementers, as a means of attracting media interest. Such stories can also be featured on agency websites and in future awards applications. Do not assume, however, that the media will be uncritically supportive. Be prepared for criticism, and see the next precept for suggestions about how to respond.

13. Advocate. Our research shows that even after an innovation has been successfully implemented it is likely to have ongoing critics. The most frequent critics are people who oppose an innovation's philosophy, as distinct from those who oppose it because it harms their interests. The best responses to criticism parallel the responses to obstacles in the course of implementation. Respond to philosophical opposition with the tools of persuasion: argue the virtues of an initiative and demonstrate that it is delivering widespread benefits. Quantitative outcome measures and external reviews can be useful ammunition here. So, too, can clients' individual case histories. Where possible, respond to arguments that an innovation harms certain groups' interests by accommodating their concerns. Failing that, offer the counterargument that the interests of those the innovation benefits are broader and more pressing than the interests of those it harms.

If you Study Innovation: New Opportunities and Directions

Armed with these precepts, future public sector innovators should be generating many more innovation awards applications. It will then be up to scholars to mine the data these programs provide. Important work has already been done, but the possibilities are far from exhausted. The challenge is to think more searchingly about the research and data-collecting opportunities awards programs offer. In the extended academic literature review that began this study, I employed a three-part conceptualization of public sector innovation research as focusing on innovations, innovators, and innovative organizations. (Much of the analysis that followed suggested how difficult it can be to separate the three.) I return now to that three-part division to consider a few of those research opportunities and, I hope, trigger thinking for still more.

Innovations: Longitudinal and Comparative Research

In the 1980s and early 1990s, applications to innovation awards were used by researchers as the bases for case studies. Researchers read the semifinalist applications and site visit reports, then followed up with documentary research and interviews of their own. A second wave of quantitatively oriented research followed, which I accept responsibility for initiating. This wave involved coding the applications to create databases and in some instances contacting applicants with a follow-up research questionnaire, then using the responses to this questionnaire to create databases. This research, initiated by academics rather than the awards programs, has been sporadic, undertaken when we have been able to secure funding from either the innovation awards programs themselves or from national research granting councils or foundations. It has undoubtedly provided extremely valuable information about both the content and process of public sector innovation.

Some innovation awards, in particular the HKS Awards, have traditionally envisioned a dual role for themselves: conducting the awards program to recognize and inspire public sector innovation and supporting research about such innovation. Yet when resources are constrained, it is inevitable that they will give higher priority to the awards themselves, not the research. By not supporting research in a systematic and ongoing way, innovation awards programs are missing an opportunity to create an invaluable research resource that could in turn support the process and diffusion of innovation. Consider, for example, the HKS Awards: Coding the comprehensive and detailed semifinalist applications is labor-intensive and expensive. The shorter initial applications gather a considerable amount of factual information that could be readily compiled and made available to researchers in an annual database consisting of the following:

—Name of the program

—Organization in which it is based

—Location

—Policy area

—Applicant and contact person

—Start date of the program

—The program's application history

—The program's current application status: "not selected"; "semifinalist"; "finalist"; "winner"

One last essential element of this database is a short description of the innovation. This could be coded from the applicant's description by HKS Awards staff or research assistants or it could be created by adding to the initial application a checklist of innovation characteristics and asking applicants to check off all that are relevant to their initiatives.

If this information were available for each year's competition, the HKS Awards would soon be able to create a longitudinal database that could identify innovation trends in the different policy areas (for example, the decline of community policing applications), as well as organizations or locations that have proved to be hotbeds of innovation through repeated applications and "serial innovators"—individuals who have been associated with a number of successful initiatives. All of these findings would identify further questions to which researchers could direct their attention and areas to investigate for answers. Gathering data from the HKS Awards, or any other innovation award, on an ongoing basis can be thought of as a sampling strategy that offers an alternative to large one-time studies such as the EC's Innobarometer. Large one-time samples deal with the innovation experience of the entire public sector but, because of their cost, are not repeated frequently, if at all. Innovation awards data include only the organizations that choose to apply, but the data would be available every year or two, hence facilitating the identification of trends. The awards program staff itself should be interested in monitoring the total number of applications, the frequency of repeat applications, and the start date of programs. A decline in the number of initial applications, too great a percentage of repeat applications, and too many very new programs would all be problematic for the sustainability of the award itself—all concerns raised in Hartley and Downe's (2007) list of measures of the effectiveness of awards programs.

One way to support the creation of an innovation database would be to charge applicants a small filing fee, explicitly justified as supporting research. If the HKS Awards were to charge an initial application fee of $50 and a semifinalist application fee of an additional $50, assuming that these small fees do not discourage applications, then with 500 initial applicants and 125 semifinalists, this would bring in $31,000 every year, which could support both the database and some research projects.

These suggestions regarding the HKS Awards are applicable to public sector innovation awards programs in other countries. Rather than waiting for academics to approach them to use their applications pool for research, they, too, could create databases for researchers to explore. The payoff would be in the enhanced research about the content and process of public sector innovation that could result. If this research were undertaken in a number of countries, it would provide the opportunity for comparative cross-national research. This research could identify both broadly based features and differences that are due to varying levels of economic development or unique national contexts.

Public Sector Entrepreneurship: Serial Innovators

Researchers on public sector entrepreneurship have looked at a wide variety of public sector populations to find and study entrepreneurs but, surprisingly, have not used applications to innovation awards to identify subjects.[6] The individuals whom a researcher on public sector entrepreneurship would want to study are those most deeply involved in initiating an innovation. The HKS Awards semifinalist applications provide considerable variability in the detail they supply about the initiator(s). In 13 out of 127 semifinalist applications in 2010, it was not possible to identify an initiator at all. In other cases, initiators were identified by position, but not by name. Thirty-nine of the 127 semifinalist applications were written by the manager of the innovative program, and in some of these the program manager was the initiator. Despite this variability, there would be sufficient identifiable initiators of innovations that a researcher of public sector entrepreneurship could contact them.

Pursuing only two such contacts culled from the 2010 semifinalist applications demonstrated to me the potential richness of such research subjects. While coding 2010 applications during the research phase of this study, I encountered two

6. In some public sector entrepreneurship studies, an entire population of politicians or public servants has been surveyed to find factors explaining why some in the population are more entrepreneurial than others. Like surveys of innovations undertaken in an entire population of organizations, these surveys are one-off, while innovation awards could continuously produce data.

key initiators whose names were familiar to me as 1990–94 HKS Awards semifinalists discussed in *Innovating with Integrity*.[7] Given the passage of two decades between their appearances in the HKS Awards, I hypothesized that the two were "serial innovators" and contacted them for semi-structured telephone interviews. Jory Wolf, the CIO for Santa Monica, California, was the initiator of its 2010 semifinalist City Net, the fiber-optic broadband infrastructure the city made available to commercial users. He also initiated Santa Monica's 1993 semifinalist program, the Public Electronic Network, a very early e-mail and discussion forum linking city councilors and interested citizens. Larry Rosenstock, the founding principal of High Tech High, a San Diego, California, charter school, was a 2010 semifinalist. He had also been the executive director of CityWorks, a program that applied the Coalition of Essential Schools' educational philosophy to technical education at Rindge School of Technical Arts in Cambridge, Massachusetts, which was a 1992 HKS Awards winner. At least as significant as the details each interviewee provided of his career as a serial innovator was the opportunity our conversations offered to compare and contrast these innovators' professional trajectories, approaches to innovation, and even their personality types. The following very brief summary of my interviews suggests something of the wealth of material such research can generate.

Wolf began his career in human resources in the Santa Monica city government. An interest in computers, at a time when mainframes were becoming accessible through terminals, led him to move to information technology. Wolf has made an extraordinary personal and professional commitment to the Santa Monica government, working for the city for thirty-three years and eventually becoming CIO. The information technology (IT) operation he heads is centralized, handles a number of functions, including asset management and geographic information systems, and has a staff of forty. Wolf knows the entire Santa Monica civic administration well, describing himself as the city's IT "reference librarian" and its general "fix-it guy." City managers and councils have trusted him and given him considerable autonomy to work on his innovations. In return, he has worked on the city's long-term IT strategy, making it consistent with the city's long-term plans. Wolf's long experience in the public sector has taught him the importance of external recognition as a motivator, and he has frequently applied for awards. Wolf's professional loyalty is clearly mirrored by a personal commitment to Santa Monica and its lifestyle, which he describes as "unique." He intends to remain with its government until he retires.[8]

7. Given how much time has passed since I wrote *Innovating with Integrity*, the psychological process involved was actually one of rediscovery. The names and contexts sounded vaguely familiar, and I then traced them in detail for confirmation.

8. Jory Wolf, interviewed by author, January 30, 2013.

Larry Rosenstock's personal and professional biographies could hardly be more different from Wolf's, yet he shares with Wolf a career-long commitment to innovation. While studying law in Boston in the 1970s, he also began teaching carpentry to inner-city vocational classes. Rosenstock felt strongly that the working-class youths he was teaching had the same natural intelligence as their middle-class counterparts but that they were being segregated by race and class and by rigid differentiations between academic and "practical" (manual) aptitude. He began to conceive a model of education that could integrate standard vocational and academic training (Rosenstock 2010). Rosenstock completed his legal training and moved to the Harvard Center for Law and Education, where he lobbied for federal legislation that broadened federal support for vocational education to include integration of vocational and academic curricula. He returned to the educational system as executive director of Rindge School for the Technical Arts in Cambridge, where he developed the CityWorks vocational education program. CityWorks applied Coalition of Essential Schools ideas such as personalized curriculum, student projects, and building links between school and community. Rosenstock counted as his achievements increases in the number of vocational students taking arts courses and vice versa, as well as CityWorks students playing a major role in designing and building a residence for senior citizens and adolescent mothers (Borins 1998, 268, 271). Rosenstock was then appointed acting principal of Cambridge Rindge and Latin School. He found the Cambridge high school system too bureaucratic, however, and resigned in October 1996.

Within days he learned that the U.S. Department of Education had put out tenders for its New Urban High School Project, which would involve studying innovations in urban high school education. Rosenstock quickly organized a group of leaders of the Coalition of Essential Schools movement and wrote a successful grant application. He then spent much of the next three years visiting schools throughout the country, refining his theories of and models for educational reform and giving presentations. At one such presentation in San Diego, he met Sol Price, the president of Price Club, a chain of warehouse stores that was ultimately acquired by Costco. Price hired Rosenstock to run his charitable foundation, which he did for some years. When a group of technology industry leaders in San Diego, concerned by the difficulty they had finding qualified engineers, came up with a plan to establish a charter school that would focus on science and technology, they hired Rosenstock as its first principal. He has spent the last decade building High Tech High, applying Coalition of Essential Schools ideas to technological education.[9]

9. Larry Rosenstock, interviewed by author, March 16, 2013.

Rosenstock's career progression is almost dizzying in terms of the number of moves he has made, yet he sees his commitment to instituting a model of integrated vocational and academic education as informing every phase of its course. He also notes that he made three apparently downwardly mobile moves—going from law school to teach carpentry to inner-city kids; leaving a position as a lawyer at a Harvard research center to lead an urban vocational school; and giving up the presidency of a foundation to launch a charter school—that ultimately defined his career as a leading educational reformer.[10]

Wolf and Rosenstock are both public sector entrepreneurs, but their career paths are vastly different. Wolf has spent his entire professional life with one employer that has been supportive of the multiple technological innovations he has launched. Rosenstock has followed an ideal; has frequently moved from one employer to another; has both created and exploited a range of opportunities; has attempted, with partial success, to reform an established academic institution; and has launched an educational startup. My telephone interviews with both men focused on their narratives of career progress. In-person interviews, using psychological assessment tools (a research methodology employed by Roberts and King (1991, 1992, 1996) in their early studies of policy entrepreneurs), likely would have revealed major differences in temperament and personality that I could only surmise on the basis of telephone interviews. The telephone interviews revealed two forcefully contrasting career paths and personality types. Yet by any standard of judgment, both men are highly effective public sector entrepreneurs. The richness and diversity of these two individuals' experiences strongly suggest the potential richness of research in public sector entrepreneurship. Scholars in this area could use the applications to innovation awards to identify individuals to study using their preferred methodologies and instruments. While such studies are unlikely to reveal a single innovator "type," or typical career path, they could afford important insights into commonalities in experiences, outlooks, and organizational contexts.

"Hotbeds of Innovation"

How can innovations awards applications be used for the third stream of innovation research, identifying innovative organizations? It can be hypothesized that the frequency with which an organization applies to the HKS Awards over a given period of time is a measure of its innovativeness. Donahue (2008) used this as an indicator of the innovativeness of the U.S. Department of Labor under Secretary Robert Reich. The HKS Awards are well known and prestigious, and the program's staff does considerable outreach. We can assume, therefore, that there are

10. Rosenstock, author interview.

Table 8-2. *Innovative City Governments*

City / Semifinalists	Number of 2010 semifinalists	Population rank
New York City	5	1
Center for Economic Opportunity (winner)		
NYC Service (finalist)		
Court-Based Homelessness Prevention Law Project (top 25)		
Bryant Park Corporation		
Re-Entry Court		
Boston	3	21
Teacher Residency (finalist)		
Citizens Connect		
Real Education Alternatives Lab		
Denver	3	23
Greenprint Denver Environmental Management System		
Human Services Work Management System		
Professional Compensation System for Teachers		
Orange County, Calif.[a]	3	3
Online Voter Information Program		
One Water One Watershed (top 25)		
SECURE Electronic Recording Delivery System		
Philadelphia	3	5
LandCare Program		
Project U-Turn		
Transit Oriented Development Gap Financing		

(continued)

not systematic differences among public sector organizations in their willingness or propensity to apply to the HKS Awards but rather that any systematic differences are a function of their innovativeness. Two ways to measure frequency are initial applications and semifinalist applications. Initial applications represent innovativeness as defined by the organization itself, while semifinalist applications measure innovativeness as defined by the judging panels.

As an exploratory exercise, I applied this approach to the 2010 semifinalist applications, recognizing that one year is a short time frame. I chose to focus on city governments, assuming that it is possible to look at a city government in its entirety to evaluate how innovative it is. Table 8-2 shows the number and names of semifinalist applications from each city or county government with more than one application. We expected the number of semifinalists to be correlated with the population of the city, as the literature suggests (Walker 2014) and as indi-

Table 8-2. *Innovative City Governments* (Continued)

City / Semifinalists	Number of 2010 semifinalists	Population rank
Detroit (Wayne County)	2	18
Juvenile Services System		
Mortgage Foreclosure Prevention Program		
San Diego	2	8
High Tech High		
Neighborhood for Kids		
San Francisco	2	14
Healthy San Francisco (finalist)		
Citywide Post-Disaster and Recovery Initiative (top 25)		
Seattle	2	22
Funders Group (top 25)		
Health Reform Program		
Somerville, Mass.	2	<300
Shape Up Somerville (top 25)		
SomerStat		

Source: 2010 applications coded by author and Kaylee Chretien; population data from 2010 U.S. Census.

a. Orange County's population of 3 million would make it the nation's third-largest city, after New York and Los Angeles.

cated by our research showing that, all else equal, a jurisdiction's population has a positive influence on its chances of being selected as a semifinalist (pp. 130–32). In fact, however, the table shows several cities of moderate size (Boston, Denver, Detroit, Seattle) "punching above their weight" with a relatively large number of semifinalists. Somerville, Massachusetts, contiguous to Boston and Cambridge, with a population of about 77,000, had two semifinalists. On the other hand, several of the ten largest U.S. cities had very few semifinalists: Los Angeles, the second largest, had one application; Chicago, the third largest, one; Houston, fourth largest, one; Phoenix, sixth largest, none; San Antonio, seventh largest, one; Dallas, ninth largest, none; San Jose, tenth largest, none.

A full statistical analysis would attempt to find independent variables explaining the number of applications by city. This would be the topic of a very different research initiative than this book. The HKS Awards program, however, has sponsored some recent case study and interview-based research looking at the factors explaining the innovativeness of the New York, Boston, Philadelphia, and

Denver civic administrations, and I conducted a telephone interview regarding Somerville.

This sponsored research includes Georges, Glynn-Burke, and McGrath's (2013a) case studies of Boston's Mayor's Office of New Urban Mechanics, a small team mandated to encourage innovation within government and engage citizens; Philadelphia's comparable Office of New Urban Mechanics; Denver's Office of Strategic Partnerships, intended to support and enhance partnerships between government and local organizations; and the New York City Department of Education's iZone, an innovation office within the department that focuses on enhancing the use of technology as well as analyzing student and program evaluation data to develop new initiatives. On the basis of these cases the authors concluded that the keys to successful innovation by urban governments are structures supporting innovation (a chief innovation officer and an innovation unit), a discrete stream of funding through that unit to support innovation, and a strong mayoral mandate or endorsement.

In a subsequent paper, based on many more interviews in a number of other cities, Georges, Glynn-Burke, and McGrath (2013b) developed a more general model of what they called "a framework for an innovative jurisdiction." This framework stresses building capacity for innovation: facilitating collaboration across sectors; encouraging volunteer service; providing funding for innovation and operational capacity, for example through a chief innovation officer and an innovation office. It also encompasses opening "space" for innovation, by utilizing and analyzing data, establishing an innovation fund, and reducing administrative hurdles to innovation.[11] And finally, it highlights the importance of developing a culture of innovation, by rewarding and protecting innovators (permission to fail), mobilizing public awareness of and support for innovation, and empowering citizens to participate in generating innovations.

These papers represent the culmination of considerable research and an important initiative in understanding the factors that are necessary for building an innovative jurisdiction. I agree that a strong mayoral mandate or endorsement can, obviously, be useful, but I would add that the political strength of or political capital built up by the mayor determines how effective his or her endorsement will be. Boston's mayor Tom Menino served from 1993 to 2013, New York's Michael Bloomberg from 2002 to 2013, Denver's John Hickenlooper served from 2003 to 2011, and Philadelphia's mayor Michael Nutter was a city councilor from 1991 to 2006 before being elected mayor in 2007. All were popular leaders who could readily spend some of their political capital to support an innovation agenda.

11. New York City's Office of Policy and Strategic Planning, which reports to the mayor's chief policy adviser, is working at the leading edge in terms of linking and analyzing large data sets and using them for problem solving. See Alan Feuer, "The Mayor's Geek Squad," *New York Times*, March 23, 2013.

Bloomberg is unique in being able to deploy his personal wealth through the Bloomberg Philanthropies to influence the urban management and policy agenda, in New York and elsewhere, for example, through its $5 million support for the recent Mayor's Challenge competition to develop innovative policy ideas.[12] Georges, Glynn-Burke, and McGrath's second paper expanded their framework for an innovative jurisdiction to generate a long list of necessary factors that resembles the complete set of characteristics of public sector innovation set forth in chapter 3 of this volume. Innovation is undoubtedly a complex phenomenon. The essential question still to be answered is the role of each of the many identifiable factors in supporting innovation. Which ones, either individually or in combination, are truly essential? Databases developed from the HKS Awards or other programs could be analyzed to provide an answer.

Somerville, Massachusetts, demonstrated, at a smaller scale, a number of the necessary factors for an innovative jurisdiction. Mayor Joseph Curtatone, first elected in 2003 after serving as a councilor for eight years, is in his fifth two-year term as mayor and is a politically secure "mayor for life." Curtatone has always been interested in the use of data for solving management problems. It was a key element of his platform when he first ran for mayor, and he has implemented it while in office. Curtatone, trained as a lawyer, has been taking his master's in public administration at the Kennedy School while in office. The two 2010 semifinalist innovations, SomerStat and Shape Up Somerville, both involve data gathering and analysis as a key element. The SomerStat office plays the role of chief innovation officer and has good access to the mayor. With three analysts in its office, one in the fire department, and two in the police department, Somerville has considerable analytical capacity for a small city. In addition, the use of analysis is deeply ingrained in the city administration's organizational culture, so much so that "stat" is used as a verb.[13]

Although Somerville city hall's organizational culture was put in place by Mayor Curtatone, it is also consistent with the city's broader civic culture. Somerville is geographically close to a number of universities, in particular Harvard and Tufts, and has a large student and young adult population. The city has a constant inflow of students on fellowships and internships and has been the site for many university-based research projects.

Looking at New York, Boston, and Somerville suggests the outlines of a common formula for an innovative jurisdiction: it incorporates the analytical interests of its mayor; is supported by the mayor's political capital; establishes permanent structures of support for innovation through the use of chief innovation officers

12. Jennifer Steinhauer, "Providence Is Top City in Contest of Ideas," *New York Times*, March 12, 2013.

13. Daniel Hadley, interviewed by the author, January 25, 2013.

and the creation of offices of innovation; allocates resources to support innovation; and creates civic cultures that are strongly supportive of public sector innovation. If Jory Wolf and Larry Rosenstock offered vivid object lessons in the highly individual nature of public sector entrepreneurship, the consonances among these three cases of innovative jurisdictions suggest the benefits of detailed comparative analysis. Researchers on innovative organizations or jurisdictions could develop a cross-sectional and time-series database on a large sample of U.S. cities, using applications to the HKS Awards as the dependent variable and a variety of political leadership, internal organizational, and external environmental characteristics as independent variables. There would likely be a good deal of variation in the data for both the dependent and independent variables. For example, city politicians are a diverse breed, including well-entrenched policy aficionados such as Bloomberg, Menino, and Curtatone; politicians who work on instinct alone; and politicians who have gone from office to jail. The value of data from the HKS Awards and other awards programs lies in the opportunity these data afford researchers studying innovative public sector organizations or jurisdictions to identify case study subjects that can be used to develop theory and to access data that can be used to test it.

Innovators, Stories, Data: Some Final Words

In the course of researching this study I had the privilege of interviewing four innovators within the public sector. As different as Larry Rosenstock, Jory Wolf, Daniel Hadley (the director of SomerStat and representative of Somerville mayor Joseph Curtatone), and Allison Hamilton (the originator of Oregon's Solar Highway) are, they share qualities of creativity, vision, enthusiasm, and, yes, persistence. Studying and celebrating their accomplishments and those of other successful innovators is often as enjoyable as it is illuminating. Innovators are generally enthusiastic and accomplished individuals, keen to inspire others with their own experience. Even the most hardened researcher, committed to the search for inconsistencies and alternative narratives, can hardly fail to be impressed and even inspired. Case-oriented innovation research regularly yields such encounters, along with the undeniable intellectual satisfaction of reflecting on why the innovations succeeded and developing broadly applicable lessons for practitioners.

This book, like *Innovating with Integrity* before it, has adopted a different approach. Rather than scrutinizing isolated case histories, I have chosen to distill the narratives innovators provide into databases. Using statistical tools I analyzed the nature and process of public sector innovation over time and space (using international comparators), as revealed by those databases. Although numbers may seem a poor substitute for personalities and regression coefficients admittedly fall short on human interest, this approach does not ignore the stories that lie behind each innovative initiative. Rather, my analysis seeks to situate them within larger frames of meaning. This process of hunting through the data to find meaningful patterns possesses its own intrinsic intellectual fascination, as my colleagues in diverse fields of the natural and social sciences and, increasingly, the humanities can attest.

What is more, by assembling, coding, and analyzing these stories of innovations, I have been able to generate a meta-story that carries an important moral. Public sector innovation is an enduring phenomenon that continually changes, a remarkably stable process whose content has shifted significantly over the course of two decades and will undoubtedly continue to do so. This book provides an opportunity to share with both academic colleagues and practitioners my observations of and insights into this process. As a scholar of public sector innovation for the last two decades and, even more, as a citizen, I am gratified to think that innovation will always be with us, that there will always be public servants and politicians seeking ways to make government better—more efficient, more responsive, more economical, more accessible, more proactive, more creative. And I sincerely hope there will always be engaged and resourceful researchers, like the colleagues I have cited throughout this study, exploring new ways to understand these future innovators' efforts. This book is directed to both those communities, in the hope of assisting them in the important work they will do.

Appendix: Initial Application and Semifinalist Application Questionnaires

Initial Application Questions

1. Please provide a two sentence summary of the innovation. This description should accurately and succinctly convey the essence of the innovation. (50 words or less).

2. Please tell the story of your innovation, including the circumstances of its conception (such as previous efforts to deal with a particular problem), the initiation of your program (for example how it was designed and launched), and the program's ongoing operations (for example how it has been modified in response to obstacles or opposition). Dates would be helpful in anchoring the narrative. (500 words or less).

3. The Innovations Awards four selection criteria are
   i. novelty, the degree to which the program or initiative demonstrates a leap in creativity
   ii. effectiveness, the degree to which the program or initiative has achieved tangible results
   iii. significance, the degree to which the program or initiative addresses an important problem of widespread public concern
   iv. transferability, the degree to which the program or initiative, or aspects of it, has been successfully transferred to other government entities or shows promise of being successfully transferred.

   Please show how your program meets each of these criteria (500 words or less).

Semifinalist Application Questions

1. Describe your innovation. What problem does it address? When and how was the program or policy initiative originally conceived in your jurisdiction? How exactly is your program or policy innovative? How has your innovation changed previous practice? Name the program or policy that is closest to yours.

2. If your innovation is an adaptation or replication of another innovation, please identify the program or policy initiative and jurisdiction originating the innovation. In what ways has your program or policy initiative adapted or improved on the original innovation?

3. How was the program or initiative embodying your innovative idea designed and launched? What individuals or groups are considered the primary initiators of your program? Please substantiate the claim that one or more government institutions played a formative role in the program's development.

4. How has the implementation strategy of your program or policy initiative evolved over time? Please outline the chronology of your innovation and identify the key milestones in program or policy development and implementation and when they occurred (e.g., pilot program authorization enacted by state legislature in February 2008; pilot program accepted first clients, June 2008; expanded program approved by legislature in February 2009).

5. Please describe the most significant obstacle(s) encountered thus far by your program. How have they been dealt with? Which ones remain?

6. What is the single most important achievement of your program or policy initiative to date?

7. What are the three most important measures you use to evaluate your program's success? In qualitative or quantitative terms for each measure, please provide the outcomes of the last full year of program operation and, if possible, at least one prior year.

8. Please describe the target population served by your program or policy initiative. How does the program or policy initiative identify and select its clients or consumers? How many clients does your program or policy initiative currently serve? What percentage of the potential clientele does this represent?

9. What would you characterize as the program's most significant remaining shortcoming?

10. What other individuals or organizations have been the most significant in (a) program development and (b) on-going implementation and operation? What roles have they played? What individuals or organizations are the

strongest supporters of the program or policy initiative and why? What individuals or organizations are the strongest critics of the program or policy initiative and why? What is the nature of their criticism?

11. If your program or policy initiative has been formally evaluated or audited by an independent organization or group, please provide the name, address, and telephone number of a contact person from whom the materials are available. Please summarize the principal findings of the independent evaluator(s) and/or auditor(s). If your program has been the subject of an article, book, or other publication (including web-based) produced by an independent organization or group, please provide a complete citation.

12. To what extent do you believe your program or policy initiative is potentially replicable within other jurisdictions and why? To your knowledge, have any other jurisdictions or organizations established programs or implemented policies modeled specifically on your own?

13. What is the program's current operating budget? What are the program's funding sources (e.g., local, state, federal, private)? What percentage of annual income is derived from each? Please provide any other pertinent budget information.

14. Has the program or policy initiative received any awards or other honors? If so, please list and describe the awards or honors and the sponsoring organizations. If no, please indicate "not applicable" below.

15. Has the program received any press or other media coverage to date? If yes, please list the sources and briefly describe relevant coverage. If no, please indicate "not applicable" below.

16. Please attach an organization chart to show the current number, responsibilities, and reporting relationships of key program employees or staff.

References

Ansell, Chris, and Allison Gash. 2008. "Collaborative Governance in Theory and Practice." *Journal of Public Administration Theory and Practice* 18, no. 4: 543–71.

Arundel, Anthony, and Dorothea Huber. 2013. "From Too Little to Too Much Innovation: Issues in Measuring Innovation in the Public Sector." *Structural Change and Economic Dynamics* 27, no. 4: 146–59.

Austen, Ben. 2013. "The Death and Life of Chicago." *New York Times Magazine.* June 2, pp. 22–29.

Avolio, Bruce, and Bernard Bass. 2009. *Multifactor Leadership Questionnaire: Third Edition Manual and Sampler Set.* Redwood City, Calif.: Mind Garden.

Bardach, Eugene. 1998. *Getting Agencies to Work Together: The Practice and Theory of Managerial Craftsmanship.* Brookings.

———. 2008. "Developmental Processes: A Conceptual Exploration." In *Innovations in Government: Research, Recognition, and Replication*, edited by Sandford Borins. Brookings.

Bartlett, Dean, and Pauline Dibben. 2002. "Public Sector Innovation and Entrepreneurship: Case Studies from Local Government." *Local Government Studies* 28, no. 4: 107–21.

Barzelay, Michael. 1992. *Breaking through Bureaucracy: A New Vision for Managing in Government.* University of California Press.

Behn, Robert. 1988. "Management by Groping Along." *Journal of Policy Analysis and Management* 7, no. 4: 643–63.

———. 1991. *Leadership Counts: Lessons for Public Leaders from the Massachusetts Welfare, Training and Employment Program.* Harvard University Press.

———. 1998. "What Right do Public Managers Have to Lead?" *Public Administration Review* 58, no. 3: 209–24.

———. 2008. "The Adoption of Innovation: The Challenge of Learning to Adapt Tacit Knowledge." In *Innovations in Government: Research, Recognition, and Replication*, edited by Sandford Borins. Brookings.

———. 2014. *The PerformanceStat Potential: A Leadership Strategy for Producing Results.* Brookings.

Bernier, Luc, and Taïeb Hafsi. 2007. "The Changing Nature of Public Entrepreneurship." *Public Administration Review* 67, no. 3: 488–503.

211

Bernier, Luc, Taïeb Hafsi, and Carl Deschamps. 2012. "Innovation in the Canadian Public Sector: The Impact of the Environment." Unpublished paper, in author's collection.

Berry, Frances, and William Berry. 2007. "Innovation and Diffusion Models in Policy Research." In *Theories of the Policy Process*, edited by Paul Sabatier. Boulder: Westview.

Borins, Sandford. 1988. "Public Choice: 'Yes Minister' Made it Popular, but Does Winning a Nobel Prize Make It True?" *Canadian Public Administration* 31, no. 1: 12–26.

———. 1991. "The Encouragement and Study of Improved Public Management: The Institute of Public Administration of Canada Innovative Management Award." *International Review of Administrative Sciences* 57, no. 2: 179–94.

———. 1998. *Innovating with Integrity: How Local Heroes Are Transforming American Government*. Georgetown University Press.

———. 2000a. "Loose Cannons and Rule Breakers, or Enterprising Leaders? Some Evidence about Innovative Public Managers." *Public Administration Review* 60, no. 6: 498–507.

———. 2000b. "What Border? Public Management Innovation in the United States and Canada." *Journal of Policy Analysis and Management* 19, no. 1: 46–74.

———. 2000c. "Public Service Awards Programs: An Exploratory Analysis." *Canadian Public Administration* 43, no. 3: 321–42.

———. 2001a. "Public Management Innovation in Economically Advanced and Developing Countries." *International Review of Administrative Sciences* 67, no. 4: 715–31.

———. 2001b. "Public Management Innovation: Toward a Global Perspective." *American Review of Public Administration* 31, no. 1: 5–21.

———. 2006. *The Challenge of Innovating in Government*. 2nd ed. Washington: IBM Center for the Business of Government (www.businessofgovernment.org/pdfs/BorinsReport.pdf).

———, ed. 2008. *Innovations in Government: Research, Recognition, and Replication*. Brookings.

———. 2011. *Governing Fables: Learning from Public Sector Narratives*. Charlotte, N.C.: Information Age Publishing.

———. 2012. "Making Narrative Count: A Narratological Approach to Public Management Innovation." *Journal of Public Administration Research and Theory* 22, no. 1: 165–89.

———. 2013. "A Private Sector Perspective on Public Management Innovation" (www.sandford borins.com/2013/07/02/a-private-sector-perspective-on-public-management-innovation).

Borins, Sandford, Ken Kernaghan, David Brown, Nick Bontis, Perri 6, and Fred Thompson. 2007. *Digital State at the Leading Edge*. University of Toronto Press.

Borins, Sandford, and Richard Walker. 2011. "Many Are Called but Few Are Chosen: Modelling the Selection Process for the Innovations in American Government Awards." Cambridge, Mass.: Harvard Kennedy School, Ash Center for Democratic Innovation and Governance (www.innovations.harvard.edu/cache/documents/26380/2638028.pdf).

Bovaird, Tony, and Elke Loffler. 2009. "More Quality through Competitive Quality Awards? An Impact Assessment Framework." *International Review of Administrative Sciences* 75, no. 3: 383–401.

Boyne, George, Julian Gould-Williams, Jennifer Law, and Richard Walker. 2005. "Explaining the Adoption of Innovation: An Empirical Analysis of Public Management Reform." *Environment and Planning C: Government and Policy* 23, no. 3: 419–35.

Carstensen, Helle, and Christian Bason. 2012. "Powering Collaborative Policy Innovation: Can Innovation Labs Help?" *Innovation Journal* 17, no. 1: 1–26 (www.innovation.cc/scholarly-style/christian_bason_v17i1a4.pdf).

Carter, Ralph, and James Scott. 2004. "Taking the Lead: Congressional Foreign Policy Entrepreneurship in US Foreign Policy." *Politics and Policy* 32, no. 1: 34–61.

Cels, Sanderijn, Jorrit de Jong, and Frans Nauta. 2012. *Agents of Change: Strategy and Tactics for Social Innovation.* Brookings.

Considine, Mark, Jenny Lewis, and Damon Alexander. 2009. *Networks, Innovation, and Public Policy: Politicians, Bureaucrats, and the Pathways to Change Inside Government.* Basingstoke, U.K.: Palgrave Macmillan.

Cyert, Richard and James March. 1963. *Behavioral Theory of the Firm.* Englewood Cliffs, N.J.: Prentice Hall.

Damanpour, Fariborz, and Marguerite Schneider. 2008. "Characteristics of Innovation and Innovation Adoption in Public Organizations; Assessing the Role of Managers." *Journal of Public Administration Research and Theory* 19, no. 3: 495–522.

Damanpour, Fariborz, Richard Walker, and Claudia Avellaneda. 2009. "Combinative Effects of Innovation Types and Organizational Performance: A Longitudinal Study of Service Organizations." *Journal of Management Studies* 46, no. 4: 650–75.

Deyle, Robert. 1994. "Conflict, Uncertainty, and the Role of Planning and Analysis in Public Policy Innovation." *Policy Studies Journal* 22, no. 3: 457–73.

Donahue, John D. 2008. "The Unaccustomed Inventiveness of the Labor Department." In *Innovations in Government: Research, Recognition, and Replication*, edited by Sandford Borins. Brookings.

Donahue, John D., and Richard Zeckhauser. 2011. *Collaborative Governance: Private Roles for Public Goals in Turbulent Times.* Princeton University Press.

Farah, Marta, and Peter Spink. 2008. "Subnational Government Innovation in a Comparative Perspective: Brazil." In *Innovations in Government: Research, Recognition, and Replication*, edited by Sandford Borins. Brookings.

Gallup Organization. 2010. *Innobarometer 2010, Analytical Report: Innovation in Public Administration.* Survey prepared for the Directorate General Enterprise and Industry of the European Commission. Flash EB Series #205 (http://ec.europa.eu/public_opinion/flash/fl_305_en.pdf).

Gertner, Jon. 2012. *The Idea Factory: Bell Labs and the Great Age of American Innovation.* New York: Penguin.

Georges, Gigi, Tim Glynn-Burke, and Andrea McGrath. 2013a. "Improving the Local Landscape for Innovation (Part 1): Mechanics, Partners, and Clusters." Research paper. Cambridge, Mass.: Harvard Kennedy School, Ash Center for Democratic Governance and Innovation (www.innovations.harvard.edu/showdoc.html?id=2849471).

———. 2013b. "Improving the Local Landscape for Innovation (Part 2): Framework for an Innovative Jurisdiction." Cambridge, Mass.: Harvard Kennedy School, Ash Center for Democratic Governance and Innovation (www.innovations.harvard.edu/showdoc.html?id=2849663).

Golden, Olivia. 1990. "Innovation in Public Sector Human Services Programs: The Implications of Innovation by 'Groping Along.'" *Journal of Policy Analysis and Management* 9, no. 2: 219–48.

Goldsmith, Stephen and William Eggers. 2004. *Governing by Network: The New Shape of the Public Sector.* Brookings.

Gore, Al. 1993. *Creating a Government That Works Better and Costs Less: Report of the National Performance Review.* New York: Times Books.

Hartley, Jean. 2008. "Does Innovation Lead to Improvement in Public Services? Lessons from the Beacon Scheme in the United Kingdom." In *Innovations in Government: Research, Recognition, and Replication,* edited by Sandford Borins. Brookings.

Hartley, Jean, and James Downe. 2007. "The Shining Lights? Public Service Awards as an Approach to Service Improvement." *Public Administration* 85, no. 2: 329–53.

Howard, Cosmo. 2001. "Bureaucrats in the Social Policy Process: Administrative Policy Entrepreneurs and the Case of *Working Nation.*" *Australian Journal of Public Administration* 60, no. 3: 56–65.

Kamensky, John. 2013. "From 'Reinventing Government' to 'Moneyball Government.'" *Public Administration Times* 36, no. 3: 8, 10.

Kanter, Rosabeth. 2000. "When a Thousand Flowers Bloom." In *Entrepreneurship: The Social Science View*, edited by Richard Swedberg. Oxford University Press.

Kelman, Steven. 2008. "The 'Kennedy School School' of Research on Innovation in Government." In *Innovations in Government: Research, Recognition, and Replication*, edited by Sandford Borins. Brookings.

Kelman, Steven, Sounman Hong, and Irwin Turbitt. 2013. "Are There Management Practices Associated with the Outcomes of an Interagency Service Delivery Collaboration? Evidence from British Crime and Disorder Reduction Partnerships." *Journal of Public Administration Research and Theory* 23, no. 3: 609–30.

Levin, Martin, and Mary Bryna Sanger. 1994. *Making Government Work: How Entrepreneurial Executives Turn Bright Ideas into Real Results.* San Francisco: Jossey-Bass.

Light, Paul. 1998. *Sustaining Innovation: Creating Nonprofit and Government Organizations that Innovate Naturally.* San Francisco: Jossey-Bass.

Lonti, Zsuzsanna and Anil Verma. 2003. "The Determinants of Flexibility and Innovation in the Government Workplace: Recent Evidence from Canada." *Journal of Public Administration Research and Theory* 13, no. 3: 283–310.

Mack, W. R., Deanna Green, and Arnold Vedlitz. 2008. "Innovation and Implementation in the Public Sector: An Examination of Public Entrepreneurship." *Review of Research Policy* 25, no. 3: 233–52.

Mintrom, Michael. 1997. "Policy Entrepreneurs and the Diffusion of Innovation." *American Journal of Political Science* 41, no. 3: 738–70.

Mintrom, Michael, and Sandra Vergari.1998. "Policy Networks and Innovation Diffusion: The Case of State Education Reforms." *Journal of Politics* 60, no. 1: 126–48.

Mintzberg, Henry, Bruce Ahlstrand, and Joseph Lampel. 2009. *Strategy Safari.* 2nd ed. Harlow, U.K.: Pearson.

Moore, Mark. 1995. *Creating Public Value: Strategic Management in Government.* Harvard University Press.

———. 2013. *Recognizing Public Value.* Harvard University Press.

Nolan, Jeremy. 2012. "Public Sector Innovation: Unlocking the Impact of Transformational Leadership in a Cross-Cultural Context." Ph.D. dissertation, Australian National University.

Osborne, David. 1990. *Laboratories of Democracy.* Boston: Harvard Business School Press.

Osborne, David, and Ted Gaebler. 1992. *Reinventing Government: How the Entrepreneurial Spirit Is Transforming the Public Sector.* Reading, Mass: Addison-Wesley.

Osborne, Stephen. 1998. *Voluntary Organizations and Innovations in Public Services.* London: Routledge.

Osborne, Stephen, Celine Chew, and Kate McLaughlin. 2008. "The Once and Future Pioneers? The Innovative Capacity of Voluntary Organisations and the Provision of Public Services: A Longitudinal Approach." *Public Management Review* 10, no. 1: 51–70.

Petchey, Roland, Jacky Williams, and Yvonne Carter. 2008. "From Street-Level Bureaucrats to Street-Level Policy Entrepreneurs? Central Policy and Local Action in Lottery-Funded Community Cancer Care." *Social Policy and Administration* 42, no. 1: 59–76.

Pollitt, Christopher, and Geert Bouchaert. 2000. *Public Management Reform: A Comparative Analysis.* Oxford University Press.

Potts, Jason, and Tim Kastelle. 2010. "Public Sector Innovation Research: What's Next?" *Innovation: Management, Practice, and Policy* 12, no. 2: 122–37.

Reich, Robert. 1997. *Locked in the Cabinet.* New York: Knopf.

Roberts, Nancy, and Paula King. 1991. "Policy Entrepreneurs: Their Activity Structure and Function in the Policy Process." *Journal of Public Administration Research and Theory* 1, no. 2: 147–75.

———. 1992. "An Investigation into the Personality Profile of Policy Entrepreneurs." *Public Productivity and Management Review* 16, no. 2: 173–90.

———. 1996. *Transforming Public Policy: Dynamics of Policy Entrepreneurship and Innovation.* San Francisco: Jossey-Bass.

Rogers, Everett. 2003. *Diffusion of Innovations.* 5th ed. New York: Free Press.

Rosenstock, Larry. 2010. "I Used to Think . . ." *UnBoxed: A Journal of Adult Learning in Schools* (online journal), no. 6 (www.hightechhigh.org/unboxed/issue6/i_used_to_think).

Sahni, Nikhil, Maxwell Wessell, and Clayton Christensen. 2013. "Unleashing Breakthrough Innovation in Government." *Stanford Social Innovation Review* 11, no. 3: 27–37.

Salge, Torsten. 2010. "A Behavioral Model of Innovative Search: Evidence from Public Hospital Services." *Journal of Public Administration Research and Theory* 21, no. 1: 181–210.

Salge, Torsten, and Antonio Vera. 2012. "Benefiting from Public Sector Innovation: The Moderating Role of Customer and Learning Orientation." *Public Administration Review* 72, no. 4: 550–60.

Schall, Ellen. 1997. "Public-Sector Succession: A Strategic Approach to Sustaining Innovation. *Public Administration Review* 57, no. 1: 4–10.

Sorensen, Eva, and Jacob Torfing. 2011. "Enhancing Collaborative Innovation in the Public Sector." *Administration and Society* 43, no. 8: 842–68.

Straussman, Jeffrey. 1993. "Management by Groping Along: The Limits of a Metaphor." *Governance* 6, no. 2: 154–71.

Teodoro, Manuel. 2011. *Bureaucratic Ambition: Careers, Motives, and the Innovative Administrator.* Johns Hopkins University Press.

Terry, Larry. 1998. "Administrative Leadership, Neo-Managerialism, and the Public Management Movement." *Public Administration Review* 58, no. 3: 194–200.

Teske, Paul, and Mark Schneider. 1994. "The Bureaucratic Entrepreneur: The Case of City Managers." *Public Administration Review* 54, no. 4: 331–40.

Thomson, Ann Marie, James Perry, and Theodore Miller. 2009. "Conceptualizing and Measuring Collaboration." *Journal of Public Administration Research and Theory* 19, no. 1: 23–56.

Vigoda-Gadot, Eran, Aviv Shoham, Nitza Schwabsky, and Ayalla Ruvio. 2008. "Public Sector Innovation for Europe: A Multinational Eight-Country Exploration of Citizens' Perspectives." *Public Administration* 86, no. 2: 307–29.

Walker, Richard. 2003. "Evidence on the Management of Public Services Innovation." *Public Money and Management* 23, no. 3: 93–102.

———. 2006. "Innovation Type and Diffusion: An Empirical Analysis of Local Government." *Public Administration* 84, no. 2: 331–35.

———. 2008. "An Empirical Evaluation of Innovation Types and Organizational and Environmental Characteristics: Towards a Configuration Framework." *Journal of Public Administration Research and Theory* 18, no. 4: 591–615.

———. 2014."Internal and External Antecedents of Process Innovation: A Review and Extension." *Public Management Review* 16, no. 1: 21–44.

Walker, Richard, Fariborz Damanpour, and Carlos Devece. 2010. "Management Innovation and Organizational Performance: The Mitigating Effect of Performance Management." *Journal of Public Administration Research and Theory* 21, no. 3: 367–86.

Walker, Richard, Emma Jeanes, and Robert Rowlands. 2002. "Measuring Innovation: Applying the Literature-Based Innovation Output Indicator to Public Services." *Public Administration* 80, no. 1: 201–14.

Walters, Jonathan. 2008. "Twenty Years of Highlighting Excellence in Government." In *Innovations in Government: Research, Recognition, and Replication,* edited by Sandford Borins. Brookings.

Wu, Jiannan, Liang Ma, and Yuqian Yang. 2013. "Innovation in the Chinese Public Sector: Typology and Distribution." *Public Administration* 91, no. 2: 347–65.

Index

Note: HKS datasets are organized by years covered below the entry for Harvard Kennedy School Innovations in American Government Awards.

Academic research: and education and training innovations, 161; and formal evaluation of innovation, 113–14, 136, 140, 184; future research opportunities, 194–204. *See also* Literature review

Access Alabama, 163

Access to health services, 166

Accommmodation, 98, 106

Accountability, 54, 59–60

Accreditation review, 114, 136, 184

Achievements, 112–13

Advisory committees, 54

Advocates, Inc., 174

Affordable Care Act, 184

Agency heads as initiator of innovation, 65, 78, 83

Agricultural Development Fund (Kentucky), 157, 158, 159

Aircraft Icing Prediction Initiative, 150–51

Alabama, education and training innovations in, 163

Alameda County, California, health and social services innovations in, 167

Alaska, education and training innovations in, 161

Alexander, Damon, 24

Alliance building, 68

Alternative dispute resolution, 175

American Recovery and Reinvestment Act of 2009, 158, 168

AmeriCorps, 47

Ancillary innovation, 47

Anderson, James, 66

Angola State Penitentiary (Louisiana), 171, 176

Ansell, Chris, 47, 90

Antipoverty initiatives, 147

Arizona, criminal justice and public safety innovations in, 171, 172

Arkansas, health and social services innovations in, 167

Arlington, Virginia, community and economic development innovations in, 156

Ash Center for Democratic Governance and Innovation, 2, 6. *See also* Harvard Kennedy School Innovations in American Government Awards

Association of Public Safety Communication Officials, 174

Attribution bias, 127, 133

Audit Commission (UK), 36

Audits, 113, 114, 136

Australia: innovation award applications from, 41; public policy entrepreneurship in, 24; statistical studies in, 38
Automatic HIV Counseling Program (Washington, D.C.), 167
Avellaneda, Claudia, 36, 38
Avolio, Bruce, 17
Awards, 117–18, 120–24

Baltimore: community and economic development innovations in, 159; management and governance innovations in, 147
Bardach, Eugene, 90
Barriers. *See* Obstacles
Bartlett, Dean, 22
Barzelay, Michael, 15, 16
Bason, Christian, 28
Bass, Bernard, 17
Beacons Scheme (UK), 18
Behn, Robert, 4, 14, 19–20, 73, 115, 187
Bend the Curve (Maine), 147
Bernier, Luc, 17, 23
Berry, Frances, 25–26
Berry, William, 25–26
Beshear, Steve, 66, 148
Biotechnology centers, 156
Bivariate correlations, 14
Blair, Tony, 29
Bloomberg, Michael, 66, 147, 148, 202, 203, 204
Borins, Sandford F., 4, 125
Boston: Citizen Connect, 146; education and training innovations in, 161–62, 163; as hotbed of innovation, 201, 202
Boston Day and Evening Academy, 162, 163
Bottom-up innovations, 64–65, 66, 67
Bouchaert, Geert, 3
Boulder, Colorado, transportation, infrastructure, and environment innovations in, 153
Boutique innovations, 55–56, 119
Boyne, George, 30, 34
Brazil: innovation awards in, 16; interorganizational collaboration in, 47, 183; reasons for innovation in, 72
Breaking through Bureaucracy (Barzelay), 15

Brown, Gordon, 29
Brown, Lee, 15
Bryant Park Corporation, 157
Budget Formulation and Execution Manager, 147
Budgets: and interorganizational collaboration, 51; as measure of scale, 55–56, 60. *See also* Funding
Bureaucracy as internal barrier, 90, 98, 106
Bureaucratic Ambition (Teodoro), 24
Bureau of Land Management (U.S.), 151
Burlington, Vermont, transportation, infrastructure, and environment innovations in, 153
Burnout, 89, 98

California: Air Resources Board, 152, 154; transportation, infrastructure, and environment innovations in, 151, 154. *See also specific cities and counties*
Cambridge Ringe and Latin School, 198
Canada: information technology use in, 6; innovation award applications from, 41; innovation awards in, 16, 17; statistical studies in, 32
CAPAM. *See* Commonwealth Association for Public Administration and Management
Careerism, 73
Carstensen, Helle, 28
Carter, Ralph, 22, 25
Carter, Yvonne, 23, 24, 25
Case studies, 12, 27–28
Causal factors for innovation, 70–73, 84
Cels, Sanderijn, 17, 72
Center for Applied Identity Management Research, 174, 176
Center for Economic Opportunity (New York City), 147, 148, 150
Central Park East Secondary School (New York City), 164
Central Station Alarm Association, 174
Centrist media, 119, 185
Champions, 22, 87
Charlotte County, Florida, management and governance innovations in, 146
Charter schools, 161, 162, 164, 178

Chew, Celine, 29

Chicago, management and governance innovations in, 148, 150

Child Psychiatry Access Program (Massachusetts), 166

Children and family services. *See* Health and social services

Child Support Enforcement System (Massachusetts), 176

China, innovation awards in, 16

Chretien, Kaylee, 42

Christensen, Clayton, 12

CitiStat (Baltimore), 147, 150

Citizen Connect (Boston), 146

Citizen empowerment, 49, 50, 59, 128–29, 136, 175, 186

City Net (Santa Monica, California), 197

City of Parks initiative (Louisville, Kentucky), 157

Citywide Post-Disaster Resilience and Recovery Initiative (San Francisco), 174, 176

CityWorks (Cambridge, Massachusetts), 162, 164, 197, 198

Civic Consulting Alliance (Chicago), 150

Civil society, 47

Cleveland: community and economic development innovations in, 159; transportation, infrastructure, and environment innovations in, 153

Clients: as critics of innovation, 99, 101; inclusion in oral presentation by finalists, 139; as initiator of innovation, 65, 83

Coalition of Essential Schools, 162, 164, 198

Code Enforcement Task Force, 175

Coding of 2010 HKS applicant data, 42–44

Collaboration process, 47. *See also* Interorganizational collaboration

Collective entrepreneurship, 21

Combs, Susan, 148

Commonwealth Association for Public Administration and Management (CAPAM), 5, 17, 41

Commonwealth International Innovation Awards: and creation stage of innovation, 61, 83; dataset analysis, 5, 40–41; and formal evaluations, 115; literature review, 16; organizational level of applicants, 64–65; and transfer of innovations, 116

Community and economic development: diversity of innovations in, 177, 184; innovation characteristics, 50; policy area narratives, 9, 144, 154–60

Community policing, 173, 175, 178, 183

Community Safety Information Grid (East Orange, New Jersey), 174, 175

Community Stabilization First Look Pilot Program (Minneapolis), 158, 159

Community Supervision Centers (Missouri), 172

Comparative research, 194–96

Competition and Costing Program (Indianapolis), 149

Consensus-building, 94

Consensus Council (North Dakota), 149

Conservative media, 119, 155

Considine, Mark, 24

Consolidated Fire Services, 175

Consultants, 75, 98, 140, 184

Consulting Alliance (Chicago), 148

Co-optation, 98

Cost reductions, 110, 111, 136, 146

Council of the Arts' Cultural Data Project (Pennsylvania), 155

Creating Public Value: Strategic Management in Government (Moore), 15, 108

Creation stage of innovation, 8–9, 61–85; causal factors for innovation, 70–73, 84; novelty, 61, 62–63; organizational level of applicants, 63–70, 76–83, 84–85; planning vs. groping along, 73–75, 84; precepts for practitioners, 189–91

Crime and Disorder Reduction Partnerships, 47

Criminal justice and public safety: diffusion of innovation in, 50, 178; policy area narratives, 10, 144, 171–77

Crisis as incitement for innovation, 70–71, 76, 84

Critics, 87, 99–105

CSX Transportation, 174, 176

Curtatone, Joseph, 148, 203, 204

Customer orientation, 37

Customize Employment Program (Labor Department), 148
Cyert, Richard, 31, 38

Daly, Tom, 148
Damanpour, Fariborz, 33, 34, 36, 37, 38
Davenport, Iowa, community and economic development innovations in, 157
Dayton, Ohio, education and training innovations in, 162
Decisionmaking approaches, 75
De Jong, Jorrit, 17, 72
Demonstration projects, 93, 98
Denmark, MindLab case study, 28
Denver, Colorado: education and training innovations in, 162; as hotbed of innovation, 201; management and governance innovations in, 147; transportation, infrastructure, and environment innovations in, 151
Denver Classroom Teachers Association, 162
Department of Defense Reorganization Act of 1986, 63
Deschamps, Carl, 17
Descriptive statistics, 14
Detroit: community and economic development innovations in, 158; as hotbed of innovation, 201
Devece, Carlos, 37, 38
Developmental innovation, 29
Dibben, Pauline, 22
Diffusion of innovations: and determinants of innovation, 8, 178; literature review, 14, 25–26, 39; and novelty, 62
Diffusion of Innovations (Rogers), 2, 25
Digital State at the Leading Edge (Borins and others), 6
Distance education, 161, 163, 178
Donahue, John D., 27–28, 90, 199
Downe, James, 18, 124, 196
Dropout recovery, 161, 162, 163, 178
Dukakis, Michael, 63

Early Neutral Evaluations program (Hennepin County, Minnesota), 175
East Orange, New Jersey, criminal justice and public safety innovations in, 174, 175

Economic and Social Research Council (UK), 29
Economic development. *See* Community and economic development
Economic Gardening (Littleton, Colorado), 155–56
Education and training: changes in policy priorities, 178, 184; innovation characteristics, 50–51; policy area narratives, 9, 144, 160–65
Education and Training Choices Program (Massachusetts), 19
Education Department (U.S.), 198
Effectiveness: coding applications for, 43, 44, 127; EC Innobarometer survey on, 111; as finalist selection criteria, 134–37; quantitative evidence for, 141; of semifinalists, 130; statistical studies, 35–36
Election mandates, 72
Electronic tolling, 153
Employee satisfaction, 111
English as a second language, 161, 163
Enhanced Enforcement Program (Massachusetts), 19
Environment. *See* Transportation, infrastructure, and environment
Environmental Protection Agency (EPA), 151, 153, 154
Envision Utah, 153
eRulemaking program, 146
e-Transparency Task Force (Kentucky), 66
Europe: and Innobarometer, 34–35; innovation awards in, 17; statistical studies in, 38. *See also specific countries*
Evidence-Based Home Visiting Initiative (New Jersey), 166, 169, 171
Evolutionary innovation, 29
Executive initiation, 66
Expansionary innovation, 29
Expert opinion ratings, 33
Expert Workshop on Measuring Public Sector Innovation (OECD), 36
External Alarm Interface Exchange American National Standard, 174, 176
External measures of value creation, 113–19

Factor analysis, 14
Family Resource Centers (Michigan), 167, 169

Family services. *See* Health and social services

Farah, Marta, 16, 47, 72, 183

Federal Highway Administration, 67

Female Offender Reentry Group Effort (FORGE, New Jersey), 172, 176

Financial audits, 114, 136

Flexibility, 91, 192

Florida: criminal justice and public safety innovations in, 171; education and training innovations in, 163; transportation, infrastructure, and environment innovations in, 151

Florida Benchmarking Consortium, 147

Ford Foundation, 15, 16

Foreign policy entrepreneurship, 22–23

FORGE (Female Offender Reentry Group Effort, New Jersey), 172, 176

Formal evaluations, 113–19, 124

Framingham, Massachusetts, criminal justice and public safety innovations in, 174, 175

Frontline staff: collaboration by, 84; education and training innovations initiated by, 160; gender distribution of innovators, 68–69; inclusion in oral presentation by finalists, 139; as innovation initiators, 63–64, 65, 76, 78, 83, 104–05, 187; management and governance innovations, 149

Funders Group (Seattle), 147–48

Funding: and interorganizational collaboration, 51, 59, 104, 183; sources for, 188; tactics for overcoming obstacles, 94, 103–04, 106; in UK, 23

Future Soldiers Program (Pendleton, Indiana), 173

Gaebler, Ted, 3, 11

Gainsharing, 149, 150

Gash, Allison, 47, 90

Gates Foundation, 115, 164, 171, 179

Gender distribution of innovators, 68–69, 83–84

Georges, Gigi, 202, 203

Georgia: health and social services innovations in, 168, 170; management and governance innovations in, 148; transportation, infrastructure, and environment innovations in, 153–54

GE Security, 174

Global financial crisis (2008–09), 119, 185

Glynn, Tom, 28

Glynn-Burke, Tim, 202, 203

Golden, Olivia, 19, 79–80

Goldsmith, Stephen, 133

Goldwater-Nichols Department of Defense Reorganization Act of 1986, 63

Gore Report (1993), 11

Governance. *See* Management and governance

Governing Fables: Learning from Public Sector Narratives (Borins), 6

Green, Deanna, 24

Greenhouse gas emissions, 154

Greenprint Environmental Management System (Denver), 151

Groundwater Replenishment System (Orange County, California), 151, 152

Hadley, Daniel, 204

Hafsi, Taïeb, 17, 23

Hamilton, Allison, 67, 68, 90, 204

Harris, Patti, 66

Hartley, Jean, 18, 124, 196

Harvard Center for Law and Education, 198

Harvard Kennedy School Innovations in American Government Awards: applicants for 2010, 40–60; initial application questions, 207; semifinalist application questions, 208–09; sustainability of, 1–2, 56–59, 60, 195–96. *See also HKS Awards datasets below by years*

Harvard Kennedy School Awards dataset (1990–94): and community and economic development innovations, 159; and creation stage of innovation, 61, 83; and criminal justice and public safety innovations, 175–76; and education and training innovations, 163–65; and health and social services innovations, 169–70; and management and governance innovations, 148–49; and transfer of innovations, 115–17; and transportation, infrastructure, and environment innovations, 153–54

Harvard Kennedy School Awards dataset (1995–98): and creation stage of innovation, 61, 83; literature review, 16; and transfer of innovations, 115–17

Harvard Kennedy School Awards dataset (2010): award selection determinants, 124–40; coding and comparing, 42–44; consistency between semifinalists and non-semifinalists, 44–52; and creation stage of innovation, 61–85; dataset analysis, 40–60; external measures of value creation, 113–19; finalist selections, 40, 133–37; funding of innovations, 51, 59; interorganizational collaboration by, 44–54, 59; narratives of innovations, 86–107; organizational structures enabling collaboration by, 53–54; policy area narratives, 143–79; recognition of, 120–24; semifinalist selections, 40, 125–33; size of projects, 54–56; and transfer of innovations, 115–17; value creation by, 108–19; winner selection, 138–40. *See also* Semifinalists for 2010 HKS awards

Harwich, Massachusetts, transportation, infrastructure, and environment innovations in, 154

Hawaii, education and training innovations in, 164

Health and social services: changes in policy priorities, 178, 184; innovation characteristics, 50; policy area narratives, 9, 144, 165–71

Healthy Families Succeed Program (Wyoming), 168, 170

Healthy Indiana, 166

Healthy San Francisco, 166, 170

Hennepin County, Minnesota, criminal justice and public safety innovations in, 175

Hickenlooper, John, 202

High-risk populations, 165

High Tech High (San Diego), 162, 164, 197, 198

Historical narratives, 139

Hong, Sounman, 47

Hotbeds of innovation, 199–204

Housing and Urban Development Department (U.S.), 158

Howard, Cosmo, 22, 25

Human Services Work Management System (Denver), 147

iJury (Travis County, Texas), 175, 176

Impacts of innovations. *See* Effectiveness

Improved Solutions for Urban Systems (Dayton, Ohio), 162, 163, 164

Incarceration rate, 171, 178, 183

Incentives, 12, 59, 91, 128

Incrementalism, 20, 84

India, innovation awards in, 16, 17

Indiana: criminal justice and public safety innovations in, 173; health and social services innovations in, 166

Indianapolis, management and governance innovations in, 149

Infant mortality, 169

Information gathering, 75

Information technology: innovation opportunities driven by, 6, 73, 197; management and governance innovations involving, 145, 149, 184; use of, 49, 59, 128, 132, 136

Infrastructure. *See* Transportation, infrastructure, and environment

Innobarometer 2010, Analytical Report: Innovation in Public Administration (Gallup), 34–35, 36, 42, 47, 68, 91, 111, 141, 183

Innovating with Integrity (Borins), 2, 6–7, 16, 20, 39, 40, 42, 45, 63, 74, 78, 79–80, 83, 104

Innovation: creation stage, 8–9, 61–85, 189–91; implementation stage, 9, 192–93; life span narratives, 56–59, 86–107; operational stage, 193–94. *See also* Public sector innovation

Innovation awards: changes in, 181–85; external reviews, 184–85; future research opportunities, 194–204; and interorganizational collaboration, 181–83; precepts for practitioners, 189–94; process consistency for, 186–89; and public recognition, 120–24; research studies on, 11–39; typology, 29; and value creation, 117–18. *See also specific award programs*

"Innovation in Public Sector Human Services Programs: The Implications of Innovation by 'Groping Along'" (Golden), 79

Innovations in American Government Awards. *See* Harvard Kennedy School Innovations in American Government Awards

Innovations in State and Local Government Awards, 15

Innovative organizations, 14, 26–38. *See also* Public sector innovation; *specific organizations*

In-Q-Tel, 147

Institute of Public Administration of Canada (IPAC), 5, 16, 17

Integrated Basic Education and Skills Training Program (Washington), 163, 164

Integrated Ethics (VA hospitals), 169

Intelligence Community Civilian Joint Duty Program, 63

Interest groups. *See* Public interest groups

International City/County Management Association, 33

International Newcomer Academy (Nashville, Tennessee), 163

Interorganizational collaboration: consistency in, 186; and criminal justice and public safety innovations, 176; and education and training innovations, 160; and funding, 51, 59, 104, 183; and health and social services innovations, 170; by HKS Awards 2010 applicants, 44–54, 59, 131–32; and internal barriers, 90; in management and governance innovations, 147–48; by semifinalists, 128

Iowa, transportation, infrastructure, and environment innovations in, 153

IPAC. *See* Institute of Public Administration of Canada

iZone (New York City), 202

Jail Diversion Program (Framingham, Massachusetts), 174

Japan, innovation awards in, 17

Jeanes, Emma, 30, 47

Joint Urban Mobility Program (San Francisco), 149

Kamensky, John, 5

Kanter, Rosabeth, 11

Kastelle, Tim, 11

Kelman, Steven, 47

Kentucky: community and economic development innovations in, 157; education and training innovations in, 164;

management and governance innovations in, 146–47, 148; political initiation of innovation in, 66. *See also specific cities*

King, Paula, 21, 22

King County, Washington, management and governance innovations in, 148

Kulongoski, Ted, 67

Laboratories of Democracy (Osborne), 3

Labor Department (U.S.), 27–28, 148, 199

Lancaster, Pennsylvania, community and economic development innovations in, 155

LandCare Program (Philadelphia), 158

Lansing, Michigan, education and training innovations in, 164

Leadership Counts: Lessons for Public Leaders from the Massachusetts Welfare, Training and Employment Program (Behn), 19

Learning orientation, 37

Legislative constraints, 90, 93

Legislative initiation, 65–66, 75

Levin, Martin, 15, 16, 19, 78

Lewis, Jenny, 24

Liberal media, 119, 185

Life Sciences Greenhouse (Pennsylvania), 156, 158

Light, Paul, 27, 29

Limited English Proficiency/Sensory Impaired Program (Georgia), 148

Literature review, 11–39; case studies, 27–28; on diffusion of innovations, 25–26; on innovative organizations, 26–38; on management by "groping along," 19–20; on public sector entrepreneurship, 20–25; on research using innovation awards, 15–19; statistical studies, 28–38

Littleton, Colorado, community and economic development innovations in, 155–56

Lobbying, 72, 79

Local and state media, 118–19, 146, 185, 193

Local hero innovators, 67–68, 83, 85

Logistical problems, 89, 93

Longitudinal research, 194–96

Lonti, Zsuzsanna, 32

"Loose Cannons and Rule Breakers, or Enterprising Leaders? Some Evidence about Innovative Public Managers" (Borins), 4

Los Angeles: criminal justice and public safety innovations in, 173, 175, 176; education and training innovations in, 164

Louisiana, criminal justice and public safety innovations in, 171

Louisville, Kentucky, community and economic development innovations in, 157

Low-income populations, 165

Lyons, Liz, 43

Ma, Liang, 16

Mack, W. R., 24

Maine: education and training innovations in, 161; management and governance innovations in, 147

Major, John, 29

"Making Narrative Count" (Borins), 105

Malaysia, innovation awards in, 16, 17

Malta, innovation award applications from, 41

Management and governance: innovation characteristics, 50; policy area narratives, 9, 144, 145–50

Management by groping along, 14, 19–20, 73–75, 84, 187, 191

"Many Are Called but Few Are Chosen" (Borins and Walker), 125

March, James, 31, 38

Marchand, Christina, 125

Marin County, California, management and governance innovations in, 151

Massachusetts: community and economic development innovations in, 158, 159; criminal justice and public safety innovations in, 176; Department of Public Welfare Education and Training Choices Program, 19; Department of Revenue Enhanced Enforcement Program, 19; education and training innovations in, 164; health and social services innovations in, 166; health insurance program in, 63; Housing Partnership, 158; management and governance innovations in, 149

Master Naturalist Program (Texas), 161

McConnell, Mike, 139

McGrath, Andrea, 202, 203

McLaughlin, Kate, 29

Media: and community and economic development innovations, 155; and creation stage of innovation, 79; and education and training innovations, 161; as evaluation measure, 99, 136, 137, 141, 185; management and governance innovations, 146; and operational stage of innovation, 193; recognition from, 118–19, 120–24, 185

Menino, Tom, 202, 204

Mental Illness project (Los Angeles), 173

Mesa County, California, management and governance innovations in, 152

Miami-Dade County Civil Citation Initiative, 173, 176

Michigan: criminal justice and public safety innovations in, 173; health and social services innovations in, 167, 168, 169, 170

Michigan Partnership for Education, 164

Middle managers: collaboration by, 84; gender distribution of innovators, 68–69; as innovation initiators, 63–64, 65, 76, 78, 83, 104–05, 187; management and governance innovations initiated by, 146

Miller, Theodore, 47

MindLab, 28

Minneapolis, community and economic development innovations in, 158

Minnesota: case studies in, 27; criminal justice and public safety innovations in, 175; educational policy entrepreneurs in, 21; education and training innovations in, 162; Striving Toward Excellence in Performance (STEP), 15; transportation, infrastructure, and environment innovations in, 153

Mintrom, Michael, 22

Mintzberg, Henry, 20, 74

Missouri: criminal justice and public safety innovations in, 172, 176; management and governance innovations in, 151

Mobile Inmate Video Visitation (Pinellas County, Florida), 171

Money Follows the Person (Texas), 167

Montgomery County, Maryland, criminal justice and public safety innovations in, 172, 176

Moore, Mark, 15, 16, 108

Mortgage foreclosure crisis, 155, 158, 184
Mortgage Foreclosure Prevention Program
 (Wayne County, Michigan), 158, 159
Motivational factors, 26
Multi-jurisdiction Assessing program (New
 Hampshire), 148
Multiple regression analysis, 14
Municipal Research and Services Center
 (Washington), 147

Narratives of life span of innovation, 86–107;
 archetypal narrative, 9, 105–07; average age
 of innovations since inception, 56–59, 86;
 critics of innovation, 99–105; obstacles, 87,
 88–99
Narratological theory, 105
Nashville, Tennessee, education and training
 innovations in, 163
National Geographic Society, 151
National Health Service (UK), 23, 31
National media: and community and economic
 development innovations, 155; and education and training innovations, 161; as
 evaluation measure, 137, 185; management
 and governance innovations, 146; recognition from, 118–19, 185, 193
National Performance Review (1993), 11
Nauta, Frans, 17, 72
Neighborhood for Kids (San Diego), 168, 170
Neighborhood Stabilization Program (HUD),
 158
Nevada, health and social services innovations
 in, 168
New England Common Assessment Program,
 161
New Hampshire: education and training
 innovations in, 161; management and
 governance innovations in, 148
New Jersey: criminal justice and public safety
 innovations in, 172, 174; health and social
 services innovations in, 166, 169
New leadership as incitement for innovation,
 70, 72–73, 84
New Markets Tax Credit Program, 156, 158, 159
New opportunities as incitement for
 innovation, 70, 73

New Organizational Vision Award (NOVA),
 169, 171
New Orleans Baptist Theological Seminary,
 171, 176
New Public Management (NPM), 2–3, 29,
 108, 115, 140
New Urban High School Project (U.S.
 Education Department), 198
New York (state), transportation,
 infrastructure, and environment innovations
 in, 152. *See also specific cities*
New York City: community and economic
 development innovations in, 157; criminal
 justice and public safety innovations in, 172;
 Department of Juvenile Justice, 27;
 education and training innovations in, 164;
 health and social services innovations in,
 165; innovation environment in, 202;
 management and governance innovations in,
 147, 148, 149, 150; political initiation of
 innovation in, 66
New York University, 27
New Zealand: innovation award applications
 from, 41; New Public Management in, 3
No Child Left Behind Act of 2001, 167
Nolan, Jeremy, 17
Nongovernmental local awards, 117–18
Nongovernmental national awards, 117–18
Non-monetary incentives, 12
Nonprofit sector: and education and training
 innovations, 160, 164; evaluations by, 140,
 184; and interorganizational collaboration,
 49, 99, 128, 131–32, 181–83
North Carolina, health and social services
 innovations in, 169
North Coast Geotourism Program (California),
 151
North Dakota, management and governance
 innovations in, 149
Northeast Regional Greenhouse Gas Initiative,
 151–52, 154
No-till planting technology, 154
NOVA (New Organizational Vision Award),
 169, 171
Novelty: coding applications for, 43, 44, 127;
 creation stage of innovation, 62–63; at

creation stage of innovation, 61, 83; and diffusion of innovations, 62; as finalist selection criteria, 134–37; quantitative evidence for, 141; as semifinalist selection criteria, 132

Nutter, Michael, 202

NYC Service (New York City), 148, 150

Oakland, California: criminal justice and public safety innovations in, 175; health and social services innovations in, 167, 169

Oakland Unified School District, 167

Obama, Barack, 66

Obama, Michelle, 170

Obesity, 170

Obstacles: external barriers, 88, 90; internal barriers, 88–89, 106; lack of resources, 88, 89–90, 91, 93, 103–04, 106; as motivational factor, 26; narratives of life span of innovation, 88–99

Office of Innovative Partnerships (Oregon), 67

Office of New Urban Mechanics (Boston), 202

Office of Strategic Partnerships (Denver), 202

Ohio, community and economic development innovations in, 156. *See also specific cities*

Ohio Association of Second Harvest Foodbanks, 168

Ohio Benefits Bank, 168, 170

Oklahoma: criminal justice and public safety innovations in, 172; education and training innovations in, 164; transportation, infrastructure, and environment innovations in, 153

Olmsted, Fredrick Law, 157

One System of Care for Grandparents Raising Grandchildren (Georgia), 168, 170

One Water One Watershed Program (Riverside County, California), 151, 152

Online Electronic Benefit Transfer Program for WIC (Michigan), 168, 170

Online Voter Information Program (Orange County, California), 146

Open Book Texas, 146–47, 148

Open Door Transparency Portal (Kentucky), 66, 147, 148

Operating budgets, 55. *See also* Budgets

Operational stage of innovation, 193–94

Orange County, California: management and governance innovations in, 146; transportation, infrastructure, and environment innovations in, 151, 152, 154

Oregon: community and economic development innovations in, 157; management and governance innovations in, 150; Solar Highway project, 67; transportation, infrastructure, and environment innovations in, 152, 154

Oregon Benchmarks, 149, 150

Organizational level of innovators, 63–70, 76–85, 128, 131. *See also* Frontline staff; Middle managers

Organizational search model, 31

Organizational structures enabling collaboration, 53–54

Organization for Economic Cooperation and Development (OECD), 36, 38

Osborne, David, 3, 11

Osborne, Stephen, 29

Park development, 157

Partnerships, 49, 65, 67. *See also* Interorganizational collaboration

Pataki, George, 152

Patton, Paul, 157

Pay-for-performance, 162, 178, 184

Payzant, Tom, 161

Pediatric Practice Enhancement Project (Rhode Island), 166–67

Peer Intervention Program (New York City), 164

Pendleton, Indiana, criminal justice and public safety innovations in, 173

Pennsylvania, community and economic development innovations in, 155, 156. *See also specific cities*

Performance measurement, 115, 147, 188

PerformanceStat, 115, 147

Perry, James, 47

Persistence, 91, 93, 98, 192

Personal narratives, 139

Petchey, Roland, 23, 24, 25

Philadelphia: community and economic development innovations in, 156, 158; education and training innovations in, 163

Pilot studies, 75
Pinellas County, Florida, criminal justice and
    public safety innovations in, 171
Planning, 14, 73–75, 84, 191
Policy analysis, 113, 136
Policy area narratives, 143–79; community and
    economic development, 154–60; criminal
    justice and public safety, 171–77; education
    and training, 160–65; health and social
    services, 165–71; management and govern-
    ance, 145–50; transportation, infrastructure,
    and environment, 150–54
Political influence as incitement for innovation,
    70, 72, 76
Political initiation of innovation, 65–66
Political opposition to innovation, 90–91, 98
Political sensitivity, 91
Politicians: as critics of innovation, 101; as
    initiator of innovation, 65, 76, 78, 83, 84
Pollitt, Christopher, 3
Population reach as measure of scale, 55–56
Portland General Electric, 67
Potomac Yards (Arlington, Virginia), 156
Potts, Jason, 11
Power politics approach, 93–94
Prehistory of innovations, 62–63
Pre-release and Re-entry Services Program
    (Montgomery County, Maryland), 172, 176
Prevention Services Law Project (New York
    City), 165
Price, Sol, 198
Prince George's County, Maryland, health and
    social services innovations in, 168
Private sector: and community and economic
    development innovations, 155, 158; and
    criminal justice and public safety inno-
    vations, 171; innovations by, 11, 20; and
    interorganizational collaboration, 49, 59,
    128, 131–32, 181–83; opposition to inno-
    vations, 90; and Oregon's solar highways, 67
Private value, 108
Problems as incitement for innovation, 70,
    71–72, 76, 84
Process improvement innovations, 59, 186
Productivity, 110, 111, 146
Professional or trade media: and education and
    training innovations, 161; as evaluation

measure, 118–19, 185, 193; management
    and governance innovations, 146
Project-based learning, 99
Project U-Turn (Philadelphia), 163
Property Code Enforcement initiative
    (Lancaster, Pennsylvania), 155
Public choice theory, 71
Public consultations, 75
Public Electronic Network (Santa Monica,
    California), 197
Public interest groups, 99, 101, 160
Public opinion, 26
Public recognition, 120–24. *See also* Media;
    specific awards programs
Public safety. *See* Criminal justice and public
    safety
Public sector entrepreneurship: hotbeds of
    innovation, 199–204; literature review,
    20–25; serial innovators, 196–99
Public sector innovation: changes in, 181–85;
    external reviews of, 184–85; future research
    opportunities, 194–204; implementation
    stage, 9, 192–93; and interorganizational
    collaboration, 181–83; precepts for prac-
    titioners, 189–94; process consistency for,
    186–89; research studies on, 11–39;
    typology, 29. *See also specific organizations
    and awards programs*
Public sector unions, 99
Public transit, 153
Public value, 108. *See also* Value creation

Quality Compensation System for Teachers
    (Minnesota), 162

Raven Island (Alaska), 161
Recognizing Public Value (Moore), 108
Recycling, 153, 154
Reentry Court (New York City), 172, 176
Reentry plans, 172
Regimented Treatment Program (Oklahoma),
    172, 176
Regional Greenhouse Gas Initiative, 49,
    151–52, 154
Regulatory constraints, 90, 91, 93
Reich, Robert, 27–28, 199
Reinventing government, 5

Reinventing Government (Osborne and Gaebler), 3, 11
Renewable energy, 67
Reno, Nevada, criminal justice and public safety innovations in, 175
Replication, 115–16. *See also* Transferability
Research studies, 11–39; case studies, 27–28; on diffusion of innovations, 25–26; on innovative organizations, 26–38; on management by "groping along," 19–20; on public sector entrepreneurship, 20–25; statistical studies, 28–38; using innovation awards, 15–19
Resource availability, 26. *See also* Budgets
Restraint/Seclusion Prevention Initiative (Rhode Island), 169
Return to Roots Program (Virginia), 157
Rhode Island: education and training innovations in, 161; health and social services innovations in, 166–67, 169
Richmond, Virginia, criminal justice and public safety innovations in, 174
Rindge School of Technical Arts (Cambridge, Massachusetts), 162, 164, 197, 198
Risk-averse organizational culture, 91
Riverside County, California, transportation, infrastructure, and environment innovations in, 151, 152
River Vision on the Mississippi (Davenport, Iowa), 157
Road pricing, 149
Roberts, Nancy, 21, 22
Robert Wood Johnson Foundation, 170–71, 179
Rogers, Everett, 2, 8, 25, 183
Romney, Mitt, 63, 152
Rosenstock, Larry, 162, 197, 198, 199
Rowlands, Robert, 30, 47
Rural development, 155

Safe Passages (Oakland), 167, 169, 171
Safe Summer (Prince George's County, Maryland), 168
St. Petersburg, Florida, criminal justice and public safety innovations in, 175
Salge, Torsten, 31, 37, 38
Salt Lake City, transportation, infrastructure, and environment innovations in, 152

San Antonio, Texas, management and governance innovations in, 152
San Diego: criminal justice and public safety innovations in, 175; health and social services innovations in, 168, 170
San Francisco: criminal justice and public safety innovations in, 174, 175, 176; health and social services innovations in, 166; management and governance innovations in, 149; transportation, infrastructure, and environment innovations in, 153
Sanger, Mary Bryna, 15, 16, 19, 78
Santa Ana Watershed Authority, 151, 152
Santa Monica, California: community and economic development innovations in, 156; information technology innovations in, 197
Schall, Ellen, 27
Schneider, Marguerite, 33, 34
Schneider, Mark, 21
Scott, James, 22, 25
Seattle: as hotbed of innovation, 201; management and governance innovations in, 147–48; transportation, infrastructure, and environment innovations in, 153
SECURE system (Orange County, California), 146, 148
Semifinalists for 2010 HKS awards: application questions, 115, 208–09; consistency between semifinalists and non-semifinalists, 44–52; duration of innovation, 126; funding for innovations, 51; organizational level of, 131; previous applications by, 58, 126, 128; selection determinants for, 124, 125–33; size of organizations, 126–27, 131
Senior Executive Service, 68
Serial innovators, 196–99
Service improvements, 110, 111, 136
Shape Up Somerville, 167, 168, 171, 203
Significance: coding applications for, 43, 44, 127; as finalist selection criteria, 134–37; quantitative evidence for, 141
Singapore, innovation awards in, 16, 17, 41
Single-payer health insurance, 170
Site visits, 138
Size of organization, 35, 126–27, 131
Size of projects, 54–56

Smart Charlotte 2050 (Charlotte County, Florida), 146
Smart Way Program (EPA), 151, 153, 154
Social marketing, 93, 98, 178
Social services. *See* Health and social services
SoftSecond loan program (Massachusetts), 158
Solar Highway project (Oregon), 67, 152
Somerville, Massachusetts: health and social services innovations in, 167, 168; as hotbed of innovation, 201, 203; management and governance innovations in, 147; SomerStat, 147, 148, 150, 203
Sonoma County, California, management and governance innovations in, 151
Spence, Harry, 15
Spink, Peter, 16, 47, 72, 183
Sponsors, 22
Staff resistance, 91
Standardized Program Evaluation Protocol (Arizona), 172
Statewide Land Use Program (Oregon), 152
Station Manager Program (New York City), 149
Statistical studies, 12, 28–38
Steering committees, 51
STOPPED program (Michigan), 173, 175
Strategic planning, 20, 84. *See also* Planning
Straussman, Jeffrey, 20
Street-level policy entrepreneurs, 24, 25, 68
Striving Toward Excellence in Performance (STEP), 15
Structural equation modeling, 14
Student Conflict Resolution Experts (Massachusetts), 164
Sustaining Innovation (Light), 27

Task forces, 75
Teacher quality initiatives, 161, 162
Teacher Residency Program (Boston), 161–62, 163
Technology, 12. *See also* Information technology
Teodoro, Manuel, 24, 73
Terry, Larry, 4
Teske, Paul, 21
Texas: education and training innovations in, 161; health and social services innovations

in, 167; management and governance innovations in, 146–47. *See also specific cities*
Thatcher, Margaret, 29
Thayer Junior/Senior High School (New Hampshire), 164
Theoretical models, 123, 124, 137, 141, 160, 191
Third Frontier Program (Ohio), 156, 158
Thomson, Ann Marie, 47
Tobacco Settlement Act of 2001, 156, 158
Top-down innovations, 66
Total innovation, 29
Trade media. *See* Professional or trade media
Training. *See* Education and training
Transferability: coding applications for, 43, 44, 127; as finalist selection criteria, 134–37; and public value creation, 115–16, 185; quantitative evidence for, 141; and recognition, 120–24; as semifinalist selection criteria, 132
Transit-Oriented Development Gap Financing Program (Philadelphia), 156, 158
Transparency, 146
Transportation, infrastructure, and environment: changes in policy priorities, 177; innovation characteristics, 50; policy area narratives, 9, 144, 150–54; watershed management, 48
Travis County, Texas, criminal justice and public safety innovations in, 175
Turbitt, Irwin, 47

Unions, 99
United Kingdom (UK): Economic and Social Research Council, 29; funding of innovation programs in, 23; information technology use in, 6; innovation award applications from, 41; innovation awards in, 18; interorganizational collaboration in, 47; local government innovation in, 22; New Public Management in, 3; statistical studies in, 29, 30, 31, 36, 37
University of Texas, 174
Urban and Rural Reserve (Oregon), 157
Urban development, 155
User resistance, 111
Utah, transportation, infrastructure, and environment innovations in, 153

Vacant Property Registration Fee Program (Wilmington, Delaware), 158
Value creation, 108–19; external measures of, 113–19; and New Public Management, 108, 115; and productivity, 110, 111; service improvements, 110, 111; and transfer of innovations, 115–17
Vanity projects, 109
Variance inflation factors, 82, 123
Vector Security, 174
Vedlitz, Arnold, 24
Vera, Antonio, 37, 38
Vergari, Sandra, 22
Verma, Anil, 32
Vermont, education and training innovations in, 161
Vertical authority relationships, 65
Veterans Administration, 169
Victoria, Australia, public policy entrepreneurship in, 24
Vigoda-Gadot, Eran, 32–33
Virginia, community and economic development innovations in, 157. *See also specific cities*
Virtual School initiative (Florida), 163
VISTA (Volunteers in Service to America), 168
Volunteers, 50, 59, 136, 148, 186

Wagner Graduate School of Public Service at New York University, 27
Walker, Richard, 30, 31, 34, 36, 37, 38, 47, 125

Walters, Jonathan, 55
Washington (state): education and training innovations in, 163, 164; management and governance innovations in, 147, 148
Washington, D.C., health and social services innovations in, 167
Watershed management, 48
Wayne County, Michigan: community and economic development innovations in, 158, 159; criminal justice and public safety innovations in, 173, 176
West Virginia Health Right, 166
West Virginia Rx, 166, 170
Wichita, Kansas, transportation, infrastructure, and environment innovations in, 153
Williams, Jacky, 23, 24, 25
Wilmington, Delaware, community and economic development innovations in, 158
Winston-Salem, North Carolina, management and governance innovations in, 148
Wolf, Jory, 156, 197, 199
Workplace Health Initiative (King County, Washington), 148
Wu, Jiannan, 16
Wyoming, health and social services innovations in, 168, 170

Yang, Yuqian, 16
Youth violence and delinquency, 169

Zeckhauser, Richard, 90